THE CRISIS OF ACTION IN NINETEENTH-CENTURY ENGLISH LITERATURE

THE CRISIS OF ACTION IN NINETEENTH-CENTURY ENGLISH LITERATURE

STEFANIE MARKOVITS

The Ohio State University Press
Columbus

Library of Congress Cataloging-in-Publication Data
Markovits, Stefanie, 1971–
The crisis of action in nineteenth-century English literature / Stefanie Markovits.
p. cm.
Includes bibliographical references and index.
ISBN-13: 978–0-8142–1040–6 (cloth : alk. paper)
ISBN-10: 0–8142–1040–6 (cloth : alk. paper)
ISBN-13: 978–0-8142–9118–4 (cd-rom)
ISBN-10: 0–8142–9118-X (cd-rom)
1. English literature—19th century—History and criticism. 2. Literature and society—Great Britain—History—19th century. 3. National character-istics, British, in literature. 4. Character in literature I. Title.
PR451.M35 2006
820.9'358—dc22
2006013139
Cover design by DesignSmith.
Type set in Adobe Garamond
Printed by Thomson-Shore, Inc.

9 8 7 6 5 4 3 2 1

For Inga and Dick

Contents

ACKNOWLEDGMENTS

This book could not have been written without aid from a number of teachers, friends, and colleagues. The ideas in it go back to thoughts I was developing as an undergraduate, in particular in a seminar with Jonathan Lear on Aristotle's *Ethics* and one on Georgic poetry led by Kevis Goodman. Joseph Bristow, Paul Fry, Pericles Lewis, Lucy Newlyn, Annabel Patterson, and Linda Peterson have read and commented helpfully on portions of the manuscript. Alexander Welsh has also been generous in sharing his thoughts with me. My friends and former fellow graduate students Molly Murray, Marco Roth, Charlotte Taylor, and Emily Wilson have sent me many a useful quotation. Sarah Bilston, not only a friend and colleague, but also a sister-in-law, has read and discussed drafts of my work and sympathized with my trials along the way. In the final stages, Sandy Crooms has been a wonderful editor to work with: friendly, prompt, and patient. I am especially thankful to my erstwhile supervisors and present colleagues, David Bromwich and Ruth Bernard Yeazell. To Ruth my debt is particularly great: her undergrad seminar on Jane Austen made me want to become an English professor; her rigor, intelligence, and kindness have kept me going since then. But above all, I would like to thank my family—Inga, Dick, Daniel, Benjamin, Julia, and Rebecca; my daughters, Nelly and Florence, born during the revision of the manuscript; and my husband, Ben. Their patience and support have been beyond measure.

An earlier version of chapter 2 appeared in *Nineteenth-Century Literature* under the same title (in vol. 55, no. 4, pp. 445–78; © 2001 by the Regents of the University of California); I would like to thank the journal and the University of California Press for permission to reprint this in extended and revised form. Similarly, an earlier version of chapter 3 appeared in *Studies in English Literature, 1500–1900* as "George Eliot's Problem with Action" (vol. 41, no. 4 [Autumn 2001]); it is reprinted in a much-extended form, with permission. Finally, I would like to thank the Frederick W. Hilles Fund of Yale University for providing assistance with the publication of this book.

Introduction

It was the dream itself enchanted me:
Character isolated by a deed
To engross the present and dominate memory
—W. B. Yeats, "The Circus Animals' Desertion"

WE THINK OF the nineteenth century as an active age—the age of revolutions and railroads, of great exploration, colonial expansion, and the Great Exhibition. Yet reading the works of Romantic and Victorian writers, one notices what amounts to a crisis concerning the role of action in literature. The crisis manifests itself regularly in authors' critical reflections: from Wordsworth's claim in the Preface to *Lyrical Ballads* (1800) to have written a new kind of poetry in which "the feeling therein developed gives importance to the action and situation, and not the action and situation to the feeling"; to Arnold's dismissal of *Empedocles on Etna* (1852) because in it "suffering finds no vent in action"; to Henry James's discussion of "nefarious" plot in his Preface (1908) to *The Portrait of a Lady* (1881), in which he explained his decision to focus on character from the first, making an "ado" out of very little to do, replacing external action with "an 'exciting' inward life."[1]

These writers were all responding to, and frequently reversing, the familiar dictum set out by Aristotle in his *Poetics:*

1

> All human happiness or misery takes the form of action; the end for which
> we live is a certain kind of activity, not a quality. Character gives us qual-
> ities, but it is in our actions—what we do—that we are happy or the
> reverse. In a play accordingly they do not act in order to portray the
> Characters; they include the Characters for the sake of the action.[2]

In the nineteenth century, Aristotle's statement about the relative importance of action and character in drama was transformed into a critical bat-
tleground. Writers involved in the struggle over these two categories
effected a revolution in literature. In what follows, I will map out the territory of the conflict by focusing on four participants in the combat—
William Wordsworth, Arthur Hugh Clough, George Eliot, and Henry
James. I will trace the course of the debate from its origins in the sea of
Romantic poetry, through the hills and valleys of Victorian narrative verse,
up into the highlands of the great Victorian psychological novel. But I will
also show how difficult the terrain proved to be and at what cost the
ground was gained.

I begin here with Aristotle because that is where so many of the writers
of the nineteenth century, trained in the classical traditions of the univer-
sities, themselves began. In *Lothair* (1870), when the General declares his
conviction that "Action may not always be happiness, . . . but there is no
happiness without action," he demonstrates Disraeli's discipleship under the
great Greek philosopher.[3] It is the very frequency of such allusions that first
led me to see the problem of action as a central concern of the post-Romantics.
The generic division of the novel into novels of plot and novels of character shows the dominance of the debate over action and character in the Victorian
age; it was in this period that these two Aristotelian categories became indispensable tools of the critical trade. But they became so for a reason—or rather,
for many reasons. So my story is also one of the hows and whys that lie
behind the crisis in action.

Aristotle's belief in the primacy of action stands behind his description
of the relative importance of character (*ethos*) and action (*praxis*) in drama.
Because action is prior to character (rather than character to action), it is
the more essential category. As his *Nicomachean Ethics* makes particularly
clear, morality cannot be achieved without action: "of all the things that
come to us by nature [such as the senses] we first acquire the potentiality
and later exhibit the activity . . . ; but the virtues we get first by exercising
them."[4] But his definition of *character* (at least in drama) as "that which
reveals the moral purpose of the agents"[5] also demonstrates his belief in the

lucidity of the moral life. We can see what a person is like by looking at what he or she does—"character isolated by a deed," to use Yeats's formulation.[6] By the time Yeats and his generation were writing, though, such clarity had become the stuff of dreams. In the modern world, the relationship between the internal and external had gained significantly in complexity, clouding over the moral mechanism.

The problem is one most famously addressed by Kant. His quest to understand the connections between things visible and invisible (phenomenal and noumenal) lies behind his most powerful thought. But in the *Foundations of the Metaphysics of Morals* (1785), Kant described an immovable veil obscuring the face of virtue: "even the strictest examination can never lead us entirely behind the secret incentives, for, when moral worth is in question, it is not a matter of actions which one sees but of their inner principles which one does not see."[7] A seemingly benevolent deed may mask vicious purposes, and those purposes—rather than the actions they result in—determine the virtue of the agent. With the increased emphasis on the role of the will in determining morality, action lost its ability to signify character; people's deeds need not fully reveal their essential selves. As Angel Clare reflects in Thomas Hardy's *Tess of the D'Urbervilles* (1891), "The beauty or ugliness of a character lay not only in its achievements, but in its aims and impulses; its true history lay, not among things done, but among things willed."[8]

In fact the source of the modern dispute about action and character can be found in the context of Romantic poetry—that is, in the context of post-Kantian thought. And for all the emphasis on Aristotle, the terms of the nineteenth-century debate have little to do, finally, with the ancient Greek distinctions. Even as they invoked the inventor of their critical tools, the writers of the period were refashioning his instruments to suit their modern needs.[9] So I want first to reflect briefly on both the process of translation and what was lost in it.

Wordsworth's Preface to *Lyrical Ballads* serves as a convenient starting point. There Wordsworth not only replaced the Aristotelian triumvirate of action, character, and situation with his own action, feeling, and situation, he also accorded the new category of feeling the eminent position Aristotle had given to action. *Character* and *feeling* would seem to fit into different categories of things, and it is hard to see how Wordsworth can have made this change. But his substitution of the more explicitly internal *feeling* for the Aristotelian *ethos* has some historical legitimacy: *ethos* is a notoriously difficult concept to translate, and the English word *character* seriously attenuates its meanings. One root of the confusion lies in the relationship between *ethos* and *pathos* (generally translated as *suffering,* a kind of feeling). According to Quintilian, the ancients divided emotions into two classes: "the one is called *pathos* by the Greeks and is rightly and correctly expressed in Latin by *adfectus* (emotion): the other is called *ethos,* a word for which in my opinion Latin has no equivalent: it is however rendered by *mores* (morals)."[10] Yet the two forms of emotion can also be thought of in terms of their relationship to external action; "*ethos* results from the successful translation of the will into an act, verbal or physical, whereas *pathos* ensues where there is failure to translate will into act."[11] So when Wordsworth chose to write poetry focusing on feeling, he may well have wished to suggest the existence of a form of character that bears the same relationship to *pathos* that *ethos* bears to *praxis;* something analogous to character can be generated by suffering (as character is generated by action for Aristotle), and this something (which I would argue comes to be called *consciousness*) is of great value to the moral life.

*In*action—both frustrated external action and heightened internal action—fascinates the writers I consider. But for Aristotle, both *ethos* ("that which reveals the moral purpose of the agents") and *pathos* ("which we may define as an action of a destructive or painful nature") are produced by action.[12] For something to matter morally, it must involve action of some sort, and that action must be external in nature. This is why in works of art, plot ranks above character in importance; if we are to learn of the good, we must see characters do good (and bad) deeds. So if one believes Aristotle's position regarding the role of action in the moral life, the elevation of character (and corresponding demotion of plot) in many works of post-Romantic literature has troubling implications. As Robert Caserio puts it in *Plot, Story, and the Novel,* "when writers and readers of novels lose interest in plot and story, they appear to lose faith in the meaning and the moral value of acts."[13] This study owes a great debt both to the ethical philosophy of Aristotle and to Caserio's translation of that philosophy into the literary realm. Its central concern is in the interplay of literature, action, consciousness, and the moral life. What creates the sense of a self, in life and in art? Must one do the right thing, or is it enough to will it? How does literary work connect to this question? Can thinking ever be doing, as so many nineteenth-century authors seem to hope? What would a character built by such thinking look like?

Examining texts that thematize versions of the struggle with action, one notices the frequent recurrence of two narrative trends: frustrated marriage plots (either courtships that fail to reach marriage, like that of Claude and

Mary in Arthur Hugh Clough's *Amours de Voyage* [written 1849, published 1858], or marriages that entrap those in them, such as Dorothea's to Casaubon in *Middlemarch* [1871–72]), and frustrated revolutionary or social reform plots. Moreover, with surprising frequency, these two plotlines are conflated— as in *Amours,* where the failed courtship plot takes place against the backdrop of the French siege of Rome in 1849. The connection between marriage and politics is an old one; *Paradise Lost* (1667) provides a model for how the marriage contract can represent the social contract. Marriage is also rife with the language of philosophy of action: intentions, proposals, "I will"s or "I do"s.[14] Such words represent paradigmatic speech acts, a feature that makes them of particular interest to writers who wish to see in their own words a potential for an alternative form of political action. Finally, in an age before easy divorce, the decision to wed forms a perfect lens through which to view the arbitrariness and irrevocability of deeds.

Revolution, on the other hand, stands for the kind of wide-scale political activity that should form a modern counterpart to the nation-building activities of the epic heroes. But all too frequently, revolutionary activity disintegrates into riots in works of the period, to be replaced by "inward revolutions" such as Wordsworth's in *The Prelude* (1805; 1850), Esther Lyons's in *Felix Holt* (1866), and Hyacinth Robinson's in *The Princess Casamassima* (1886).[15] Alternatively, revolution becomes a dramatic presentation viewed by tourists standing on the sidelines: Wordsworth in Paris or Clough in Rome. In the works of Clough and Arnold, heroic combat devolves into versions of the Battle of Epipolie (described by Thucydides), where "ignorant armies clash by night."[16] While the plotlines of marriage and revolution are traditionally representative of specifically gendered activity—marriage for women, heroics for men—many nineteenth-century authors reverse this pattern. The hero of *Amours de Voyage* finds himself entangled in the marriage plot, while James's Princess Casamassima, having given up on her marriage, seeks the thrill of revolutionary activity. All in all, marriage and revolutionary plots provide convenient mechanisms through which to explore aspects of the crisis of action.

I must state up front a few general positions, although I hope my reasons for assuming them will become clearer in what follows. First, what do I mean by *action?* Kenneth Burke calls "the human body in purposive motion" the basic unit of action, and this seems to capture the externality of action that is its Aristotelian (and epic) core.[17] I choose the word advisedly—*agency* is the more favored academic term—because I intend to invoke explicitly the connections between actions of characters and the structures of plot used

by authors. Moreover, while I am interested in passivity (and its relationship to passion), I will often refer instead to *inaction* (the *OED*'s first cita-
tion is from 1707) in order to stress the link between not doing and inner
doings, between inaction and character. My claim is that on some level, in
literature at least, if not in life, we are who we are, not by virtue of what
we do, but by what we have failed to do. Frustrated action—inaction—is
character building. The "growth" of "one's imagination"[18] (the phrase is James's
in the Preface to *The Portrait of a Lady*, but naturally harks back to
Wordsworth's *Prelude*) is produced when the chance for outward action is
stunted. Conversely, an excess of action can endanger the development of
consciousness. So, for example, Dickens's highly engaged and active plots
can be seen to result in his famously flat characters. The "round" excep-
tions, such as Arthur Clennam in *Little Dorrit* (1857) or Pip in *Great Expectations*
(1861), tend to be marked by their passive, will-less natures.[19]

I also want to emphasize the political implications of the word *action*:
many of the authors I treat are deeply concerned with the relationship between
a poetics, a plot, and a politics. I should stress, though, that the political
valence of the crisis is never straightforward: the increased emphasis on character in the period is neither strictly liberal nor conservative as an impulse;
how it functions depends very much on the circumstances. So, for example, it opened the door to a variety of action that was available to women,
even as it closed off the possibility for more radical forms of change that
could enlarge their sphere of opportunity. I may argue that Wordsworth's
politics become more conservative in response to his disavowal of action,
but George Eliot's conservatism merely serves as a kind of fire shield, pro-
tecting her from the effects of a fundamentally liberal understanding of the
world. And a writer like Joseph Conrad will be labeled as liberal by one critic
and reactionary by the next, in part as a result of the ambiguities produced
by his participation in the crisis of action. Similarly, the desire to view literature ethically has no particular political valence: it is suggestive that both
conservative (Charles Taylor, Alasdair MacIntyre) and liberal (Martha
Nussbaum, Jil Larson) philosophers and critics of today have insisted on
the relationship between narrative (that is, plot) and ethics.[20]

Second, what do I mean by *character*? Like most of the writers I am considering, I take the term from translations of Aristotle. But as I have suggested, both they and I mean something different from Aristotle,
something more like that "surplus of humanness" recognized by Bakhtin as
an essential product of the conflict between character and situation in the
novel,[21] something more like what we would call *consciousness*. It is that which

makes us believe in the life of a character, at times even outside of the text, in the way one thinks of some Shakespearean characters. The move from *character* to *consciousness* is, I would argue, an essential corollary to the redefinition of action (especially heroic action) that occurs in the literature of the nineteenth century—one nicely suggested by Wordsworth's revision of the epic in *The Prelude*. Whereas the emphasis with character is on acts, the emphasis with consciousness is on thoughts. But there is a continued moral charge that is implied in the close etymological ties between consciousness and conscience. Nevertheless, this revision of heroism internalizes morality in a way that can—and, I think, should—be deemed suspect.

Although many have noticed the passive drift of nineteenth-century fiction before, approaches tend not to focus on historical circumstance.[22] As Caserio acknowledges, "it is possible to argue that in every literary era narrative and antinarrative impulses coexist, so that the conflict over plot and story is atemporal and formal, not in fact timely and historical."[23] But while the many references to Milton and Hamlet that appear in the texts I consider demonstrate this atemporality, I want to emphasize the historicity of the struggle over action. The very frequency of nineteenth-century writers' allusions to works from the past that exhibit tendencies toward internal action (or inaction) suggests that there is something particular to the age's obsession with the debate.[24] So does the constant attention given to Aristotle's proclamation about the status of action; Wordsworth's Preface can be thought of as groundbreaking in this respect, as in so many others. While (as I go to some pains to emphasize) it is true that both narrative and antinarrative impulses can be found in the period—there are as many Victorian novels of plot as there are novels of character—the presence of the contest is particularly strong. For each "Ulysses," there must be a "Lotos-Eaters" (1842).

Moreover, most critics interested in the phenomenon of internalization choose to concentrate on novels and prose.[25] Studies of Romantic and Victorian poetry often note poets' complicated attitudes toward action in general and political engagement in particular, but they do not look forward to draw links between the verse and the subject matter of novels. By disregarding the connection between Romantic poetry and novels of consciousness demonstrated by their mutual concern with inaction, critics have underplayed the relationship between inaction and consciousness.[26] Theorists of genre like Lukács and Bakhtin (who discusses the novelization of poetry in "Epic and Poetry") may have hinted at the kind of links I am suggesting, but they did not address them in any detail. My analysis is structured in a chronological fashion (somewhat artificially: Richardson's *Clarissa* [1747–48], the first great novel of consciousness, predates Wordsworth's poetry) in order to emphasize its generic thrust, to show how the novel of consciousness develops in part out of Romantic poetry and its concerns with inaction. The corollary to this claim is my argument that the debates over Victorian verse narrative—which I treat in the chapter on Clough—act as a visible locus of generic unease. While most of the poetry considered here is either narrative or closet/monodrama, I ultimately wish to suggest that those most antithetical of genres, lyric and the novel, actually share concerns; Pound's desire to reproduce the complexity of a Henry James novel in verse in *Hugh Selwyn Mauberley* (1920) resembles George Eliot's efforts with regard to Wordsworth.

Naturally, I have chosen the four authors on whom I concentrate because I believe them to hold particularly revealing stances toward action. But they are also representative. There are many more writers that have been left out of this study than have been included. For every Wordsworth there is a Byron, who fights actively for his causes even as his characters (most famously, Don Juan) drift passively through his narratives. For every Clough there is an Arnold, for every Eliot a Hardy, for every James a Conrad. This abundance of examples only strengthens my sense of the usefulness of action as a category through which to approach writers of the period. Of course, as the example of Byron shows, the two camps of action and character are not always easily distinguished. Indeed, works can be as hard to place as authors: a novel with a passive hero (Pip, say) can display a particularly active plot. So when I speak of writers as belonging to one or the other side, I am talking about how they have generally been considered by their audiences, and in particular by many of the contemporary critics that I quote in my discussions.

And while the writers with whom I engage tend to belong in the camp of character rather than of plot, they have been selected in part for the ambivalence of their allegiances. This ambivalence resonates not only publicly (through their work) but also privately (in their lives), and what follows is historical in part by being biographical. By examining the cases of these four writers, we can see how reactions to a series of specific historical contingencies—including the response to the French Revolution, laissez-faire economic practices, changes in religious belief and scientific knowledge, and shifts in the role of women in society—made people in the nineteenth century particularly sensitive to the status of action and its reflection in the literary realm. Note that the focus of this study will be on reaction rather than action, on what was thought about what was done rather than on what was done. I do not mean to suggest so much an argument about the level of actual activity in the period as about the perceived state of action. Yet by concentrating on the dispute over action, connections between many of the major critical debates about the period become clearer: about individualism and doubt, internalization, sensation, and repression, the epic and the domestic. My claim is that in fact "action" spans all these categories. The crisis of action can be seen as the crux of nineteenth-century anxieties.

⚏

I begin by looking at Wordsworth's prototypically Romantic internalization of action through his engagement (both his actions and—crucially—his inactions) with the French Revolution. Nowhere is this strange, double-edged quality more apparent than in the fraught treatments of action in Wordsworth's 1796–97 drama, *The Borderers,* and in his 1807 narrative poem, *The White Doe of Rylstone; or, The Fate of the Nortons.* While neither of these works, which span the period of Wordsworth's greatest poetic production, is explicitly autobiographical, both are steeped in an atmosphere of revolutionary involvement that cannot be divorced from their author's experiences during the French Revolution. In fact, I read the poems as part of Wordsworth's grand revisionary autobiographical scheme. Moreover, in each work the interest in revolution broadens into a general concern with problems of action, in particular with what Wordsworth thinks of as betrayals into action. And in both this concern has generic consequences, not only for the poem in question, but also for Wordsworth's wider project—and for the course of English literature.

Chapter 2 turns to Victorian narrative verse and to the case of Arthur Hugh Clough and his poem *Amours de Voyage.* I show how the work's generic hybridity (it is a mock epic, five-act epistolary novel-in-verse, written in hexameters punctuated by lyrical elegiacs) is rooted in Clough's complicated relationship with action, manifested both in his well-known crisis of faith and his battle against laissez-faire government (what Carlyle called "Donothingism"). Its struggle with genre underlying an obvious concern with issues of action in its subject matter, *Amours de Voyage* provides a particularly revealing lens through which to explore the crisis in action in mid-nineteenth-century thought and its influence on the literature of the period. The chapter also explores the debate surrounding Clough's friend Arnold's programmatic Preface to *Poems* (1853) and the issue of contemporary critical responses to the question of action in literature.

The novelistic aspects of Clough's poetry offer a transition into the realm of the Victorian psychological novel. Chapter 3 looks at George Eliot, whose oeuvre demonstrates her ongoing—and largely unsuccessful—struggle to envision a safe and useful form of political action. Once again, the argument is biographical as well as generally cultural; I consider Eliot's position as a woman, her philosophical and scientific beliefs, and her interest in such risk-free substitutes for action as duty, habit, and will. The novels show her increasing sense of urgency with regard to the question of how to handle action. While her early works suggest she felt relative complacency about internalizing and suppressing action, her later works are much more ambivalent about the ethics of doing. Eliot's struggle culminates in *Daniel Deronda* (1876), in which the nature and potential of action become the dominant subject.

Chapter 4, on *The Portrait of a Lady* (1881) and *The Princess Casamassima* (1886), shows how Henry James builds upon Eliot's realizations by using the dangerous and obscured nature of action in modern society to construct his own novel forms. In *The Portrait,* James subtly revises Eliot's position through his emphasis on freedom over duty, on consciousness over the more deed-derived or Aristotelian character, and, above all, through his self-consciously formal treatment of what he calls "nefarious plot." The concept is substantiated in the anarchist "plot" that stands at the center of Hyacinth Robinson's adventure in *The Princess.* I argue that this plot can be seen as emblematic of the status of action toward the close of the century, and that the oddly marital "vow" by which Hyacinth enters into it demonstrates just how intimate is the link between the two kinds of action (political and domestic) I have been examining. Moreover, James's treatment of a real underground plot in this work from his "middle period" anticipates the way in which his later works hide more ordinary happenings through stylistic innovations. A coda on James's late story, "The Beast in the Jungle" (1902), offers a warning: taken to extremes, the demise of action entails the demise of character.

Finally, I turn in conclusion to the other side of the story, to a brief consideration of the role of the adventure novel or romance in the period. I focus my discussion on Robert Louis Stevenson's *Treasure Island* (1883), which I read as a true example of the genre. But, I argue, this pure form is achieved only by jettisoning morality and, indeed, the wider concerns of adulthood.

❦ 1 ❧

Wordsworth's Revolution:
From *The Borderers* to *The White Doe of Rylstone*

> Thus conscience does make cowards of us all,
> And thus, the native hue of resolution
> Is sicklied o'er with the pale cast of thought,
> And enterprises of great pitch and moment
> With this regard their currents turn awry,
> And lose the name of action.
> —William Shakespeare, *Hamlet*

IN THE PREFACE to *Lyrical Ballads* (1800), Wordsworth describes what makes his poems different from "the popular Poetry of the day; it is this, that the feeling therein developed gives importance to the action and situation, and not the action and situation to the feeling."[1] His ballads, a genre usually associated with the bold adventures of knights, damsels, and supernatural agents, will be *lyrical,* that is, nonnarrative and descriptive of emotions rather than events, of inner reactions rather than outer actions. The new emphasis is genuinely revolutionary—how much so can perhaps be registered when one considers the internalization of epic that occurs in *The Prelude,* the unnamed work referred to by Coleridge as "an unpublished Poem on the Growth and Revolutions of an Individual Mind."[2]

Revolution, in its specific historical sense, also lies behind Wordsworth's poetic endeavors. In 1798 Coleridge wrote to Wordsworth, requesting the production of the work that was to become *The Prelude:* "I wish you would

11

write a poem [reviving the spirits of those who] in consequence of the complete failure of the French Revolution have thrown up all hopes of amelioration and given themselves over to [solitude] and the cultivation of the domestic affections."[3] Yet if the poem Wordsworth finally delivered brings hope to its readers, it does so precisely by suggesting the powerful benefits to be gained by cultivating the domestic affections. Here, as with the other works I will explore, the most important revolutions turn out to be internal ones, like the "turn of sentiment—that might be named / A revolution" experienced by Wordsworth when he discovered that England had declared war on France.[4] Robert Browning's judgment of "The Lost Leader," the youthful radical poet who subsequently forsook political action in favor of establishment reactionism, demonstrates the strength of the myth of revolutionary disenchantment coming out of involvements with France.

The nature of Wordsworth's own involvement remains a mystery.[5] While his presence in France, first on an early walking tour with a Cambridge friend in 1790 and then for a longer stay in both Paris and Orleans for most of 1792, is sufficiently documented, the extent of his active work for revolutionary causes is unclear. Undoubtedly Wordsworth's friendship with Beaupuy, the man so admiringly represented in *The Prelude* as one whom "circumstance / Hath called upon to embody his deep sense / In action, give it outwardly a shape" (*Prelude* IX.407–9), led at least to some impassioned conversation. But for all Wordsworth's later descriptions of himself as an "active partisan" (*Prelude* IX.737), his only traceable act of solidarity—*A Letter to the Bishop of Llandaff* (1793), an inflammatory extended apology for regicide—was never published during his lifetime.

Moreover, Wordsworth carefully fostered the mystery of his activities during the revolutionary years by his close editorial control over his past, both in his writing and outside of it. So, for example, the now-infamous affair with Annette Vallon, the royalist Frenchwoman who bore him a child, Caroline, in the heady atmosphere of Orleans in 1792, is translated in his poetry into the narrative of "Julia and Vaudracour" in *The Prelude* (which he subsequently excised from the autobiographical poem, although he published it separately).[6] The affair remained the well-kept secret of a select few during Wordsworth's lifetime. Wordsworth's reticence—even concealment—is of course especially apparent and especially relevant because of the autobiographical nature of much of his work. When an admirer asked him in 1801 to provide an account of his life, he responded with a brief paragraph outlining the various places he had lived, notably amending his year-long sojourn in revolutionary France to "travel[s] on the Continent." Then he added a disclaimer: "but in truth my life has been unusually barren of events, and my opinions have grown slowly and, I may say, insensibly."[7]

Such an organic, even Burkean, model of development accords well with the poetics of the Preface to *Lyrical Ballads*. But is it true? Had Wordsworth really avoided the dangers of involvement in those "great national events" that produced an unhealthy addiction to plot, a "craving" for "incident" in literary work, or had he rather reacted against an overdose of events?[8] Kenneth Johnston's recent and adventurous biography, *The Hidden Wordsworth: Poet, Lover, Rebel, Spy*, suggests the latter version of the story, as its title implies. Yet even if one discards Johnston's theory of youthful sexual indiscretions and belief that the poet acted as a spy for the British government during his 1799 stay in Germany, Wordsworth's life in the 1790s could hardly be described as uneventful. That "revolution" "in sentiment" mentioned in *The Prelude* resulted from Wordsworth's actions during a political Revolution, and the depths of his despair back in England must have stemmed in part, as Johnston argues, from his recognition that the declaration of war between England and France would prevent a reunion with his lover and daughter.[9] Wordsworth had known the excitement of event; he is, after all, the author of the paradigmatic description of youthful revolutionary fervor: "Bliss was it in that dawn to be alive, / But to be young was very Heaven!" (*Prelude* X.693–94).

Yet whatever his actions may have been, Wordsworth's experiences with the French Revolution also anticipate the two plotlines concerning inaction on which this study will concentrate: the failed revolutionary plot (as the Terror set in and Wordsworth's faith began to falter) and the failed marriage plot (Wordsworth eventually abandoned his attempts to marry Annette—although Johnston is but the most recent and most ardent proponent of the theory that he returned to France in September of 1793 in an effort, aborted by the escalation of the Terror, to "rescue" Annette and their baby).[10] In what follows, rather than pondering any specific actions or inactions Wordsworth may have committed, I shall look at the way in which his sense of guilt about the revolutionary period of his life affected his treatment of action in his writing. But we should note that Wordsworth's guilt seems to have been as much about what he did not do as what he did do, on both political and personal fronts.

Nowhere is this strange, double-edged quality more apparent than in the fraught handling of action in Wordsworth's 1796–97 drama *The Borderers* and in his 1807 narrative poem *The White Doe of Rylstone; or, The*

Fate of the Nortons. These works were written at the beginning and end of what can be thought of as Wordsworth's great decade of poetic production, a fact that in itself suggests a connection between their concerns over action and the development of Wordsworth's poetic talents. While the poems are considered minor in comparison to the greater achievements of the *Lyrical Ballads* and *The Prelude,* I believe that their troubled surfaces reveal depths that are concealed by the polished aspects of the more canonical texts. Although neither work is autobiographical (perhaps in part *because* neither work is autobiographical), both are steeped in an atmosphere of revolutionary involvement and guilt that cannot be divorced from their author's experiences during the French Revolution. Moreover, in both texts the interest in revolution broadens into a general concern with problems of action, in particular with what Wordsworth thinks of as betrayals into action, and in both this concern has generic consequences, not only for the poem in question, but for Wordsworth's wider project.[11]

Wordsworth was himself the first to note the thematic connection between the two works when in 1836 he appended as an epigraph to *The White Doe of Rylstone* the most famous lines from *The Borderers:*

> Action is transitory, a step, a blow—
> The motion of a muscle—this way or that—
> 'Tis done—and in the after vacancy
> We wonder at ourselves like men betray'd
> Suffering is permanent, obscure and dark,
> And has the nature of infinity.[12]

I cannot think of six consecutive lines in the collected works that contain as characteristic a resonance. The passage, though not cited by Arnold, has something of the quality of an Arnoldian touchstone. Hazlitt, when recalling *The Borderers* in writing his 1825 essay on Wordsworth as a "spirit of the age," quoted it from memory, and Coleridge, as we shall see, also lifted the lines from their context for the purposes of criticism.[13] Yet the context is all important. For while the important terms remain the same—action, suffering, the permanent and the transitory, infinity, betrayal, wonder, and the peculiar "after vacancy" that stands at the very center of the quotation—how they relate to one another shifts subtly but crucially by the end of the decade.

When Wordsworth took these words out of the mouth of his youthful antihero, Rivers, and placed them at the head of a very different kind of work, he implied an authorial continuity—a stable poetic project—that resembles the organically slow, insensible growth of the autobiographical self Wordsworth described to his readers. Again, he kept the revolution well under wraps; "I still stand now by what I said then" is the claim. Of course, the addition represents but one small instance of Wordsworth's great revisionary scheme, his obsessive reworking of old texts, often with the object of bringing them into accordance with his present lines of thought.[14] But it is an especially revealing example. At stake is the relationship between action and suffering and, more particularly, the relationship between action and consciousness, the self-directed wonder that fills the "after vacancy" of action. Is action necessary for the development of human consciousness, or does suffering suffice? When Geoffrey Hartman wonders whether "self-consciousness and Wordsworth's lyricism are connected in an intrinsic and more than occasional way," he asks a version of this question.[15] Wordsworth himself pondered the connection, and as we shall see in what follows, he came up with different answers for different times.

The Borderers

Wordsworth sets *The Borderers,* his first and only drama, during the unrest of the Barons' Wars in the north of England in the thirteenth century, when bands of robbers controlled the land. Among these bands is that headed by Mortimer, the hero of Wordsworth's play.[16] Its antihero, Rivers, tricks the benevolent Mortimer (who had saved his life in events preceding those depicted by Wordsworth) into believing that the blind old Baron Herbert, the father of Mortimer's beloved Matilda, is not her real father. Rather, Rivers contrives to suggest that Herbert has adopted Matilda with the intention of selling her to the evil Baron Clifford. Mortimer is convinced and, in the absence of ordered government, feels it his duty to enforce justice himself. After much hesitation—mainly due to the confusion generated by the old man's seeming goodness—he abandons Herbert upon a heath, crucially forgetting to give him his scrip of food. Herbert dies from the ordeal. In the meantime, Rivers reveals his plot to Mortimer. He explains that he had himself been betrayed into the commission of a similar deed in his youth, when he was persuaded by his shipmates to mutiny against their captain and leave him stranded on an island to perish. Only later did his mates inform him that the captain was innocent of the crime with which he had been charged. After this autobiographical interlude, Mortimer's band arrives and kills Rivers as punishment for his treachery. Finally, Mortimer resigns his leadership of the band, promising to embrace a life of Cain-like wandering.

The idea of a betrayal into action stands at the center of the plot of *The Borderers* and also at the center of Wordsworth's relationship to his own political doings. In *The Prelude,* Wordsworth tells Coleridge of his romance with Godwinian rationalism during the early years of the Revolution in France:

> Time may come
> When some dramatic story may afford
> Shapes livelier to convey to thee, my Friend,
> What then I learned of truth,
> And the errors into which I was betrayed
> By present objects and by reasoning false. (*Prelude* X.878–83)

Most critics take this as a reference to what will be the Solitary's tale in *The Excursion* (1814),[17] but Wordsworth's only truly "dramatic story"—his only play—had already addressed the topic of Wordsworth's "betrayal" into the error of revolution. While *The Borderers* reads in many ways like a bastardization of Shakespeare's tragedies and a few other famous works, the startling originality of the play has to do with the character of Rivers. Wordsworth was himself so fascinated by his antihero that he felt compelled to write a kind of apologia for him: the essay "On the Character of Rivers." The language of betrayal he uses there of Rivers reveals a reason for Wordsworth's investment: "Let us suppose a young Man of great intellectual powers, yet without any solid principles of genuine benevolence. His master passions are pride and the love of distinction. He has deeply imbibed the spirit of enterprize in a tumultuous age. He goes into the world and is betrayed into a great crime."[18]

The obvious autobiographical reading of the drama would see Mortimer (the hero facing a moral crisis) as Wordsworth's stand-in. But Mary Moorman has suggested that the opening lines of the essay on Rivers are self-descriptive.[19] The conflict resolves itself, though, when we recognize that the two characters are versions both of each other and of their poet. The complex nature of Wordsworth's activity during the 1790s forced him to create not only a "second" but also a third "self" through which to reenact his experiences.[20] This proliferation of selves should come as no surprise from the poet who requires four narrators—the Solitary, the Wanderer, the Pastor, and the Author—to negotiate the autobiographical terrain of *The Excursion.* But what Charles Rzepka has called "the extended, but hardly suspenseful psychomachy" of the later narrative pales in comparison with the profound self-searching that characterizes *The Borderers.*[21]

Wordsworth himself provides us with another clue to the autobiographical impulse behind his play. Many critics have noticed how the Godwinian rhetoric of Rivers's rationalist creed,

> You have obeyed the only law that wisdom
> Can ever recognize: the immediate law
> Flashed from the light of circumstances
> Upon an independent intellect (III.v.30–33),

turns up again almost unaltered in *The Prelude* in reference to the poet's own romance with Godwinianism:

> The freedom of the individual mind,
> Which, to the blind restraints of general laws
> Superior, magisterially adopts
> One guide, the light of circumstances, flashed
> Upon an independent intellect. (*Prelude* X.826)

In the Fenwick Note to *The Borderers* (1843), Wordsworth recalls that he wrote the essay on Rivers in part to show the kinds of thoughts that could lead a character like Rivers to act as he does, "but still more to preserve in my distinct remembrance what I had observed of transition in character & the reflections I had been led to make during the time I was a witness of the changes through which the French Revolution had passed."[22] One must ask, whose "transition in character"? Part of the answer must be, I think, Wordsworth's own.

The burden of the passage from the essay on Rivers, and of *The Borderers,* too, rests on the threat posed by forgetting how to trace the changes in character that occur during a "tumultuous age" marked by "a spirit of enterprize," a period of what the Preface to *Lyrical Ballads* will call "great national events."[23] In other words, such times demand actions that endanger the very idea of a knowably coherent identity. "I cannot paint what then I was," Wordsworth laments in "Tintern Abbey," another poem that obliquely retraces his involvements in France.[24] But in the essay, we are told how a character who has once been seduced into committing a great sin will discover autobiography as a form of coping mechanism: "in sudden emergencies when he is called upon by surprise and thrown out of the path of his regular habits, or when dormant associations are awakened tracing the revolutions through which his character has passed, in painting his former self he really *is* great."[25] It is hard to read the emphasis on that "is" as entirely ironic. The revolution through which Wordsworth passes enables revelations of character. Rivers's autobiographical tirade to Mortimer in IV.ii, in which he shows his disciple how they share a bond in their crimes, may represent the raving of an egomaniac, but it is also proof of a solidly constructed ego, for whom past, present, and future form a coherent picture.

For Wordsworth action almost always takes the form of transgression: just think of the early stealing episodes in *The Prelude* or of poems like "Nutting." Rivers's sense of his own agency connects ineluctably to what he calls a "salient spring of energy," with which he "mounted / From action up to action" (IV.ii.119–21). One is reminded of what Coleridge famously termed Iago's "motiveless malignity." Iago considers virtue to be "a fig," a hindrance to that true freedom of will by which, as he puts it, "'Tis in ourselves that we are thus or thus," and Wordsworth indicates his debt to Shakespeare's archvillain in the essay.[26] But the rhetoric also resembles that of Milton's Satan, who notoriously asserts the connections among sin, agency, and selfhood.

Wordsworth clearly means to portray Rivers as fallen, yet he implies that his loss of innocence may be accompanied by some form of gain. Suggestively, he again echoes Rivers's discourse about the "light of circumstances" flashing upon an "independent intellect" in his description of the operations of the Imagination in the crossing of the Alps passage of *The Prelude*: "in such visitings / Of awful promise, when the light of sense / Goes out in flashes that have shown to us / The invisible world, doth greatness make abode" (*Prelude* VI.535). Sense replaces circumstance, indicating the shift in the paradigm from action to vision, but the point in both passages is the flash of recognition, a recognition of an imaginative power that can exist even within the limiting structures with which we are surrounded. Such recuperation forms the second movement in the Kantian experience of the sublime: after we face up to our inability to comprehend the phenomenal world, we grasp the existence of a noumenal self superior in its freedom to such circumscription.[27] The resemblance between the Godwinian intellect and Wordsworth's hallowed Imagination, the fount of his poetry, supports David Bromwich's claim that Mortimer can reconstruct his own fall, so similar to that of Rivers, as a happy one on the basis of an argument about selfhood. Bromwich posits that because the fall is *his* (because it has made Mortimer who he is) and because "he is interested in having a continuous identity," "a devious logic may bind his self-love to any act he finally chooses to perform." In other words, "Any act whatever may be supposed partly good for the agent who has come to associate it with himself."[28]

Bromwich's argument rests on a sequential reading of the "Action is transitory" passage. Transitory action may be inferior to infinite suffering, but it also *causes* it. There is an inherent connection between doing and being. When "we wonder at ourselves like men betray'd," the "after vacancy" of action fills up with self-consciousness. Compare the often-quoted "two consciousnesses" passage from *The Prelude*:

> A tranquilizing spirit presses now
> On my corporeal frame, so wide appears
> The vacancy between me and those days
> Which yet have such self-presence in my mind,
> That sometimes when I think of it, I seem
> Two consciousnesses, conscious of my self
> And of some other being. (*Prelude* II.27–33)

In these lines, a wider temporal gap takes the place of the "after vacancy" of action, but both passages describe a threat to the concept of continuous identity. Yet it is only because of his ability to recognize the connection between those two seemingly separate consciousnesses that Wordsworth is able to have self-knowledge—hence that strange phrase, "self-presence," which stands up against the sense of divided consciousness. The thought process resembles Descartes's central meditation on the wax: precisely because Descartes knows that the wax is one and the same piece of wax, regardless of the change in form over time, he can posit the existence of a coherent self connecting the two observations. Without some change, the implication is, we cannot see what remains the same. Tellingly, Wordsworth goes one step beyond Descartes by suggesting that he does not require the external evidence of some object like the wax but can generate the same sense of identity of the basis of memories of himself.[29]

But the process is not always as tranquil as in this early childhood passage from *The Prelude*. In "Tintern Abbey," which returns Wordsworth to the period of his closest involvement with the Revolution, when like Mortimer he was twenty-three and right in the thick of things,[30] Wordsworth needs the memory aid of Dorothy's presence as a vessel of his former self (in whose voice he may still hear "The language of [his] former

heart" and in whose eyes he can see his "former pleasures") in order to ensure
his sense of continuity. Similarly, Rivers's investment in Mortimer comes
from the younger man's resemblance to his own earlier self. In the later version of the play, he says as much to Mortimer when he reveals his plot:

Know then that I was urged,
(For other impulse let it pass) was driven,
To seek for sympathy, because I saw
In you a mirror of my youthful self. (1862–65)

But Mortimer has not had the life-changing experience of having been
betrayed into action. It is as though this difference between them poses a
threat to Rivers's continuous identity; he needs to watch Mortimer commit a version of his own crime in order to close the gap between his "two
consciousnesses," his past and present selves. "I would have made you
equal with myself," Rivers declares (IV.ii.200). If he can witness Mortimer
do the same thing he did and still remain the same person, then by analogy he will be assured of his own coherence.

Yet only great acts, such as those necessitated by periods of revolution,
cause a break in identity, what both the Fenwick Note and Mortimer himself (II.i.92–93) call a "transition" in character. Habitual action, on the
other hand, ensures our sense of a continuous self. Some lines from "The
Old Cumberland Beggar," a poem composed in early 1798 (just a year
after the completion of *The Borderers*), suggest that Wordsworth was
thinking about the relationship between large and small actions. In the
later poem Wordsworth writes of the benefits brought to his community
by the presence of an old beggar:

Where'er the aged Beggar takes his rounds,
The mild necessity of use compels
To acts of love; and habit does the work
Of reason, yet prepares that after joy
Which reason cherishes. And thus the soul,
By that sweet taste of pleasure unpursued
Doth find itself insensibly disposed
To virtue and true goodness. (lines 90–97)

These small, habitual acts of love, because they are repeated over time,
stand in contrast with the transitory action portrayed by *The Borderers*.
They replace the "work of reason," the labors of the "independent intel-

lect." Correspondingly, the "after joy" that results from such deeds
markedly opposes what the drama describes as the "after vacancy" of
action. In part, the emphasis on habitual action, which we shall see repeated in the works of Arthur Hugh Clough and George Eliot, represents a
conservative response to the kind of unconstrained activity characteristic
of revolutionary France, a place where, in the words of Mary
Wollstonecraft, "vice, or, if you will, evil, is the grand mobile of action."[31]

While Wordsworth often links action to vice, he also commonly connects virtue to habit.[32] In the Preface to *Lyrical Ballads,* Wordsworth
argues that poetry can provide a moral education by fostering habitual
contemplation in a process analogous to the acts of charity described by
"The Old Cumberland Beggar": "by the repetition and continuance of
this act feelings connected with important subjects will be nourished, till
at length, . . . such habits of mind will be produced that by obeying blindly and mechanically the impulses of those habits, . . . the understanding
of the being to whom we address ourselves . . . must necessarily be in some
degree enlightened, his taste exalted, and his affections ameliorated."[33]
Just think of those "little, nameless, unremembered acts / Of kindness and
of love," which in "Tintern Abbey" are said to make up the "best portion
of a good man's life" (lines 34–36). Yet the fact that such acts are "unremembered" should make us pause, given the cult of memory that
Wordsworth embraces. Unremembered acts cannot be reflected upon and
so cannot provide the basis of self-consciousness. Wordsworth implies as
much in the essay on Rivers: "Perhaps there is no cause which has greater
weight in preventing the return of bad men to virtue than that good
actions, being for the most part in their nature silent and regularly pro-
gressive [like the unremembered acts of "Tintern Abbey"], they do not
present those sudden results which can afford a sufficient stimulus to a
troubled mind."[34] If one asks, "What needs stimulating?" the only satis-
fyingly Wordsworthian answer is self-awareness.

The Borderers suggests that while uncharacteristic acts, such as those we
are betrayed into by revolutionary times, may pose a threat to our sense of a
continuous self, they also set off their own healing mechanism: reflection.
Macbeth, right after the murder of Duncan, lets out a cry of shame for his
act: "To know my deed, 'twere best not know myself."[35] Wordsworth reverses this formula; his claim is rather: "To know myself, 'twere best to know my
deed." The reversal comes with his recognition that action causes suffering,
and suffering entails self-consciousness. This is why right after having abandoned Herbert, Mortimer can describe an odd feeling of succumbing to a
vast sense of calm: "I could believe that there was here / The only quiet heart

on earth.—In terror, / Remembered terror, there is love and peace"
(III.v.2–4). If one capitalizes those *t*'s one can transform Mortimer's statement
into Wordsworth's response to his revolutionary involvement.

Yet the emphasis this argument places on the role of action in the production of self-consciousness leads me to another question: If action is so
important, where is the action in this play? The center of the drama regis-
ters this ambivalence. It portrays a great crime that is hardly a crime at all,
not only because Mortimer has been betrayed into it, but also because it is
at most a crime of omission, an abandonment rather than a stabbing, a failure to do rather than a doing. Even the omission is twofold; that strange
insistence on the forgotten scrip of food—and surely to abandon Herbert
even with it would have been to consign him to death—must in part be
intended to further narrow the gap between Mortimer's guilt and innocence.[36] Consider Mortimer's own analysis of his deed:

> A hideous plot, against the soul of man:
> It took effect—and yet I baffled it,
> In *some* degree. (2113–15)

Note the passive construction applied to the crime: the plot "took effect."
Mortimer reserves the active voice for his partial baffling of Rivers's plan, presumably referring to his decision to desert Herbert on the heath rather than
kill him. Yet Wordsworth knew that crimes of omission are still crimes. In fact,
in *A Letter to the Bishop of Llandaff* he made precisely this point in reference
to the lack of action on issues of reform that prevailed in English politics:

> As a teacher of religion your lordship cannot be ignorant of a class of
> breaches of duty which may be denominated faults of omission. You pro-
> fess to give your opinions upon the present turbulent crisis, expressing a
> wish that they may have some effect in tranquilizing the minds of the peo-
> ple. From your silence respecting the general call for a parliamentary
> reform, . . . what can be supposed but that you are a determined enemy
> to the redress of what the people of England call and feel to be grievances?[37]

Still, Wordsworth himself maintained his silence with regard to reform, not
least by withholding the publication of this very pamphlet. Crimes of inaction play as great a role in his story in France as those of action: just think
of his abandonment of Annette and Caroline. This failure to act must have
stood as one of the psychologically most devastating aspects of his involve-

ment in France and must in part lie behind the crime of abandonment in *The Borderers.*

Many critics have compared *The Borderers* to *Othello,* and Wordsworth (as the essay on Rivers makes clear) has Iago in mind when forming his antihero's character. But his play also bears traces of reflection on *Hamlet,* and the parallels between Mortimer and the Prince of Denmark, who both believe they must murder to secure justice and do so only after much hesitation, bring to the foreground a new set of concerns. While Rivers's relation to Iago makes sense of Wordsworth's position regarding his revolutionary *actions,* Mortimer's similarity to Hamlet provides a better entrance into an exploration of his guilt about his revolutionary *inactions.* Looked at through the lens of *Hamlet, The Borderers* urges audiences to reconsider their understanding of action in a manner that will allow Wordsworth to redefine its nature, with important consequences for his poetic project. Wordsworth's play hovers between asserting a connection between action and self-consciousness and asserting a connection between inaction and self-consciousness. To say this is to claim that Wordsworth was not resolved in his attitudes toward action when he wrote the play. But it is also to suggest that the process of writing *The Borderers* helped him to formulate the question as one concerning action.

Wordsworth greatly admired *Hamlet.* The poet who claimed "the mind of Man" as his "haunt and the main region of [his] song" said of the tragedy, "There is more mind in Hamlet than in any other play, more knowledge of human nature."[38] Hamlet's infamous "conscience"—really his *consciousness,* the quality of mind that here refuses to embrace that which it cannot know—causes the currents of enterprise to "turn awry, / And lose the name of action."[39] But critics since Coleridge have argued that Hamlet's self-consciousness is both product and cause of his delay. Coleridge actually quotes the "Action is transitory" passage from *The Borderers* in a lecture on *Hamlet,* after noting the Prince's "great, enormous, intellectual activity, and a consequent proportionate aversion to real action, with all its symptoms and accompanying qualities."[40] While Coleridge sees inaction as a consequence of Hamlet's reflectiveness, we get the soliloquies that give us such a powerful sense of Hamlet's identity largely because of his inaction. So if we saw previously how action could lead to self-consciousness, the connection of *The Borderers* to *Hamlet* suggests that inaction can foster reflection.

The comparison to Hamlet can also help make sense of the crime at the heart of *The Borderers.* In Wordsworth's tale, Mortimer's hesitation at killing Herbert involves conscience in its modern sense:

I cannot do it:
Twice did I spring to grasp his withered throat,
When such a sudden weakness fell on me,
I could have dropped asleep upon his breast. (II.iii.195–98)

The image is startlingly vivid: the enraged Mortimer, about to pounce on the fatherly figure of the old man, collapses into a desire to return to the comforts of infancy. This wish to regress to the natural state of dependence upon the parent supplants the unnatural act of parricide. Faced with the need to serve as Herbert's judge and executioner, Mortimer desires the escape of sleep. While Hamlet fears his dreams, Mortimer embraces them, almost narcoleptically. Hamlet's situation is of course different: he is required to kill the unnatural father in order to avenge the natural. Yet each man refuses to act, attempting to avoid the pressures of political account-ability. Moreover, for both protagonists, the act of parricide relates to issues of memory—not least because as David Erdman has pointed out in relation to *The Borderers,* it stands in place of regicide (in *Hamlet,* the "par-ricide" is literally also a regicide).[41] The father represents the past, so for Wordsworth, parricide represents the ultimate crime: a break with one's own past, a refusal of memory.

A casual allusion in *The Prelude* emphasizes how Wordsworth uses *Hamlet* to demonstrate his personalized sense of history and accountability:

I thought of those September massacres,
Divided from me by a little month,
And felt and touched them. (*Prelude* X.63–66)

That "little month" refers to the small space of time between Hamlet's father's death and his mother's remarriage. Like Hamlet, Wordsworth is horrified by how much can change in a brief period, about how easily the rest of the world can forget.[42] As Hamlet must watch helplessly while Claudius takes from him, in the month following his father's death, both crown and mother, Wordsworth waits powerlessly on the sidelines dur-ing the French Revolution, divided by accidents of time and the fact of his foreignness from the history that rages about him.[43] And like Mortimer, Wordsworth is unable to act, but his very impotence becomes a form of action for which he holds himself liable—he should have *done* something. Although the danger for Mortimer lies in a temptation to action (that is, to the murder of Herbert), his eventual crime is one of inaction. Incapable of attacking the old man physically, he leaves

Herbert to the elements, abdicating responsibility by declaring him God's victim, not his own:

> Here will I leave him—here—All-seeing God!
> Such as *he* is, and sore perplexed as I am,
> I will commit him to this final *Ordeal!* (1391–93)

Mortimer stands with Hamlet on the border between action and inaction. In this way, he expresses the duality of Wordsworth's guilt: on the one hand, the complicity in action he feels for having supported the Revolution; on the other, his shame of inaction for not having worked to stop the Terror and for the abandonment of Annette and Caroline.

By making the action that lies at the very heart of his drama a kind of nonaction, Wordsworth, even as he writes *The Borderers,* has already aligned himself with the inward focus of his later poetry, in which concern for the "moving accident" is replaced by an interest in "silent suffering."[44] Wordsworth cares as much about inaction—internalized action—as about action, as his play's well-documented relationship to closet drama (that favorite Romantic genre) indicates.[45] While he seems originally to have intended the play for production, in the 1842 Note about the work, he (rather defensively) insists that "it was first written . . . without any view to its exhibition upon the stage."[46] Wordsworth's one drama thus presents a fitting contribution from one who will later disparagingly dispense with "sickly and stupid German Tragedies."[47]

Charles Lamb argued that the Romantic love of closet drama stemmed from a fear of closure, from a longing for an infinitude that is incommensurable with the transitory nature of action. He described his response to having seen a great performance of a play by Shakespeare in his youth:

> It seemed to embody and realize conceptions which had hitherto assumed no distinct shape. But dearly do we pay all our life after for this juvenile pleasure, this sense of distinctness. When the novelty is past, we find to our cost that instead of realizing an idea, we have only materialized and brought down a fine vision to the standard of flesh and blood. We have let go a dream, in quest of an unattainable substance.[48]

Wordsworth expresses the same sense of disappointment upon first seeing Mont Blanc, when he "grieve[s] / To have a soulless image on the eye / Which had usurped upon a living thought" (*Prelude* VI.453–55). The sublime is incompatible with embodied action, the province of the theater.

Lamb wrote of the characters of Shakespeare (and he might well have had Rivers and Mortimer in mind, too) that they

> are so much the objects of meditation rather than of interest or curiosity as to their action that while we are reading any of his great criminal characters,—Macbeth, Richard, even Iago,—we think not so much of the crimes which they commit, as of the ambition, the aspiring spirit, the intellectual activity, which prompts them to overleap these moral fences. . . . But when we see these things represented the acts which they do are comparatively every thing, their impulses nothing.[49]

Intellectual activity is what matters, not action. Self-consciousness represents the ultimate human experience, and self-consciousness is an act of mind, not of body.

So the mind can be a center of its own kind of drama—a psychic one. In the nightmare trial sequence from *The Prelude,* Wordsworth describes his response to his involvements in France as an internalized dialogue in which he plays the roles of accused and judge, defense and prosecution:

> Through months, through years, long after the last beat
> Of those atrocities . . .
> I scarcely had one night of quiet sleep.
> Such ghastly visions had I of despair,
> And tyranny, and implements of death,
> And long orations which in dreams I pleaded
> Before unjust tribunals, with a voice
> Labouring, a brain confounded, and a sense
> Of treachery and desertion in the place
> The holiest that I knew of—my own soul.[50] (*Prelude* X.371–72, 374–81)

What he recounts bears some resemblance to the two-in-one of thinking that Hannah Arendt discusses in *The Life of the Mind:*

> Nothing perhaps indicates more strongly that man exists *essentially* in the plural than that his solitude actualizes his merely being conscious of himself . . . into a *duality* during the thinking activity. It is this duality of myself with myself that makes thinking a true activity, in which I am both the one who asks and the one who answers. Thinking can become dialectical and critical because it goes through this questioning and answering process.[51]

Thinking is a "true activity" because soliloquy is dialogue. Out of this dialogue, both consciousness and conscience develop.[52] For Wordsworth, the activity often has to do with memory—a conversation takes place between present and past selves—as in "Tintern Abbey" or the "Two consciousnesses" passage of *The Prelude*. Bromwich has remarked that "About the time that he completed his work on the *Lyrical Ballads,* [Wordsworth] began to see that the link between one moment and another in a single mind could have the resonance, and oddly something also of the moral weight, of a revelation between moments in two minds."[53] I believe that he realized this even earlier, when he was working on *The Borderers.* In this play, as in *Hamlet,* the dialogue between me and myself—soliloquy—stands behind much of the dramatic dialogue. The conversations between Rivers and Mortimer, Rivers's "shadow" (V.i.33), are versions of a deeper conversation Wordsworth is having with both past and present selves.

And this conversation has lasting consequences for both Wordsworth's poetry and his politics. In 1798, Coleridge sent a letter to his brother, concerning his dismissal of politics: "I wish to be a good man & a Christian—but I am no Whig, no Reformist, no Republican." He had retired to the country "to muse on fundamental & general causes." Then he added an extraordinary claim:

> I love fields & woods & mounta[ins] with almost a visionary fondness—and because I have found benevolence & quietness growing within me as that fondness [has] increased, therefore I should wish to be the means of implanting it in others—& to destroy the bad passions not by combating them, but by keeping them in *inaction*.[54]

Coleridge sounds much more like Wordsworth than himself here. The letter testifies to his friend's remarkable powers of influence. Yet inaction can be a public virtue as well as a private one—in fact, it can be public by virtue of its privacy, by virtue of its independence. Consider Hannah Arendt's thoughts, arising out of the ashes of a Holocaust so much more devastating than the Reign of Terror. She sees thinking as being able to "prevent catastrophes" caused by the bureaucratization of cruelty by providing us with a stopping point. Paradoxically, thought becomes a form of action precisely in its tendency to oppose action:

> When everybody is swept away unthinkingly by what everybody else does and believes in, those who think are drawn out of hiding because their refusal to join in is conspicuous and thereby becomes *a kind of action.* In

such emergencies, it turns out that the purging component of thinking . . .
is political by implication.[55]

For Wordsworth, though, thinking has as much to do with suffering as
with action. When Rivers reveals his plot to Mortimer, he tells him that
his sin will be his salvation: "Enough is done to save you from the curse /
Of living without knowledge that you live. / You will be taught to think"
(IV.ii.204–6). The later version of the play replaces the final line quoted
with "Now you are suffering," as though thought and suffering were
equivalent processes. In the Preface to *Lyrical Ballads,* Wordsworth reflects
on the symbiotic relationship between thought and feeling: "our continued influxes of feeling are modified and directed by our thoughts, which
are indeed the representatives of our past feelings."[56] Emotions (and suffering in particular), Wordsworth seems to want to argue, can be composed
of ideas as forceful—as difficult and worthy of consideration—as those of
any "independent intellect." It is a belief worth keeping in mind when we
consider his attitude toward characters like Johnny, the idiot boy, or
Margaret, or the Leech Gatherer. And as Lionel Trilling points out, "if
between sentiments and ideas there is a natural connection so close as to
amount to a kind of identity, then the connection between literature and
politics will be seen as a very immediate one."[57] The idea must have struck
Wordsworth, also.

Yet while Wordsworth's interest in internalization in *The Borderers*
seems to suggest the moral possibilities of inaction and suffering in a time
of revolutionary fervor, at the same time he is critical of such a stance.
Because Mortimer does nothing, he kills a good man. Wordsworth's confusion yields inevitable frustration. If we are not to act, what are we to *do?*
Unlike Coleridge or Keats or Shelley, Wordsworth rarely strikes a con-
vincingly sustained note of self-criticism. Usually, moments of doubt are
quickly followed upon by compensatory recognition, as in "Resolution
and Independence"; often, one gets the sense that Wordsworth is secretly
proud of what he presents as a flaw. But in *The Borderers,* the critique feels
very real, a fact that stands behind the genuine force of the work.
Wordsworth articulates his frustration through Mortimer's awareness of
the apparent impotence of verbal appeals—like, for example, those made
by poetry:

Why may we speak these things, and do no more,
Why should a thrust of the arm have such a power,
And words that tell these things be heard in vain? (2237–39)

Hence Mortimer's envy of the worm

> that, underneath a stone whose weight
> Would crush the lion's paw with mortal anguish,
> Doth lodge, and feed, and coil, and sleep, in safety. (1794–96)

The intensity of Mortimer's desire to be outside of the political fray must have some source in Wordsworth's experiences in France. Note again the longing that Mortimer expresses for sleep, the ultimate in (living) physical inactivity.

 At the end of *The Borderers,* when Rivers expresses his wish to go with Mortimer to Palestine, where they will find a less "paltry field for enterprise" (2251), Mortimer proves that he has learned his lesson:

> Men are there, millions, Rivers,
> Who with bare hands would have plucked out thy heart
> And flung it to the dogs: but I am raised
> Above, or sunk below, all further sense
> Of provocation. (2260–64)[58]

This is not simply Christian quietism, a "turn the other cheek" mentality. Mortimer now recognizes his capacity for action, but he also knows his duty: "there lies not now / Within the compass of a mortal thought, / A deed that I would shrink from;—but to endure, / That is my destiny" (2267–70). The field of action no longer appeals to him, although Mortimer seems unsure whether the change in him is a noble one— whether he has been "raised above" action or has "sunk below" it—as I have argued that Wordsworth is unsure in this play as to whether action or inaction is the best route toward self-consciousness. The play concludes appropriately with a final bow and flourish to *Hamlet.* Mortimer calls on Lacy, his Horatio, to "Raise on that dreary Waste a monument / That may record my story" (2294–95). Words take over from deeds as the curtain falls on the scene. It is as though Wordsworth were fulfilling the prophesy of the epigraph from Pope that he appended to his play:

> Of human actions reason though you can,
> It may be reason, but it is not man;
> His principle of action once explore,
> That instant 'tis his principle no more.[59]

Having explored the principle of action, Wordsworth abandons it.

The White Doe of Rylstone; or, The Fate of the Nortons

If *The Borderers* allows for two mutually exclusive and yet coexistent analy-
ses of the relationship between action and consciousness, *The White Doe of
Rylstone* also incorporates two perspectives on issues of action, indicated
already by the titles Wordsworth offers for his poem. The preferred title
suggests a lyrical treatment similar to "Hart-leap Well," another poem by
Wordsworth about a place in which a deer is the genius loci. But the alternative title hints at the action-filled ballad "The Rising in the North" that
served as Wordsworth's source for his tale, which he notably (given the epic
intents of his poem) considers to be "much better than Virgil had for his
Aeneid."[60] The split parallels the narrative's two strands, one of which stays
with Emily (whom the story associates with the Doe) in her sufferings at
home, while the other follows her brother Francis's participation in the
revolt that brings on his family's fate. Wordsworth's ordering of his titles
should be taken as a normative judgment about the relative importance and
success of both the two plot lines and the kinds of action—or inaction—
they portray.

Like *The Borderers*, *The White Doe* takes on the theme of revolution by
representing a conflict far in the past, in this case the Catholic uprising
against the Protestant Queen Elizabeth. Again, the locale is northern, and
again we are presented with two main characters—here a brother and sister—who are versions not only of one another but also (as we shall see) of
their poet. The opening canto of the poem provides a frame to which
Wordsworth never returns that introduces the reader to the Doe and her
environment in Bolton Priory and describes, in the manner of "The
Thorn," a series of interpretations of her presence offered by a collection
of churchgoers.[61] The narrator then promises an accurate interpretation,
and the tale proper commences with a description of Emily, the sole
daughter of the Norton household, who has been forced against her religious conscience to embroider a banner for the Nortons to take into battle. While her father and most of her brothers are Catholic, Emily, like
Francis and their deceased mother, is Protestant. Francis also faces a crisis
of conscience. At first he refuses to join his father and brothers in the
revolt, trying instead to persuade Norton of the folly of his cause. But
when this attempt proves unsuccessful, he succumbs to his sense of loyalty to family and decides to follow them into battle. He insists, however,
that Emily stay at home, despite her desire to join the rest of her family;
"*Her duty is to stand and wait,*" Francis declares, invoking Milton's reflection that "They also serve who only stand and wait."[62]

The remaining five cantos alternate loosely between relating the story as Francis experiences it on the field of battle and as Emily hears it told back in Rylstone-hall by an old man whom she sends out as scout. Francis finds that his family has been imprisoned. His father makes of him one request: that he take from the enemy the banner that Emily had embroidered and return it to Bolton Priory. While Francis rescues the banner, he is killed before he can fulfill his mission. The final canto tells Emily's response to the tragedy. Initially, she succumbs to complete despair and—like Mortimer—"wander[s], long and far" (1630). Eventually Emily returns to the Priory, where she reencounters the White Doe. The Doe becomes her constant companion, giving her a renewed feeling of kinship with the world, to which she is again "tied" until her death (1883). The poem concludes by describing the Doe's loyal vigilance over Emily's grave.

As readers have argued from the start, Wordsworth ran into problems balancing the two strands of his narrative. In the initial version of the poem, Emily's role seems to have been much more limited in the opening cantos. For Coleridge, advising his friend in 1808 on the draft he had been sent, the imbalance was linked to what he called "a disproportion of the Accidents to the spiritual Incidents" in the work; in other words, Wordsworth's interest in the "filial Heroism" of Francis and his brothers was too divorced from the almost "separate (& doubtless most exquisit Poem) wholly *of* [Emily]."[63] While Coleridge's complaint about disproportion in the poem targets its lack of outward action (what he calls "Accidents"), he seems nevertheless to prefer Emily's lyrical, "spiritual" portion of the narrative. Compare Geoffrey Hartman's assessment of Coleridge's comment: "Coleridge saw at once that there were really two stories: the ballad of Emily (almost totally Wordsworth's own) and the ballad of the revolt (based on historical tradition)."[64] Both Coleridge and Hartman imply that there is something un-Wordsworthian about Francis's story. In part, in what follows, I am trying to revise this estimation of especially that latter "part" of the poem by suggesting that in *The White Doe of Rylstone*, we have in fact not two but three very Wordsworthian narratives (adding the story of the Doe herself, with whom the poem begins and ends): the first, of Wordsworth of the period of the French Revolution, as he actually had been; the second, of Wordsworth as he wished to be known, as he came to mythologize himself; and the third, of Wordsworth as he would strive (almost incomprehensibly) to become.

An earlier letter to Coleridge suggests Wordsworth would have been prepared for his friend's objection:

> I also told Lamb that I did not think the Poem could ever be popular . . .
> because the main catastrophe was not a material but an intellectual one; I
> said to him further that it could not be popular because some of the prin-
> cipal objects and agents, such as the Banner and the Doe, produced their
> influences and effects not by powers naturally inherent in them, but such as
> they were endued with by the Imagination of the human minds on whom
> they operated.[65]

In both of these points, Wordsworth calls attention to his poem's interest
in the inner life—the intellectual, the imaginative—rather than its outward
manifestations. In this, it represents a narrative parallel to the closet
drama. Note how no mention is made at this point of his human actors.
Instead, Wordsworth writes first of two things at the center of the narrative that are important not because of their material nature but because of
their effect on the subjects who encounter them.[66] Moreover, Wordsworth
describes the banner and the Doe as not just objects, but also "agents," as
though the agency of the people in his tale had been displaced onto them.

This choice of words makes sense, as Wordsworth recognized that the
problem with his poem was one of action. He continues his letter:

> further, that the principle of action in all the characters, as in the Old Man,
> and his Sons, and Francis, . . . was throughout imaginative; and that all
> action (save the main traditionary tragedy), i.e., all the action proceeding
> from the will of the chief agents, was fine-spun and inobtrusive, conso-
> nant in this to the principle from which it flowed, and in harmony with
> the shadowy influence of the Doe, by whom the poem is introduced, and
> in whom it ends.[67]

In calling his principle of action "imaginative" and his action "fine-spun
and inobtrusive," Wordsworth suggests that the Doe, in her very ghostli-
ness, represents the principle of action expressed by the narrative as a
whole. In part, Wordsworth wanted to distinguish the action of the poem
from the action of traditional ballads—his own ballads are *lyrical*. As a
reviewer in *The Eclectic* put it, in terms remarkably similar to
Wordsworth's description of his work, the reader expects "some busy narrative of lofty adventure, such as Walter Scott's tales had led us to associate with the metre," but instead is "forced to stand in Rylstone
Church-yard and look all the while at a White Doe, and listen all the
while to a rhapsody . . . upon its whiteness, and brightness, and famous-
ness, and holiness."[68] In other words, the poem forces us to assume

Emily's position in regard to its events; like hers, our duty is to stand and wait—and think.

So when in 1843, in the Fenwick Note to the poem, Wordsworth reflected back on his work, his comments contain a certain ambiguity. "Everything that is attempted by the principal personages in 'The White Doe' fails, so far as its object is external and substantial," he admitted, but "So far as it is moral and spiritual it succeeds."[69] On the one hand, Wordsworth is giving us an assessment of his poem as a literary work: like Coleridge, he seems to have thought he had succeeded with Emily's plot but failed with that of the Norton uprising. But on the other hand, the passage can be read as an indictment of outward action in the world: "moral" in this analysis is the opposite of "external," in the same way that "spiritual" obviously stands in contrast with "substantial." So attempts at external acts will necessarily fail, because the structure of action contains inherent flaws. Consider, for example, the bind in which the narrative places Francis: he must betray either his family or his God; anything he does will involve him in sin. Wordsworth's remark calls to mind an observation from *The Convention of Cintra* (1808) (ironically, a political pamphlet arguing for English activism in fighting French oppression of the Spanish): "The true sorrow of humanity consists in this;—not that the mind of man fails; but that the course and demands of action and of life so rarely correspond with the dignity and intensity of human desires."[70] Both passages point to the necessary failure of action in comparison to possible successes in the mind of man. Action inadequately represents the mind, just as Wordsworth's poem inadequately represents action. Thus when in 1836 Wordsworth declared that *The White Doe* was "in conception, the highest work he had ever produced," he was really arguing for its achievement in the only realm in which genuine success is possible: the mind.[71] As *Hamlet's* Player King declares, "Our thoughts are ours, their ends none of our own."[72]

In the Fenwick Note, Wordsworth related his success in the poem to its interest in the will rather than action: "The mere physical action was all unsuccessful; but the true action of the poem was spiritual—the subduing of the will and all inferior passion, to the perfect purifying and spiritualizing of the intellectual nature."[73] The subduing of the will is the subject of Wordsworth's great "Ode to Duty" (composed 1804–7), which resonates deeply in Wordsworth's treatment of Emily, as we shall see. But the comment also recalls the sonnet Advertisement to *The White Doe,* added in 1820, only to be removed in 1827. The sonnet begins:

"Weak is the will of Man, his judgement blind;
Remembrance persecutes, and Hope betrays;
Heavy is woe;—and joy, for human kind,
A mournful thing, so transient is the blaze!"
(p. 76; Wordsworth's quotation marks)

Wordsworth somewhat counters this view in the rest of the sonnet, where he discourses on the healing powers of Imagination and Faith that are so central to his narrative. But in 1832, he replaced the prefatory poem with the lines from *The Borderers* (followed immediately by their own parallel religious appendix, describing the solace for suffering to be found by "toil-ing" with "patient thought" or being "wafted" on "wings of prayer"). I repeat them here for comparison:

Action is transitory—a step, a blow,
The motion of a muscle—this way or that—
'Tis done; & in the after-vacancy
We wonder at ourselves like men betrayed:
Suffering is permanent obscure & dark,
And has the nature of infinity. (p. 77)

The betrayal of action replaces that of hope, the transience of action stands in for that of joy, and the persecution of remembrance gives way to won-der at the after-vacancy of action.

Yet action differs from volition by its externality, by, to be precise, "the motion of a muscle." Only in a narrative in which the will is allowed so little outlet in action can these passages be substituted for one another without a shift in meaning; it is as though Wordsworth—and the poem as a whole—forces volition and action to be equated: to will something (or even to hope for it) is as much as to do it.[74] To say this is to claim that *The White Doe* works to push action off its narrative surface by internalizing it. I have argued for a sequential reading of the above passage: action is transitory, but it causes per-manent suffering, and hence self-consciousness. I have also shown how the role of inaction in *The Borderers* complicates the connection between action and self-consciousness by suggesting that an act of omission can also gener-ate reflection. But now, I shall demonstrate that in *The White Doe of Rylstone*, Wordsworth attempts to do away with the need for action altogether—just as he kills off the Norton men, including even the Mortimer-like Francis—and in the process rewrites his own history of involvement with the Revolution. Action is transitory and suffering permanent. Why then act at all?

ᴇᵈ

If one were to search for a real proponent of action in Wordsworth's *White Doe of Rylstone,* it would be found in old Norton, a figure of patriarchal heroism. Willard Spiegelman has argued that "thematically, the poem concerns types of heroic behavior, one active, the other passive, and refuses to acknowledge the superiority of either."[75] But Norton (whom Spiegelman properly takes to be the work's advocate of action) seems to represent the impossibly simple, and therefore dangerously outmoded, virtue of a past era, and his bold action leads his family to its disastrous fate, the "traditionary tragedy" of which Wordsworth wrote. Moreover, from the perspective of the poem, his Catholicism links his virtue inseparably to superstition. So Wordsworth lacks interest in Norton; his real concern is reserved for the comparison between the forms of action—or, rather, inaction—proposed by Francis and Emily, the poem's two protagonists.[76]

The first thing to notice is just how similar the state of affairs in the poem is to that Wordsworth faced during the French Revolution. Consider Old Norton's remarks about the failure of the revolt:

> Might this our enterprise have sped,
> Change wide and deep the Land had seen,
> A renovation from the dead,
> A spring-tide of immortal green. (1276–79)

Such utopian hope was characteristic of France in the early 1790s, as experienced by the young Wordsworth. Yet Wordsworth's position soon became complicated by conflicting loyalties. In a scenario represented in *The White Doe* by the split in the Norton family's religious affiliations, Wordsworth's republican beliefs stood in opposition to those of his royalist lover, who was increasingly endangered as the Terror progressed. Moreover, Wordsworth's loyalty to France alienated him from his fellow citizens upon his return to England, as *The Prelude* movingly recounts. Tempestuous times sever the organic self from its well-rooted past:

> I, who with the breeze
> Had played, a green leaf on the blessèd tree
> Of my belovèd country, nor had wished
> For happier fortune than to wither there,
> Now from my pleasant station was cut off
> And tossed about in whirlwinds. (*Prelude* X.254)

Francis suffers just such alienation from his family and northern country-
men. They label him a "coward" (928) for standing by his beliefs and
avoiding the battle. And his religious brethren offer no alternative community. One recalls how in *The Borderers* Herbert had branded Mortimer
a "wild Freebooter," one who "upon the borders of the Tweed, / Doth prey
alike on two distracted countries, / Traitor to both" (207, 208–10). Francis
soon discovers that Elizabeth's soldiers despise him for his disloyalty to his
family:

> *He* did not arm, he walked aloof!
> For why?—to save his Father's Land;
> Worst Traitor of them all is he,
> A Traitor dark and cowardly! (1482–85)

The sense of "treachery and desertion" (*Prelude* X.380) affects both
Wordsworth and Francis strongly as they find themselves taking sides in a
struggle against their compatriots.

So just as Wordsworth sits silently in church "like an uninvited guest . . .
/ Whom no one owned" (*Prelude* X.273–74), surrounded by his fellow
Englishmen but feeling only more strongly for that the divide between him
and them, Francis watches alone from above the field of battle, like

> One
> With unparticipated gaze;
> Who 'mong these thousands friend hath none,
> And treads in solitary ways. (760–63)[77]

The idea of "unparticipated gaze"—marvelous phrase—hints at the curse
of spectatorship that Wordsworth must have experienced while witnessing
the whirlwind of revolutionary activity surrounding him. It also calls to
mind what William Jewett has described in relationship to *The Borderers*
as "the failure of the specular mechanism of moral discourse"—that is, the
distinction between sympathetic spectatorship and action.[78] Or as David
Marshall puts it, Wordsworth's play "insists that the eyewitnesses of its
tragedy acknowledge their roles as eyewitnesses: in acting the role of an eye-
witness who cannot cross the border of the stage and leave the silence and
inaction, the audience enters the scene of the crime that the theater itself
compulsively returns to and repeats night after night."[79] Wordsworth
exhibits the compulsion of repetition in his work. He attempts to compensate for his own "inaction" by filling the "silence" with his obsessively

recurring memories. When he places Francis alone atop that hillside, gazing down upon the battle that rages below him, he is reliving the experience of his own Revolution.

Given that both Mortimer and Francis resemble Wordsworth, it should
come as no surprise they also resemble one another. The connection
between Wordsworth and his two heroes is hinted at by the fact that
Francis is almost able to persuade one of his brothers, suggestively named
Marmaduke—the name Wordsworth gives to Mortimer in the revised version of *The Borderers*—of the hopelessness of the Nortons' cause. The
"pensive" Marmaduke, who of all the Norton men is most like Francis,
seems at first to be "yielding inwardly" to his brother's arguments (495).
The resemblance appears most distinctly, though, in the description of
Francis's chief action in the drama: his retrieval of the banner. With "a look
of calm command," Francis takes the banner from a soldier's hand. But it
is not until later that he realizes his deed:

> He marked not, heard not as he fled;
> All but the suffering heart was dead
> For him abandoned to blank awe,
> To vacancy, and horror strong:
> And the first object which he saw,
> With conscious sight, as he swept along—
> It was the banner in his hand!
> He felt—and made a sudden stand.
>
> He looked about like one betrayed:
> What hath he done? (p. 129)[80]

Once again, the by-now-familiar collection of terms: the vacancy, the
blank awe, the suffering, and, above all, the betrayal into action.
Somewhere between unconsciously being swept along and consciously seeing the banner in his hand (the source and locus of action), Francis has
shared Mortimer's experience in *The Borderers*. Wordsworth has com-
pressed the crisis of action explored by his earlier work into a few lines, and
his decision to annex the corresponding lines from the play to this new
poem shows his conscious recognition of the connection between the
texts.

Like Mortimer's forgetting of Herbert's scrip of food, Francis's
"crime"—if in fact crime it be—is involuntary. And in a way, this excuses
it. Given that his loyalties are divided and that his duties to family and to

his religion are irreconcilable, anything he could do would have to go against his conscience. Again, we can see how Wordsworth's revolutionary experiences would have made him acutely aware of this difficulty. But to do nothing would be a choice in itself, as Wordsworth would have recognized. Wordsworth "saves" Francis by letting him act involuntarily. By dividing action from intention, Francis can remain in some sense "true" to both sets of responsibilities. Appropriately, he responds with his acts of body to the demands of his father, the poem's chief advocate of action, and with his intentions to his religion, the internally driven Protestantism.

Wordsworth had already emphasized the involuntary nature of Francis's actions at an earlier point in the text—as in *The Borderers,* it becomes clear that we are witnessing a tragedy of repetition. A remarkable sequence shows just how complicated the path from intention to action can be and demonstrates how the conflict Francis faces tears him apart, body and soul. Wordsworth tells us how Francis "unknowingly" grabs a lance to himself only seconds before declaring his inability to join his father and brothers: "With theirs my efforts cannot blend, / I cannot for such cause contend" (511–12). But pulled by love for his family, he revises his position by drawing on the distinction between will and deed: "Their aims I utterly forswear; / But I in body will be there" (513–14). Only *after* declaring his intention to follow his family with "an empty hand" (519) does he notice his hold on the lance. Immediately, he throws the weapon away: "Spurned it, like something that would stand / Between him and the pure intent / Of love on which his soul is bent" (522–24).

Both passage and poem demonstrate that pure intent and action can never coincide, precisely because intentions necessarily become muddied in the impure medium of the world; "the course and demands of action and of life so rarely correspond with the dignity and intensity of human desires" (as Wordsworth noted in *The Convention of Cintra*). Action fails to represent intent. So we need some better source for the self than in deeds—something more essential to it, less liable to the corruption that comes from external circumstances. Robert Langbaum makes this point in relation to *The Borderers* when he notes that although Rivers and Mortimer "do" the same thing, our moral judgment of them differs: "The difference depends not on what the characters *do* but on what they *are.*"[81] Or consider Kant's observation: "even the strictest examination can never lead us entirely behind the secret incentives, for, when moral worth is in question, it is not a matter of actions which one sees but of their inner principles which one does not see."[82] For Kant, the problem of recognizing moral worth is rendered almost impossible because of the difficulty in seeing behind the mechanism of action. Real worth lies veiled behind the accidents of the phenomenal world. The incompatibility of ends—like Francis's desire to maintain loyalty to both his religion and his family—further obscures our ability to see character through action. Whether or not he joins in the battle, his actions will conceal an essential aspect of his character.

Hence the uneasy split we see in Francis between his active Norton self and his willing Protestant self. But the division between action and intention, while it rescues Francis from the dilemma in which he finds himself, proves costly. After retrieving the banner from the enemy, Francis is left wondering: "How has the Banner clung so fast / To a palsied and unconscious hand" (p. 130)? As in *The Borderers,* a sense of self-consciousness develops out of the wonder: "No choice is left, the deed is mine—" (1448). His act is constitutive of his self—it is *his.* But divorced from intention, it also creates a kind of emptiness in Francis, a loss of agency: "No choice is left." Instead of acting for himself, Francis seems to be providing the body for the enactment of the wishes of his dead relatives. When earlier Francis had unconsciously grasped hold of the lance, he had simultaneously remarked (twice) on the departure of his father and brothers: "Gone are they" (459, 466). Now, as if to emphasize the parallels between the two moments of unconscious action, Wordsworth repeats the inverted word order. Francis turns from his admission of responsibility for his act, "the deed is mine—," immediately to his next task, "Dead are they, dead!—and I will go" (1449). With his family "gone" in a deeper sense, Francis must "go" himself. And the odd slippage of vowel sounds between *deed* and *dead* proves prophetic. Having already relinquished his will, he now must relinquish his body; having done, he now must die. In his final act, appropriately committed "instinctively" (1505)—that is, once again, without conscious volition—Francis seizes a lance from a pikeman who has advanced to regain the banner only to be brought down in the general onslaught.

I want to suggest that in killing Francis, Wordsworth attempts to lay to rest the ghost of his revolutionary self and all that self's involvements, however ambivalent, with the world of action. In place of that self he offers us another, revised version of who he was during the last decade of the eighteenth century: Emily. This might seem a curious claim, but we have seen already how closely Wordsworth affiliated himself with the poetics of her strand of *The White Doe.* The "passive stillness" (1090) she displays should be compared to the "wise passiveness" Wordsworth argues for in "Expostulation and Reply." Moreover, for anyone acquainted with the odd sense of removal from his fellow men so characteristic of much of Wordsworth's mature poetry, his description of Emily's self-containment should resonate strongly:

> Her soul doth in itself stand fast,
> Sustained by memory of the past
> And strength of Reason; held above
> The infirmities of mortal love;
> Undaunted, lofty, calm and stable,
> And awfully impenetrable. (1642–47)

Wordsworth shares his heroine's capacity for radical disinterestedness and her tendency to retreat into memory. Like Emily, he has been "taught to feel, perhaps too much, / The self-sufficing power of Solitude" (*Prelude* II.78–79). Self-sufficiency puts, after all, a premium on the very selfhood that has been so threatened by the turmoil of revolution.

The connections between Emily's narrative and the "Ode to Duty," a poem so clearly written in Wordsworth's own voice and completed at roughly the same time he wrote *The White Doe,* emphasize the link between the author and his creation. In the dedicatory poem to *The White Doe,* Wordsworth compares Emily's story to that of Spenser's Una; both tell "Of female patience winning firm repose" (p. 50). But in the Ode, in "long[ing] for a repose which ever is the same," Wordsworth proves his own desire for such patience. In lines later excluded from the published poem, he puns on the meaning of his Christian name: "Denial and restraint I prize / No farther than they breed a second Will more wise"—wise, that is, in passiveness. With Emily, as with Dorothy in "Tintern Abbey," the vessel for Wordsworth's second self turns out to be female, and a sister. In "Tintern Abbey," Wordsworth depicted Dorothy as possessing an animal-like innocence curiously like that of the Doe, who seems to serve in the final canto of the work, like Dorothy in the earlier poem, as a vessel for memories—"This lovely Chronicler of things / Long past, delights and sorrows" (1694–95). In contrast, Emily's womanhood does not detract from her rationality. Furthermore, her gender constrains her action in a fashion that saves her from the kind of the dilemmas in which Francis finds himself embroiled; her place cannot be on the battlefield with her brothers.[83] So in choosing a female self, Wordsworth helps distance himself from his revolutionary actions and excuse his revolutionary inactions. Because *"Her duty is to stand and wait,"* Emily can reflect on the horrible events occurring around her without being implicated in them. Instead, she can focus on her suffering and the suppression of her will to act.[84]

In the "Ode to Duty," Wordsworth quotes Raphael's injunction to Adam to be "lowly wise."[85] Milton's influence is also pervasive in *The White Doe,* in spite of the Dedication's reference to Spenser. And this makes sense if we consider that Wordsworth was thinking about his revolutionary experiences. Milton's belief that "They also serve who only stand and wait" can be read to reflect and anticipate his own complicated relationship to political activity during a period of civil war and unrest. Emily's heroism exhibits Miltonic ideals of restraint and denial, of resistance to the temptation of action. And like Milton, Wordsworth believes that such heroism can be figured as epic. In fact, in the Fenwick Note he quotes from Milton's Invocation to book IX of *Paradise Lost* when referring to the superiority of mental struggle like Emily's to the bodily battles that make up standard epic fare: "How insignificant a thing, for example, does personal prowess appear compared with the fortitude of patience and heroic martyrdom."[86] Wordsworth begins his epic quest of self-exploration, *The Prelude,* by alluding to the closing lines of *Paradise Lost:* "The earth is all before me" (*Prelude* I.17), but Emily's epic more closely resembles Milton's greatest poem of inaction: *Paradise Regained.* Geoffrey Hartman compares the "triumph of privacy" in *The White Doe* to Christ's at the end of Milton's poem.[87] Like Christ, Emily must repeatedly resist temptations—"Ah tempt me not!" (1104)—first to act, by joining her brothers, and finally, shockingly, to hope for their well-being (recall how the Son must avoid even the temptation to charity). As Evan Radcliffe has shown, her suffering—and Wordsworth frequently refers to her as "the Sufferer" (1024, 1579, 1721)—emphasizes the degree to which her role should be perceived as an "*imitatio Christi.*"[88]

Yet Emily does do something: she embroiders the banner. Like Wordsworth, she is an artist.[89] Wordsworth actually invokes Miltonic creation ("Thou from the first / Wast present, and with mighty wings outspread / Dove-like satst brooding on the vast Abyss / And mad'st it pregnant"[90]) in Old Norton's representation of his daughter at work:

> A maid o'er whom the blessed Dove
> Vouchsafed in gentleness to brood
> While she the holy work pursued. (673–75)

In implicitly comparing the banner to the poem on which so much of his own epic writing is based, he also compares Emily's art to his own.

But Emily's work also parallels the more overt deed of her brother in rescuing the banner. Like Francis, she acts out of loyalty to her family, not from internal conviction. The will behind her deed comes from her father: "She did in passiveness obey, / But her Faith leaned another way" (876–77). Her completion of the task set her is subjected to narrative criticism; we are told she fulfills her father's "headstrong will" "Too perfectly," as though she should have indicated her resistance more forcefully (353–54). Yet in a way, this resistance is encoded in the banner itself. As we shall see, "the banner of battle"[91] becomes a standard emblem for writers who wish to resurrect the possibility of heroic action or lament its passing. But the symbolism of Emily's banner is much more mixed. In another example of the way Wordsworth links Emily to Christ, the banner's embroidered picture—the five wounds of Christ—represents the Passion. The *OED*'s second definition for *passion* is "The being passive." Wordsworth's choice of image confuses the symbolic value of the banner by making it combine a subject closely affiliated with a suffering passivity with an object that signifies military action. In a way, then, the banner can be aligned more properly with Francis, who, like it, is caught between alternate impulses to action and inaction, than with the other Norton men, who stand firmly in the camp of action. Hence the graphic mingling in death of Francis's blood with that of Christ's wounds on the banner; as Martin Price points out, "They are not stained with Francis's blood but 'tinged more deeply,'" as though to suggest a reciprocal ministering of a sacrament.[92]

Yet the conflation between active and passive significations of the banner need not indicate in Emily, as it does in relation to Francis, the presence of a lasting internal conflict. In fact, Wordsworth intends us to see a more positive paradox in Emily's passivity, which, he wishes us to feel, is very much active. In the April 1808 letter to Coleridge, he told his friend that Emily "is intended to be honoured and loved for what she *endures,* and the manner in which she endures it; accomplishing a conquest over her own sorrows."[93] Conquest implies activity. As Radcliffe puts it, her resignation "appears as a willed choice, not as an abdication of will and choice"[94]; recall how Wordsworth, in the "Ode to Duty" declares "That [his] submissiveness was choice." Wordsworth argues for a connection between passion and action in his "Essay, Supplementary to the Preface" (1815):

> Passion, it must be observed, is derived from a word which signifies, *suffering;* but the connection which suffering has with effort, with exertion, and *action,* is immediate and inseparable. . . . To be moved . . . by a passion, is to be excited, often to external, and always to internal effort; whether for the continuance and strengthening of the passion, or for its suppression. [95] (original emphasis)

In Emily's case, her passion leads to an internal effort of suppression, as we have seen, and—after some years of very Wordsworthian wandering—yields the reward of her "lofty, calm, and stable, / And awfully impenetrable" consciousness. Emily's more resolute form of inaction, which finds outlet only in artistic (as opposed to bodily) deeds, allows her to survive intact the revolution that brought Francis to his death. Wordsworth dissociates himself from the kinds of autobiographical conflicts he presented through characters such as Rivers, Mortimer, and Francis, while Emily becomes the true representative of the poet's past: a revised "second self" who like her author has lived a life that "has been unusually barren of events."[96]

And her conquest proves to have generic ramifications. Wordsworth defended Emily's actionless story in the 1808 letter to Coleridge:

> When it is considered what has already been executed in Poetry, strange that a man cannot perceive . . . that this is the time when a man of genius may honourably take a station upon different ground. If he is to be a Dramatist, let him crowd his scene with gross and visible action; but if a narrative Poet, if the Poet is to be predominant over the Dramatist,—then let him see if there are no victories in the world of spirit, no changes, no commotions, no revolutions there, no fluxes and refluxes of the thoughts which may be made interesting by modest combination with the stiller actions of the bodily frame, or with the gentler movements and milder appearances of society and social intercourse, or the still more mild and gentle solicitations of irrational and inanimate nature.[97]

Wordsworth's Revolution is finally completed. Gone are the days of flirtation with action, of forays into the dramatic; he has chosen the color of his flag, and it is to be white, like the Doe after whom he entitles his poem. From now on, his struggles, like Emily's, will take place in the world of spirit. Yet the letter suggests a greater revolution already set into play, for in those "gentler movements and milder appearances of society and social intercourse," one can glimpse an opening onto a new domain: the world of the novel.

⁂

This is the world to which I wish to travel, although not before exploring a darkened passageway leading up to it: that inhabited by Arthur Hugh Clough and described in his "novel-in-verse," *Amours de Voyage.* It is important to recognize, though, that for all the usefulness of his ideas to the Victorian novelists, for all his influence upon them, Wordsworth has little of their everyday familiarity. If we are to see in Emily Wordsworth's revisionist history of his revolutionary self, then the Doe herself surely must represent some form of further apotheosis toward which he strives: "the still more mild and gentle solicitations of irrational and inanimate nature." From human to animal ("irrational" nature), and even further to mineral ("inanimate nature"), Wordsworth seems to be trying to extend to its utmost limits our comprehension of what can solicit from us a moral interest.

Emily already exhibits some of the genuine strangeness of Wordsworth's moral vision as it develops in response to his revolutionary experiences: his sense that those who care about those who do are in some way more admirable—and perhaps also more truly themselves—than those who do. Initially, on her return from her wanderings, Emily is "held above / The infirmities of mortal love" (1625–26). Wordsworth recognizes a sinister element to her awful impenetrability that leads him to demand of her the Mariner-like salvation in tears brought on by the ministrations of the Doe, tears that once again tie her, albeit but "faintly, faintly," to earth. Those ties, and their connection to tears, matter to him; as Wordsworth tells us at the start, he wishes to present us with "A tale of tears, a mortal story!" (336). After all, he is the poet for whom happiness must be found "in the very world which is the world / Of all of us, . . . / . . . or not at all" (*Prelude* X.726–28), who wishes to show his readers how the "Love of Nature" can "lead" to the "Love of Mankind," as the subtitle to book VIII of *The Prelude* puts it, and as the Doe, presumably, teaches Emily. Yet Wordsworth's morality can often appear a rather inhuman commodity. The Wanderer of *The Excursion* (the Pedlar of "The Ruined Cottage"), Wordsworth's greatest purveyor of the milk of human kindness, can "*afford* to suffer / With those whom he saw suffer" precisely because he has felt "No piteous revolutions" (*Excursion* I.370–71, 359; original emphasis).[98] It is a strange vision of sympathy, one that lacks the reciprocity of emotional experience one would expect from the poet who calls himself "a man speaking to men."[99]

Wordsworth seems to struggle over Emily's humanity in a way that he need not struggle with the Doe herself. As a creature of nature the Doe requires no emotional ties to connect her to the earth; her very being belongs to it. Nevertheless, Wordsworth clearly intends her to represent a form if not of sympathy, at least of comfort. The Doe first appears to Emily just after Francis has admonished her, twice, to "Hope nothing"

(530, 532). We can think of her as a representative of a kind of pure hope, one divorced from any potential for action—a passive hope that stands in the same place in the building of the self that will and action might otherwise have occupied. She is also a symbol of memory, as her ghostly presence in the poem, her lingering over Emily's grave, attests. In *The Excursion,* the Solitary expresses his desire for "The life where hope and memory are as one" (*Excursion* III.400), a life without revolutionary transitions in character. Yet such a life would also lack the genuine sense of time, of possible change, of action as an enabler of change. Where hope and memory are as one, can either be said truly to exist?

Wordsworth concludes *The White Doe of Rylstone* by musing on the Doe's "smile" as she looks down upon Emily's resting place: "Thou, thou art not a child of time, / But Daughter of the Eternal Prime!" (1928–29). Presumably, Emily's humanity renders her time bound—that is, subject to a death from which the Doe is protected by her lack of a distinct self. I am reminded of Keats's wonderful vision of "The vale of Soul-making":

> Call the world if you Please "The vale of Soul-making" Then you will find out the use of the world . . . I say 'Soul making' Soul as distinguished from an Intelligence—There may be intelligences or sparks of the divinity in millions—but they are not Souls till they acquire identities, till each one is personally itself. I[n]telligences are atoms of perception—they know and they see and they are pure, in short they are God—how then are Souls to be made? How then are these sparks which are God to have identity given them—so as ever to possess a bliss peculiar to each ones individual existence? How but by the medium of a world like this?[100]

Keats's humanism stands in stark contrast to Wordsworth's moral vision. Wordsworth suggests that death is desirable precisely because it presents a release from human individuation as we understand it. He may yearn to have his voice preserved in perpetuity upon the earth by a whole chorus of "second selves," but one feels that this is in part to compensate for the fact that identity in the Keatsian sense has no place in Wordsworth's conception of the afterlife. Think of Lucy, being "Rolled round in earth's diurnal course / With rocks and stones and trees." Here lies Wordsworth's most elementary understanding of the concept of Revolution.

Many of Wordsworth's more memorable human figures seem almost to have returned to the state of nature. Consider the much-discussed simile in "Resolution and Independence," where the Leech Gatherer melts first into the rock and then the sea beast, to which he is compared: "Such seemed this Man, not all alive nor dead, / Nor all asleep" (71–72). Again we are presented with what the Solitary in *The Excursion* calls "the universal instinct of repose" (*Excursion* III.397), like Wordsworth's longing in the "Ode to Duty" for "a repose which ever is the same," like Emily's tale of "female patience winning firm repose"—and also like Mortimer's desire for sleep. Note that in each of these cases, Wordsworth has no interest in the standard romantic ideology of the dream as a space of freedom and imagination. Rather, he is concerned with a form of self-containment, a selfhood strangely divorced from the activity of life: "A slumber did my spirit seal." While Wordsworth calls the Leech Gatherer "more than human," he is so in part because he is less than human. He demonstrates what Lionel Trilling has called "the morality of inertia," the morality of the lesser celandine, who withstands the storm not from "courage" nor from "choice," but by "Its necessity in being old." As Trilling reminds us, "How often the moral act is performed not because we are we but because we are there! This is the morality of habit, or the morality of biology."[101] Wordsworth, though, would contest Trilling on one point: "because we are we" and "because we are there" need not represent such separate motivations. It is possible to be most oneself by standing still on a spot, by rooting oneself to it, by simply being there.

⚜2⚜

The Case of Clough:

Amours de Voyage and the

Crisis of Action in Victorian Verse

Trust in nothing but in Providence and your own efforts. Never separate the two.

—Charles Dickens, *Bleak House*

IN A LECTURE on Wordsworth's poetry written in the early 1850s, the poet
Arthur Hugh Clough qualified his great admiration for his predecessor by
remarking on his conservative tendencies, singling out for particular
scrutiny his aversion to action. Quoting Wordsworth, Clough noted that
"The moving accident, as he says, was not his trade; of event and of action
his compositions are perfectly destitute."[1] Rather, according to Clough's
Wordsworth, "Blue sky and white clouds, larks and linnets, daisies and
celandines—these . . . are 'the proper subject of mankind'; not, as we used
to think, the wrath of Achilles, the guilt and remorse of Macbeth, the love
and despair of Othello." Clough ended his review with a warning:

> Nevertheless, we fear that the exclusive student of Wordsworth may go
> away with the strange persuasion that it is his business to walk about this
> world of life and action, and avoiding life and action, have his gentle
> thoughts excited by flowers and running waters and shadows on moun-
> tain-sides.

47

This we conceive is a grievous inherent error in Wordsworth. (*PPR* I: 324, 325)

Clough's comments are part of a larger debate in Victorian criticism concerning the appropriate role for action in poetry. The discussion often took the form of a comparison between subjective and objective poetry. Subjective poetry, essentially Romantic in origin and psychological in nature, is concerned with interior processes such as thought and emotion. Objective poetry, in contrast, is classical and corresponds to a poetry of action, action being defined by its external, bodily nature. The Victorian debate most famously centered on Matthew Arnold's programmatic Preface to his *Poems* (1853).[2] As much a manifesto for his times as was Wordsworth's Preface to *Lyrical Ballads,* Arnold's essay was also written as a response to Aristotle's dictates in the *Poetics* concerning the proper roles for action and character in drama. But the Preface to *Poems* came directly out of Arnold's conversations with his close friend Clough. The two poets were responding to what they perceived to be the dangerously subjective tenor of the age, in fact and in literature: its tendency to look inward rather than outward, to explore thoughts rather than deeds.

And in the middle of the nineteenth century, the battle over action became particularly visible in the generic tensions of narrative verse. Poets writing at a period of decline for Romantic poetry—and trying to engage with the subject matter of the increasingly popular Victorian novel—struggled with action as a necessary result of their struggles over genre. The result was the phenomenon of the long Victorian poem, frequently incorporating elements from a variety of genres. The question of generic hybridity and its relationship to the place of action and character in literature comes to the fore in one such poem: Arthur Hugh Clough's *Amours de Voyage* (written 1849, published 1858). Clough referred to *Amours* as his "5 act epistolary tragi-comedy, or comi-tragedy."[3] Moreover, the work, written as a series of letters composed in (mock) epic hexameters punctuated by lyrical elegiacs in a narrative voice, is also in many respects novelistic. Victorian critics were quick to point out this quality, largely on the basis of its presentation of character.[4] Its struggle with genre underlying an obvious concern with issues of action in its subject matter, *Amours de Voyage* provides a particularly revealing lens through which to explore the crisis in action in nineteenth-century thought and its influence on the literature of the period.

THE LIFE

To see how *Amours* relates to the wider atmosphere of crisis, it helps first to look at the story that developed around the life of its author. In doing so I follow in the footsteps not only of contemporaries of Clough, but also of modern critics, most of whom find it difficult to separate analysis of Clough's works from that of his life—for excellent reasons, as I hope will become clear.[5] While the following biographical material is by now familiar to scholars of Clough, I want to emphasize the degree to which "the myth of Clough's 'failure'" (as Michael Timko has referred to it) gained such a strong hold on the Victorian critical imagination because of its relationship to what I call the crisis of action.[6]

The popular version of Clough's life, most famously represented (albeit rather turgidly) by his friend Matthew Arnold in his elegy "Thyrsis" (1866), is of a man whose overacute sensitivity and hyperactive consciousness inhibited his ability to get things done:

> What though the music of thy rustic flute
> Kept not for long its happy, country tone;
> Lost it too soon, and learnt a stormy note
> Of men contention-tost, of men who groan,
> Which task'd thy pipe too sore, and tired thy throat—
> It fail'd, and thou wast mute![7]

Although Clough produced three major poems (*The Bothie of Tober-na-Vuolich* [1848],[8] *Amours de Voyage,* and *Dipsychus and the Spirit* [written 1850, first published, in an edited version, in 1862]) as well as numerous short works of great merit, his is a story of anticlimax. As G. H. Lewes wrote when reviewing his posthumous *Poems* (1862), "he was one of the prospectuses which never became works: one of that class whose unwritten poems, undemonstrated discoveries, or untested powers, are confidently announced as certain to carry everything before them, when they appear. Only they never do appear."[9] To a great extent, the myth is the product, ironically, of a single defining act. In 1848, after a few years of holding an Oriel Fellowship, Arthur Hugh Clough found himself unable to subscribe to the Thirty-nine Articles and relinquished his post. This decision prevented him from achieving the success both he and his contemporaries had expected. Clough's deed and its consequences undoubtedly led to his great sensitivity to problems surrounding action in the modern world, a sensitivity that his poetry dramatically reflects.

The favorite student of Dr. Arnold at Rugby, Clough was marked out
to be the great man of his generation at a time when the mantle of greatness was handed down like a crown from generation to generation.[10] He
was known by his friends at Oxford as "Citizen Clough" for his radical political beliefs—in particular, for his arguments against laissez-faire policies (what
Carlyle tellingly translated as "Donothingism"[11]). On a more practical level,
he acted as a distributor of meal tickets and administrator of a hospital and
soup kitchen for the Oxford Mendicity Society. But when Clough was infected
with skepticism in Oxford's heavy atmosphere of religious doubt, the disease crippled him. He wrote to his sister, "Until I know, I will wait: and if
I am not born with the power to discover, I will do what I can, with what
knowledge I have."[12]

Yet just how much one can do without belief is at issue. Perhaps, until
we know, all we can do is wait. As an anonymous reviewer pointed out in
reference to Clough's early poem, "Qui Laborat, Orat" ("he who labors, prays"),
this is "a beautiful thought concerning one who has never been taught to
pray, [but] a pernicious falsehood about one who has rejected the practice.
With such a one it will soon be *Qui non orat, nec laborat!*"[13] Clough's mentor Carlyle bewailed the crisis in faith by linking it to the passing of an age
of natural action:

> Action, in those old days, was easy, was voluntary, for the divine worth of
> human things lay acknowledged. . . .
>   How changed in these new days! . . . Heroic Action is paralysed; for what
> worth now remains unquestionable with [the youth of these times]? At the
> fervid period when his whole nature cries aloud for Action, there is noth-
> ing sacred under whose banner he can act; the course and kind and con-
> ditions of free Action are all but undiscoverable. Doubt storms-in on him
> through every avenue; inquiries of the deepest, painfulest sort must be
> engaged with; and the invincible energy of young years wastes itself in
> sceptical, suicidal cavillings; in passionate 'questionings of Destiny';
> whereto no answer will be returned.[14]

Without belief in an end (what Carlyle called a "banner," using a
metaphor that brings to mind the banner in *The White Doe of Rylstone*) to
give some kind of narrative intelligibility to effort, the idea of action
becomes meaningless. As Hazlitt put it in his *Principles of Human Action*
(1805), "without a power of willing a given end for itself, and of employ-
ing the means immediately necessary to the production of that end,
because they are perceived to be so, there could be neither volition, nor

action, neither rational fear nor the pursuit of any object . . . : all would be left to the accidental concurrence of some mechanical impulse with the immediate desire to obtain some very simple object."[15] Why do any one thing instead of another if you cannot know what is right, or even whether such a thing as "the right" exists?

The problem is one that has long confronted intellectuals and continues to do so to this day. Contemporary philosophers such as Alasdair MacIntyre and Charles Taylor, responding to the current wave of skeptical thought contained in the relativist discourse of multiculturalism, have addressed the need in our society for goals that can impose structures of significance onto a life's narrative. Not incidentally, both these thinkers approach the issue from the perspective of their Catholic backgrounds—the same perspective John Henry Newman turned to in an attempt to find meaning in action. They argue that without an end that can give agents a sense of direction, life narratives lack a kind of plot coherence.[16] With his loss of faith, Clough seems to have lost his understanding of the trajectory of his life. His religious doubt contributed to his failure to get the first expected of him. Then in 1848, he made the crucial decision to give up his post; as he told his provost, his "objection *in limine* to Subscription would be that it is a painful restraint on speculation."[17]

After leaving Oxford, Clough traveled to the Continent, visiting revolutionary France in 1848 and Rome in 1849. But on returning home, he found that many doors to employment had been closed to him by his act of renunciation. Eventually, he departed for a sojourn in America, where he tried to find literary work through the help of his friend Ralph Waldo Emerson. As Clough wrote, "for a man to act—there are no places so hopeless, so unnerving" as the European capitals; perhaps America would provide him with a blank slate of experience, untouched by the consequences of his previous deeds.[18]

Nevertheless, he was to face a second (and oddly analogous) major decision that would eventually bring him home: whether to marry. A letter written at the height of his post-Oxford depression (to Matthew Arnold's brother Tom in New Zealand, commenting on Tom's recent marriage) shows how the vocational and domestic choices that Clough made became conflated in his mind in rather revealing ways. Clough announced: "I, like you, have jumped over a ditch for the fun of the experiment and would not be disinclined to be once again in a highway with my brethren and companions."[19] Yet the language makes unclear precisely to which pair of actions the "jump over a ditch" refers: is it to Tom's emigration coupled with his own decision to give up the Oriel Fellowship? Or is it to Tom's marriage coupled with Clough's relationship to Blanche Smith (his future wife), to whom he was not yet officially engaged but with whom his ties were strengthening?

Such connections between questions of marriage and of broader action recur throughout Clough's writings. Given that there is "little opportunity for elevated *action*" in marriage, he acknowledged in a letter to Blanche of January 1852, the "single life . . . has some superiorities." The limited scope of domestic life "does look at times a little ignoble, or at any rate unchivalrous" (*PPR* I: 172). Note how for Clough, this struggle with the shape that he felt his life should take had generic implications: married life, while not quite the "ignoble ease" feared by Virgil in the *Georgics,* precludes the possibility of epic deeds. Its usefulness struck Clough as being sadly self-contained, not reaching outside the family circle, the realm of the novel.

But his decision to marry was also couched in terms of its ability to aid him in action. Consider this remarkable statement to Blanche:

> To a certain extent it seems to me that the whole world is apt to wear a mere pictorial aspect, that it must be by an effort that I accept anything as fact. This is the meaning of what I have often told you that I "believe in you"—I do not think that I can say the same to anyone else, though I can with less effort or with no effort talk and get on with old familiars . . . but if I am to make a choice, to act . . . I cannot turn, I think, except to you. There has never been in my whole life I may say *any act* of mine, sealing either friendship or love, up to this time. It has seemed to me a great thing (a thing that at times I doubt the truth of myself) to have done this at all.[20]

Blanche, then, fills the void of absent (or at least tenuous) religious belief, allowing Clough "to make a choice, to act." She is his banner. Clough's faith in his wife became the point from which he could begin to draw other lines of belief; she was proof against a demon deceiver and would let him build out from the morass of the cogito into which he had sunk.[21]

Blanche herself related in the biographical note to her edition of his works how Clough's intellect was naturally subject to "a certain inertia, a certain slowness of movement, [which] constantly made it hard for him to get over the initial difficulties of self expression" (*PPR* I: 40). Yet, she added pointedly, during their years of marriage, "his mind turned more and more to action as its natural relief; and in his family circle his gentle wisdom and patience and great tenderness of feeling caused him to be constantly appealed to" (*PPR* I: 47). But the actions left open to him were markedly opposed to the great deeds—poetic and otherwise—he had envisioned himself doing, as Blanche's comment suggests.[22] In fact, the poet's life reads like that of a character in a George Eliot novel: we may think of him as a kind of Lydgate, whose grand visions of career became tangled in a web of domesticity; or more positively, as a Dorothea, who was able to temper her original enthusiasm for plans and content herself with the "incalculably diffusive" effects of her domestic actions.[23]

After returning from America to marry, Clough took a job in the Education Office, allowing him to support his wife. In his spare time, he worked laboriously on a translation of Plutarch's *Lives,* a slow, steady process in comparison with the more creative work of writing original poetry ("It is odd how much better I like this Plutarch than I do anything which requires distinct statement of opinion or the like"[24]). And while Clough may have exercised his domestic virtues as a model husband and father—his wife went to some pains to emphasize this[25]—duty to wife and family did not suffice. He satisfied his social conscience with his dedicated service to Florence Nightingale (Blanche's cousin) and her cause, activity bitingly summarized by Lytton Strachey:

> Though the purpose of existence might be still uncertain and its nature still unsavoury, here, at any rate, under the eye of this inspired woman, was something real, something earnest: his only doubt was—could he be of any use? Certainly he could. There were a great number of miscellaneous little jobs which there was nobody handy to do. For instance, when Miss Nightingale was travelling, there were the railway-tickets to be taken; and there were proof-sheets to be corrected; and then there were parcels to be done up in brown paper, and carried to the post.[26]

For all their sting, Strachey's comments were not harsher than Clough's own in his more critical moments: his foil Dipsychus, the "hero" of his unfinished Faustian dialogue *Dipsychus and the Spirit,* remarks that "We ask Action, / And dream of arms and conflict; and string up / All self-devotion's muscles; and are set/ To fold up papers."[27] The "modern Hotspur," Dipsychus recognizes,

> Shrills not his trumpet of To Horse, To Horse
> But consults columns in a railway guide;
> A demigod of figures; an Achilles
> Of computation. . . . (3.2.108–11)

But the work of the modern Hotspur offers a limited kind of heroism: if (and it is a big if) the end were one's own, "One's choice and the correlative of the soul, / To drudge were then sweet service" (3.2.116–17). Presumably, Clough sought such "sweet service" in folding papers and consulting timetables for Florence Nightingale. "This that I see is not all," Strachey imagines him as having comforted himself, "and this that I do is but little; nevertheless it is good, though there is better than it."[28]

"All things become clear to me by work more than anything else," Clough wrote in March 1852 to his future wife. "Any kind of drudgery will help one out of the most uncommon sentimental or speculative perplexity; the attitude of work is the only one in which one can see things properly" (*PPR* I: 174). The message also belonged to Carlyle: "Man is sent hither not to question, but to work: 'the end of man,' it was long ago written, 'is an Action, not a Thought.' In the perfect state, all Thought were but the picture and inspiring symbol of Action."[29] Or again, "Hence, too, the folly of that impossible Precept, *Know thyself.* Till it be translated into this partially possible one, *Know what thou canst work at.*"[30] Carlyle's admonition was to act as relief to burdened skeptics like Clough; setting oneself small, doable tasks provided an escape from self-consciousness. "*Solvitur ambulando,*" reads one of Clough's mottoes for *Amours de Voyage:* "it is solved by walking." Take it one step at a time; or, as Carlyle put it, "'*Do the Duty which lies nearest thee,*' which thou knowest to be a Duty! Thy second Duty will already have become clearer."[31] Work then, with its mundane, rather inglorious connotations, takes the place of grander action in a process we will see repeated in George Eliot's writings. It is this diminishment of the scope of activity that allowed Clough to continue his letter to his wife: "One may be afraid sometimes of destroying the beauty of one's dreams by doing anything, losing sight of what perhaps one will not be able to recover: it need not be so" (*PPR* I: 174). That is, the clue need not be lost if the things we choose to do are limited enough in their range. The latter years of Clough's short life passed uneventfully. He died in Florence, where he had gone to nurse his failing health, in 1861.

CLOUGH IN CONTEXT

Clough's life shows why a concern with action manifests itself so strongly in the poetry (most of which stems from 1848–50, the years directly following the renunciation of his fellowship and preceding his marriage); as Joseph Bristow argues, Clough's work is so infused with an interest in action that "the very word 'action' becomes a personification of sorts."[32] In *Adam and Eve,* for example, which is written over the span of this period,

Clough explores the original myth of the fall into sin as a fall into action. The speculative Adam ponders at the start of the play over the "irretrievable act" that resulted in his expulsion from Eden (2.5). Adam's son Cain closely resembles the figure of Wordsworth's Rivers (and, for that matter, Milton's Satan): he is the consummate actor, and both a sinner and a sympathetic figure for being so. Like his antihero precursors, he is driven to action by his desire to assert his identity:

> a strange impulse struggling to the truth,
> Urges me onward to put forth my strength,
> No matter how—Wild curiosity
> Possesses me moreover to essay
> This world of Action round me so unknown
> And to be able to do this or that
> Seems cause enough, without a cause, for doing it—
>
> Something I must do, individual
> To vindicate my nature, to give proof
> I also am, as Adam is, a man. (7.10–16, 22–24)

He shares in the Aristotelian conviction that deeds define the man. The act Cain commits, though, is the murder of his brother, and after it, his father reveals to him the most basic truth about action: "One step you stirred, and lo! you stood entrapped" (12.14). It is a truth of which Clough's decision to give up his post must have made him heartbreakingly aware.

Yet the focus on action becomes particularly apparent in *Amours de Voyage,* not least because of its generic confusions. While tension arises from the odd conjunction of the hexameters with the lyrical elegiacs that open and close each canto of the poem, the same kind of tension manifests itself in the hexameters themselves. The epic poem, Goethe and Schiller tell us, "represents man as an external agent."[33] In *Amours,* part of the satire comes from Clough's adoption of a traditionally active meter to tell the story of a failed love affair between two British tourists during the French siege of Rome in 1849. Moreover, Clough's "heroes"—the intellectual, somewhat priggish, and highly speculative Claude, and Mary Trevellyn, the similarly sensitive daughter of a well-to-do mercantile family—are markedly unheroic and even ordinary, in the tradition of the realist novel. With his choice of subject, Clough was responding to his sense (expressed a few years later in a review entitled "Recent English Poetry") that to be popular, modern poetry, like the novel, must learn to deal with "general want, ordinary feelings," the stuff of "every-day life."[34] So here, Clough novelistically reverses the standard epic hierarchy by making the love story the major plotline of the work. The siege (in marked contrast with that of Troy in the *Iliad*) acts as counterpoint.

What is perhaps most notable about the plot of *Amours* is how the love affair fails: anticlimax characterizes the poem as forcefully as it did the life of its author. The punctilious Claude cannot be quite certain of his feelings for Mary: "I am in love, you say; I do not think so exactly" (II.x.263). So Claude chooses to stay in Rome (ostensibly to explore the Vatican marbles) when Mary and her family leave. But after Mary's departure, Claude finds he has underestimated his emotions and decides to follow her. Cantos IV and V relate the pursuit, showing how crossed communications, missed opportunities, and lost letters confound the lovers. Claude and Mary's travels across Italy can be mapped out as a mental image of the real complexity of action and plot, providing a kind of antidote to the neatly plotted Victorian novel, where the hero and heroine find each other in the grand finale. *Amours* sputters quite shockingly to its nonconclusion: Claude gives up the pursuit and continues on alone eastward to Egypt; Mary regretfully goes home to England with her family.[35]

While the most overt objection on record to this ending belongs to Emerson ("I cannot forgive you for the baulking end or no end of the *Amours de Voyage*"[36]), Matthew Arnold seems to have been similarly disappointed by his friend's production: "as to the Italian poem, if I forbore to comment it was that I had nothing special to say—what is to be said when a thing does not suit you."[37] Entering into the century's debate about the role of action in literature, Arnold lamented the absence of "great human action" in the work of modern poets in the Preface to *Poems* (1853).[38] Implicit in this view was a critique of Clough, whom he felt to be infected by a "morbid conscientiousness" that "spoil[ed]" his "action"[39]—nowhere more so than in his construction of the plot of *Amours*. The diagnosis was made around the period Arnold was drafting the Preface, and it is probably fair to assume, as Lionel Trilling does, that the tension that developed in the friendship of the poets came in part from Arnold's fears of catching the speculative infection.[40] He believed he had already succumbed to it in *Empedocles on Etna*, the poem now pointedly withheld from the new volume. "You certainly do not seem to me sufficiently to desire and earnestly strive toward—assured knowledge—activity—happiness," Arnold wrote, invoking the great Aristotelian telos. And he continued by implying a lack of masculine fortitude in his friend: "You are too content to *fluctuate*—to be ever learning, never coming to the knowledge of the truth. This is why, with you, I feel it necessary to stiffen myself—and hold fast my rudder."[41] The tenor of these comments shows how close the prescriptions Arnold made to his friend for a healthy life were to his prescriptions for a healthy literature in the Preface.

Part of what makes the Preface so interesting as a statement for its times is the way in which Arnold sought to place it within a tradition of such statements. As I have suggested, this tradition begins with Aristotle's *Poetics*. The belief in the primacy of action stands behind Aristotle's description of the relative importance of character and action in drama: "In a play accordingly they do not act in order to portray the Characters; they include the Characters for the sake of the action."[42] In his Preface to *Lyrical Ballads* (1800), Wordsworth, for reasons discussed in the previous chapter, revised the claim to favor feeling—that is, an internal quality affecting character—over external action: "Another circumstance must be mentioned which distinguishes these Poems from the popular poetry of the day; it is this, that the feeling therein developed gives importance to the action and situation, and not the action and situation to the feeling."[43]

Now Arnold strove to revert to the Aristotelian hierarchy. Under the influence of the Wordsworthian model, poets, including Arnold himself, had forgotten the healthy lessons of the ancients:

> the calm, the cheerfulness, the disinterested objectivity have disappeared; the dialogue of the mind with itself has commenced; modern problems have presented themselves; we hear already the doubts, we witness the discouragement, of Hamlet and of Faust.[44]

The solution to this state was action, but not any action; rather, the deeds aimed at were those of "great human action," either modern or (more probably, given the usual "smaller human action of today") ancient. Such actions would appeal to the "permanent passions," to the "elementary feelings," to the "great primary human affections."[45] The language is almost exactly that of Wordsworth's Preface, although Wordsworth used those same phrases ("elementary feelings," "primary laws of our nature") to support his decision to write of the "beautiful and permanent forms of nature" in the "permanent" language of "humble and rustic life"[46]—that is, of what Clough termed, in his lecture on Wordsworth, "blue skies and white clouds, larks and linnets, daisies and celandines." Arnold argued with Wordsworth by using his own words against him.

In fact, though, as their mutual opposition to Wordsworth suggests, Clough also accused Arnold of a dearth of epic energy. In his discussion of Arnold's work included in "Recent English Poetry" (also 1853), Clough singled out Arnold's poetry for some of those same criticisms he had himself received.

Ironically, he did so by contrasting "A's" work with that of the Glasgow mechanic poet, Alexander Smith, whose volume *A Life Drama* (1853) would be labeled "spasmodic" by the critic and poet William Edmonstoune Aytoun. Aytoun coined the term in the early 1850s to refer to what he perceived to be the dangerously subjectivist poetry—overly speculative and lacking in plot and action—that was prevalent at the time. His worries closely resembled those of Matthew Arnold in the Preface.[47]

Actually, Clough had to misread Smith's poem drastically in order to achieve the required contrast with Arnold. *A Life Drama* tells the tale, singularly lacking in drama, of a lovelorn, Werther-ish young man, who eventually overcomes the loss of his lady to pursue a career in poetry. Yet this is Clough's description of Walter, the rather milksoppish hero of Smith's poem:

> Eager for action, incapable of action without some support, yet knowing not on what arm to dare to lean; not untainted; hard-pressed; in some sort, at times, overcome,—still we seem to see the young combatant, half combatant, half martyr, resolute to fight it out, and not to quit this for some easier field of battle,—one way or other to make something of it. (*PPR* I: 363)

We can sense why Clough found the character sympathetic. It was, however, only by learning, with Walter, to prize what the poem calls "the *quiet* lightning deed," that Clough could find in Smith's *Drama* a model for active engagement, and the rhetoric he used to defend his hero is surely inappropriate given the magnitude and type of that engagement (*PPR* I: 367; emphasis added). And when Clough turned his attention in the review to Arnold's volumes, he did so with the obvious intent of emphasizing precisely those qualities in his friend's poetry that were singled out by Arnold as flaws in his own character:

> But now, we are fain to ask, where are we, and whither are we unconsciously come? Were we not going forth to battle in the armor of a righteous purpose, with our first friend, with Alexander Smith? How is it we find ourselves here, reflecting, pondering, hesitating, musing, complaining with "A[rnold]?" (*PPR* I: 376)

Moreover, like Arnold in the Preface, Clough saw the problem as characteristic of his times: "for the present age, the lessons of reflectiveness and the maxims of caution do not appear to be more needful or more appropriate than exhortations to steady courage and calls to action" (*PPR* I: 377).

The similarity between the friends runs deep. It is emphasized further by the fact that critics have compared both Arnold and Clough to the "*shilly-shally*" Claude (II.xv.335), the hero of *Amours*. Contemporaries insisted on biographical readings of *Amours,* no doubt fueled by knowledge of the poet's experiences in Rome during the siege (Clough's letters home actually repeat Claude's lines in his own voice), the popular version of Clough's life as a failure, and the handy alliteration between the poet's and his protagonist's names.[48] More recently, though, Eugene R. August has suggested—on the basis of Park Honan's evidence that "the real-life counterpart of Marguerite [the lady in Arnold's series of poems commemorating a failed love affair in Switzerland] was a young woman named Mary Claude"—that Clough actually had Arnold in mind when composing *Amours*.[49] Yet to anyone who has read the materials surrounding Arnold's Preface, this confusion should come as no surprise. Rather, it demonstrates how much alike Clough and Arnold were, at least as far as concerns the crisis in action in which both participated; Claude resembles both Arnold and Clough because they resembled each other.

One can see this in the way the friends shared the use of certain metaphors favored by writers of the period to describe their sense of aimlessness. In "Blank Misgivings of a Creature moving about in Worlds not realized," Clough expressed the need for something that could lead him like Ariadne's thread out of the labyrinth of action and change the wanderings of a Cain or a Don Juan to the purposeful motion of a modern Ulysses or Aeneas:

> How often sit I, poring o'er
> My strange distorted youth,
> Seeking in vain, in all my store,
> One feeling based on truth;
> Amid the maze of petty life
> A clue whereby to move,
> A spot whereon in toil and strife
> To dare to rest and love.[50]

Arnold turned to the same phrase in *Culture and Anarchy:* "our habitual causes of action seem to be losing efficaciousness, credit, and control, both with others and even with ourselves. Everywhere we see the beginnings of confusion, and we want a clue to some sound order and authority." His clue would be Hellenism, a "going back" to obtain a "sounder basis of knowledge on which to act";[51] in contrast, Clough desired not to go back but to go forward, however modestly—this difference was the source of the debate between the friends. But the idea of a "clue" of life took hold of the Victorian imagination. George Eliot, as we shall see, used the same metaphor to describe her characters' sense of confusion and purposelessness, their need for some rule of action that would guide them.

More strikingly, both poets addressed the failure of epic in their works via the trope of the "battle by night." Taken from Thucydides' account of the Battle of Epipolie, where the Athenians, in the confusion of darkness, mistakenly fought one another, the image vividly represents the difficulties associated with action in the contemporary world. Clough used the metaphor first, in *The Bothie* (1848), in a letter from Philip to his tutor and mentor, Adam, who had recommended his pupil place his faith in the workings of Providence. Philip's reply shows his mistrust of the distinction between Providence and Circumstance:

> Where does Circumstance end, and Providence where begins it?
> What are we to resist, and what are we to be friend with?
> If there is battle, 'tis battle by night: I stand in the darkness,
> Here in the mêlée of men, Ionian and Dorian on both sides,
> Signal and password known; which is friend and which is foeman?[52]

He returned to it in "Say not the struggle naught availeth," which was written during the siege of Rome in 1849. In this instance Clough imagined that the darkness could hide progress rather than confusion: "If hopes were dupes, fears may be liars" (1.5). The third, most famous, use of the battle by night, by Arnold in "Dover Beach" (probably written in 1851), again took a depressing view of the picture, but Arnold notably countered the public disarray with a vision of contrasting private consolation:

> Ah, love, let us be true
> To one another! for the world, which seems
> To lie before us like a land of dreams,
> So various, so beautiful, so new,
> Hath really neither joy, nor love, nor light,
> Nor certitude, nor peace, nor help for pain;
> And we are here as on a darkling plain
> Swept with confused alarms of struggle and flight,
> Where ignorant armies clash by night. (lines 29–37)

That the two latter variations on the theme are from, respectively, by far the most famous short poems produced by Clough and Arnold is not a coincidence, as the image (like that of the lost clue of life) partakes of the spirit of the age.

So what made the battle by night such a potent metaphor in the Victorian period, and in particular such an important one for these two poets? Isobel Armstrong has noted that "for both poets, action is figured as combat or battle."[53] But battle no longer consists of the ordered string of events we are familiar with from the Greek and Roman epics—lists of single combat, with the outcomes monitored by (admittedly squabbling) gods and goddesses. Neither is it the haphazard but still nicely consecutive sequences of adventures undertaken by the heroes of romance as they progress toward their goals. Rather, battles have been replaced by revolutions that disintegrated into Reigns of Terror. As Walter Bagehot (who had come under Clough's influence while completing a Master of Arts at University College London in 1848) argued in an 1859 review of Tennyson's poetry, Arnold's preference in his Preface for antique subjects reflected his sense of the illegibility of modern action. After detailing the difference between ancient and modern warfare, Bagehot concluded that "the events of the chivalric legend are better adapted to sustained and prolonged poetry than the events of recent times and of the present day . . . because they . . . present human actions in a more intelligible shape [and] give us a sort of large-hand copy of life which is comparatively easy to understand and imitate."[54] The Battle of Epipolie, while it belonged to the world of "great human actions" for which Arnold felt such nostalgia, was in fact the first "modern" war: it anticipated the impenetrability of deeds in the contemporary world, the way in which motives and consequences ricochet and are redirected under a cloud of confusion. Hence the prevalence of the motif.

The battle by night also figured in a sermon preached by John Henry Newman at Oxford on 6 January 1839 (and published in 1843), with which both Clough and Arnold were likely to be familiar:

> Controversy, at least in this age, does not lie between the hosts of heaven, Michael and his Angels on the one side, and the powers of evil on the other; but it is a sort of night battle, where each fights for himself, and friend and foe stand together.[55]

Armstrong has seen in this passage ("where each fights for himself") a reference to "the aggressive language of economics and competitive *laissez-faire* individualism," used here to describe a "spiritual individualism" more and more threatened by association with the economic society of contemporary England.[56] In other words, the Battle of Epipolie could also stand for the laissez-faire marketplace in which an invisible hand was the only vestige of government control. (Matthew Arnold's *anarchy*, or "doing as one likes," is a related concept.) In contrast to the political engagements of poets of the previous generation, such as Wordsworth and Byron, who had firsthand experience of revolution, Clough's early political involvement took the form of a series of writings against laissez-faire policies. The legacy of the Reign of Terror had frightened off the activists. In *Amours,* when Claude thinks he witnesses the murder of a priest who had been seen fraternizing, he echoes Wordsworth in *The Prelude*[57]: "I began to bethink me of Paris Septembers, / Thought I could fancy the look of the old 'Ninety-two" (II.vii.203–4). So instead of fighting, as he wrote to his friend J. P. Gell in July of 1844, Clough intended "to set to work at Political Economy," "to see if I cannot prove 'the Apostle of Anti-laissez-faire.'"[58] He knew that his was a debased revolutionary age, where real change occurred on the Exchange.

Not only did the Revolution of 1789 loom as a specter, but the less grand failure of 1848 also stood as a recent reminder of the uncertainties of revolutionary action. Clough's attitude toward revolution took on a pronouncedly dilettantish aspect, as his letters from France in 1848 show:

> I do little else than potter about under the Tuileries Chestnuts and here and there about bridges and streets, pour savourer la republique. I contemplate with infinite thankfulness the blue blouses, garnished with red, of the garde mobile.
>
> Ichabod, Ichabod, the glory is departed. Liberty, Equality, and Fraternity, driven back by shopkeeping bayonet, hides her red cap in dingiest St. Antoine. Well-to-do-ism shakes her Egyptian scourge to the tune of Ye are idle, ye are idle.[59]

"Well-to-do-ism" had taken the place of doing in this atmosphere of Donothingism. In a letter to Tom Arnold, Clough quoted his friend's brother Matthew: "I think we rash young men may learn from the failure and discomfiture of our friends in the new Republic. The millennium, as Matt says, won't come this bout."[60] From Rome, he repeated the lament over a past glorious age of revolutionary possibility: "It is funny to see how like any other city a besieged city looks. Unto this has come our grand Liberty-Equality-and-Fraternity Revolution."[61] And in the battle by night passage from *The Bothie* I referred to above, Philip arrives at the same conclusion; given the apparent "infinite jumble and mess and dislocation," "Let us get on as we can, and do the thing we are fit for; / Every one for himself, and the common success for us all" (IX.64, 67–68). The passage neatly demonstrates the nexus of overlapping metaphors: the battle by night, the glancing allusion to laissez-faire ("Let us get on as we can"), and the tantalizing preview of Darwinism ("fit").

But I would wish to shift the emphasis from what Armstrong describes as a "crisis in individualism"—the idea that "self-culture" had become tainted by its relationship to a culture of the pursuit of private gain—to what I call a crisis in action. Clearly, Adam Smith's vision of the market radically changed our understanding of useful activity. On the one hand, Smith's market economy is a tremendously empowering construct for the average person; it suggests that the labors of the farmer in the field and the shopman in his shop are what keep the country going.[62] On the other hand, all such activity not only lacks the heroic scope, but also it occurs under the banner of self-profit. "Let me sing the song of the shopman," Claude ironically declares in a canceled paragraph of *Amours* echoing the opening line of the *Aeneid,* where the song is one of "arms and the man."[63] Industrialization obviously added to the problem of knowing what to make of the new form of action by turning workers into "hands" severed from their thinking minds (not to mention the rest of their laboring bodies) or cogs in a machine. Even the epic action of warfare had been mechanized; as Carlyle lamented, "Battles, in these ages, are transacted by mechanism; with the slightest possible development of human individuality or spontaneity."[64] Clough's concern over the mechanization of labor appears in *Dipsychus and the Spirit:*

> The earth moves slowly, if it move at all
> And by the general, not the single force.
> At the [huge] members of the vast machine
> In all those crowded rooms of industry
> No individual soul has loftier leave
> Than fiddling with a piston or a valve. (2.3.118–23)

So the emphasis on collective force took away from individuals those very powers that it had seemed so generously to bestow upon them; the broad range of individual acts that were heroicized by the new system could prove significant only when bound into group activity. As Bagehot remarked, "For this is the odd peculiarity of commercial civilization. The life, the welfare, the existence of thousands depend on their being paid for doing what seems nothing when done."[65] As a result of this paradox, the rhetoric of agency in the Victorian period can often strike one as rather convoluted. Writers were forced to juggle with various understandings of words like *freedom* and *action;* their meanings could be crucially altered depending on whether they were viewed from the perspective of the individual or the collective.

John Stuart Mill's reflections on the modern status of action demonstrate his awareness of the need for specificity, for qualifications. Of what Armstrong calls the "crisis in individualism," he declared: "One of the effects of a high state of civilization upon character, is a relaxation of individual energy: or rather, the concentration of it within the narrow sphere of the individual's money-getting pursuits."[66] Yet the first formulation of Mill's statement would have been as troubling to Clough as the latter. I say this because it seems to me that the real focus in Clough's poetry is not so much on the eighteenth-century problem of benevolence we associate with Mandeville's *Fable of the Bees* (1714), but rather on the question of whether it is really feasible to do anything meaningful at all, given how obscured the ground of action is. Clough's characters are not selfish in the money-grubbing market sense; but even though they would like to do good, they cannot seem to figure out how to do it. So they end up doing little or nothing. The epic intent is still there—hence the hexameters—but the reality of modern life is that the epic must be a mockery and that hexameters can be read only through the filter of a lyrical narrative consciousness.

Obscurity lies at the heart of the problem of modern action, which is why the battle by night became such a potent image. The Invisible Hand had replaced the Hand of God in the grand scheme of things: Elspie, Philip's beloved in *The Bothie,* dreams of a "great invisible hand" that will drop the keystone into the bridge being built between her and Philip (7.68); in *Amours,* Claude depends on the strength of "invisible arms" to hold him up over the chasm of his uncertainty (I.xii.243). But given the close relationship between "seeing" and "believing" in a culture built at least in part upon empiricist values, invisibility turns out to create trouble. (The Catholic Church has long suspected as much, and the very visibility of God in Catholicism was surely a large part of its attraction to nineteenth-century intellectuals.) Hence the overwhelming prevalence of darkness as a metaphor, as here in Carlyle:

> For young Valour and thirst of Action no ideal Chivalry invites to heroism, prescribes what is heroic: the old ideal of Manhood has grown obsolete, and the new is still invisible to us, and we grope after it in darkness, one clutching this phantom, another that; Werterism, Byronism, even Brummelism, each has its day.[67]

Carlyle's list incorporates various postures that the modern protagonist could adopt in lieu of the traditional heroic stance: the suicidal cavilings of Werther, the outcast wanderings of the Byronic hero, and the dilettantish dandyism of Beau Brummel. Clough and his heroes flirted with these attitudes but ultimately found them dissatisfying. Middle-class masculinity could discover little foothold on such uncertain ground. With the domestication of heroism, in fact, the most comfortable heroes seem to have been the heroines. Clough's admiration for Florence Nightingale reflected his recognition that her activity (including her struggle against constraints placed on her by gender) was more glorious than that of the soldiers for whom she cared. Moreover, as we shall see with George Eliot's work, women had at least an arena in which their conventionally more restricted battles could be naturally depicted: the novel.

In "The Ethical Current," the final essay of *The Gay Science* (1866), E. S. Dallas, one of the pioneers of psychological criticism, made precisely this point while considering the fate of the hero and the literary consequences of contemporary market and social structures: noting both the preeminence of biography as a genre and the fact that "a novel is but a fictitious biography," he asserted that "now all the more important characters seem to be women."[68] Not incidentally, Dallas touched in this essay on many of the issues I have raised and will raise, including, for example, "the question of Hamlet."[69] He also expressed his admiration for Plutarch's *Lives,* the very work Clough spent the last years of his life translating. Dallas described how the contemporary vogue for biography indicated the Victorian interest in a history that revealed "the inner life as well as the outer"—that is to say, a novelistic history.[70] Clough's introduction to his translation shows just how novelistic his attitude to the *Lives* was: "In reading Plutarch, the following points should be remembered. He is a moralist rather than a historian. His interest is less for politics and the changes of empires, and much more for personal character and individual actions and motives to action."[71] As Dallas quoted Plutarch remarking, "the most glorious exploits are not always the most characteristic."[72] Such a distinction between great actions and a sense of individual character is at the heart of what the writers I am looking at are exploring.

Dallas recognized all these tendencies as resulting from transformations in the perceptions of action that accompanied the shift in its quality and scope. The following passage, written in the context of an argument about the preponderance of ordinary men and women serving as the heroes and heroines of biographies, shows his awareness of how difficult it is to chart the course of individual acts through history:

> Just as philosophers tell us that every word we utter, every breath we
> inhale, has, through a million of intermediate links in the chain of cause
> and effect, a definite influence on the dancing of the leaves in an
> American forest or on the course of a hurricane in the Indian seas, so we
> recognise the fact that the action of every unit of a nation or party tells
> upon the total result of human achievement, and we insist on tracing that
> action, no matter how infinitesimal, throughout all its ramifications.[73]

But rather than interesting himself in the ramifications of the spreading of
consequences (like, we shall see, novelists such as George Eliot did), Dallas
emphasized the effect of an awareness of causal structures on the idea of
the heroic. A newly scientific age was unwilling to give up the concept of
achievement, but, pace Carlyle, the most effective action need not be that
done by the great men of history. Who could tell what mode of life actually did the most good? And given how impossible it was to track consequences, what was the point of trying to do the great deeds? Might not the
small ones have as vast impact in the end?

What I find most notable in Dallas's account, though, is his great mistrust of the process of writing such histories. The passage continues:

> We have nothing to do with the question whether this be right or
> wrong—whether to trace the influence of every little emmet on society
> may not be as worthless a task as would be an attempt to calculate the
> effect of the blast of a trumpet on the weather of to-morrow. Right or
> wrong, there is the fact that we do seek to estimate the influence on soci-
> ety of every petty individual whom we happen to like. A Dissenting gro-
> cer, who makes money and extends his operations till he is regarded as a
> marvel by the country-side, has his life written by a very able man in a
> very ornate style as the pattern of a British and Christian merchant; a sick-
> ly undergraduate who never does anything, but makes up for his noth-
> ingness by writing in his diary all his good intentions, is paraded before
> the world as a favourable specimen of the earnest and evangelical stu-
> dent.[74]

Perhaps the "Dissenting grocer" and the "sickly undergraduate" (who
could be Clough, in the less sympathetic versions of his life story) were
actually helping the nation. But history of this sort cannot be written out
as a sequence of intentions followed by events. For all his democratic values (he was an advocate of the ability of art to provide pleasure to the masses), Dallas did not seem quite to believe in the usefulness of "infinitesimal"

deeds, because the path of cause and effect is too complicated to trace. The invisible hand writes in an invisible—or at least indecipherable—script.

Clough's erstwhile disciple Walter Bagehot, in his evolutionary model of government in *Physics and Politics* (1872), was also interested in the change in the idea of heroism: how the "fighting age" had passed, to be taken over by an "age of discussion," led ideally by a government characterized by what he called (somewhat paradoxically but rather wonderfully) "animated moderation."[75] Offering a typically pragmatic salve to the popular perception of abdication on the part of the rulers, Bagehot alluded in *The English Constitution* (1867) to the same problem of legibility found in Dallas. In his description of the advantages of monarchy, he wrote: "The nature of a constitution, the action of an assembly, the play of parties, the unseen formation of a guiding opinion, are complex facts, difficult to know and easy to mistake. But the action of a single will, the fiat of a single mind, are easy ideas." Hence his conclusion: "royalty is a government in which the attention of the nation is concentrated on one person doing interesting actions. A republic is a government in which that attention is divided between many, who are all doing uninteresting actions."[76] The close resemblance of this argument to the one that Bagehot made in the review of Tennyson's poetry (concerning the intelligibility of antique versus modern actions as poetic subjects) demonstrates the connections between literary and political modes of action. It is as though Bagehot were arguing here that monarchies make for more compelling plot lines: by allowing for popular comprehension, they keep the masses appeased. Legibility is necessary to safety.

But Clough was looking for a ruler more substantive than Bagehot's figurehead of a monarch. In a discussion of laissez-faire policy in his "Sixth Letter to Parapedimus" (to the editor of *The Balance,* 20 March 1846), he argued that while the system of the free market may be the best we have, and may indeed work in nine cases out of ten, it is "an instrument demanding perpetual superintendence; a sort of ruthless inanimate steam-engine, which must have its driver always with it to keep it from doing mischief untold."[77] We hear the longing for genuine leadership. Carlyle had earlier expressed the same doubt as Clough, in almost the same language (note the frequent recurrence to industrial metaphors): "What sound mind among the French, for example, now fancies that men can be governed by 'Constitutions'; by the never so cunning Mechanising of Self-interests, and all conceivable adjustments of checking and balancing; in a word, by the best possible solution of this quite insoluble and impossible problem, *Given a world of Knaves, to produce an Honesty from their united action?*"[78] It may be good engineering, but it does sound rather like alchemy; again, the obscurity of the process renders it suspect.

⊰

So we can think of the failure of plot in *Amours de Voyage* as a gesture toward realism: in a laissez-faire world, one ruled by countless individuals, heroes are hard to find, and the courses of actions are to a great degree impossible to read. When the action of plot fails we are left with the subject of Claude's letters: his reflections on the problem of action in the modern world. It is precisely through Claude's inaction (in the sense of both impeded external action and heightened internal action) that we come to know his character so well. As Henry Sidgwick noted, Clough's presentation of character was admirable: "To say that Clough's dramatic faculty was strong might convey a wrong impression, as we imagine that he was quite devoid of the power of representing a scene of vivid action; but the power of forming distinct conceptions of character, and expressing them with the few touches that poetry allows, is one of the gifts for displaying which we may regret that he had not ampler scope."[79]

Sidgwick's comments should be located within the context of what Isobel Armstrong has recognized as a midcentury debate concerning the proper definition of the *dramatic*.[80] Following in the wake of Romantic poetry's concern for feelings, critics began to lay down hints for a new understanding of drama that placed greater emphasis on character and less on action—an understanding (Armstrong argues) derived from the idea of romantic projection, or sympathy, found in Keats's letters. The important action thus becomes a mental rather than a physical one, a process of identification that seems central to both the experience of reading lyric poetry and that of reading novels.

We can see this turn away from Aristotelian *action* toward something closer to novelistic, or at least lyric, *character* in William Caldwell Roscoe's tinkering with the meaning of the term *drama*. In an 1854 review, he wrote in response to Arnold's Preface:

> Without venturing to contradict Aristotle, we may certainly say that the poetic art is not limited to the representation of human actions, in however wide a sense we may employ the term. We have poems to the Lesser Celandine, to a Mouse, to the Skylark— . . . And an action is not only not the sole, it is not the highest, subject of the poetic art. Man is higher than his actions, and it is in the representation of the whole man that the romantic drama soars far beyond its classical rival.[81]

Roscoe seems to have been suggesting a link, via inaction, between what he called "romantic" dramas and the Romantic lyric, as the reference to poems by Wordsworth, Burns, and Shelley (and the resemblance of his argument to that of the Preface to *Lyrical Ballads*) indicates. Such use of the word *drama* and its cognates was quite common in the reviews of the period. In *The Eclectic*, C. Edmunds wrote of Browning's genius as "essentially dramatic, but not in the sense which the word vulgarly bears. Mr. Browning's is mostly the drama of character, not of incident, or scenic effect."[82] Browning's dramatic monologues, like the monologues (or letters) that make up Clough's "five-act epistolary tragi-comedy, or comi-tragedy," typify the shift in interest from incident to the revelation of character through the description of states of mind; as Richard Simpson described Browning in his review of *The Ring and the Book* (1868–69), the monologues "are eminently lyric, because their chief interest is reflective, lying not in the deed or narrative itself, but in the psychological states of the speakers."[83] It is as though drama were being filtered through lyric in order to cleanse it of action, so leaving a pure residue of character.

According to Isobel Armstrong, by the 1860s critics' interest in psychology had taken over from their nostalgia for great actions.[84] W. J. Fox's groundbreaking review of Tennyson's *Poems, Chiefly Lyrical* (1830) already showed the beginnings of this trend—and demonstrated its links to the romantic project, especially as represented by Wordsworth. Fox pointed to "our ever-growing acquaintance with the philosophy of mind and of man, and the increasing facility with which that philosophy is applied":

> This is the essence of poetic power, and he who possesses it never need furbish up ancient armour, or go to the East Kehama-hunting or bulbul-catching. Poetry, like charity, begins at home. . . . The most important department in which metaphysical science has been a pioneer for poetry is in the analysis of particular states of mind. . . . [It has provided a] new world for him [the poet] to conquer. The poets of antiquity rarely did more than incidentally touch this class of topics; the external world had not yet lost its freshness; situations, and the outward expression of the thoughts, feelings and passions generated by those situations, were a province so much nearer at hand.[85]

The review predates the publication of *The Prelude*, but that poem's interior epic seems to be what Fox was calling for.

The new psychological poetry often focused on depictions of character. Fox argued in his review of Tennyson that works of literature were enjoyed for the characters portrayed in them: "What is the vitality of the *Iliad?* Character; nothing else. All the rest is only read either out of antiquarianism or of affectation."[86] Critics frequently compared poets to portraitists when praising them for their ability to create characters. Fox had noted in particular Tennyson's talents at drawing women: "Mr. Tennyson sketches females as well as ever did Sir Thomas Lawrence. His portraits are delicate, his likenesses . . . perfect, and they have life, character, and individuality."[87] He implied that because of the circumscribed nature of their activity, women were especially suitable subjects for the new psychological school of writing: they would sit still more naturally while they were painted. In his review of *The Princess* (1847) in the *Christian Remembrancer,* Charles Peter Chretien alluded to early photographic methods: "The Daguerreotype process gives the whole of a landscape faithfully, except figures in quick motion, or the leaves of a tree which are trembling visibly in the wind. Like it, Mr. Tennyson requires all but a dead calm to display his powers to advantage."[88] Chretien was in fact critical of Tennyson's unwillingness to take full advantage of his chosen medium's ability to describe objects in motion. But perhaps activity and the accurate rendition of a consciousness are incommensurable.

As the century progressed, praise for the psychological emphasis became commonplace. An anonymous reviewer in *The Eclectic* demonstrated how the changing attitudes toward the role of action in poetry reflected awareness of the changing needs of the age. Again, the argument was posed in opposition to Arnold's tenets in the Preface:

> The sweetest songs ever sung do not necessarily relate an action, they chronicle a thought, or a sentiment. . . . how shall we deal with this wondrous living age of ours, so transitory, so full of hopes and fears; its fettered energies, its phases of faith, its mental revolutions, if we are to have actions alone represented? For our own part we believe there is a world of unuttered thought yet to be uttered subjectively, and that it affords as great and glorious a field for the poet as all the great actions of the past.[89]

Those "mental revolutions," like Claude's in *Amours,* replaced the external revolutions of epic poetry. They are essentially Romantic ground; again, *The Prelude* seems to provide the model. Indeed, in many of these discussions the epic appears to have dropped off the literary map altogether. Still, we can see in the arena of Victorian poetry—and specifically in the context of the debate concerning the appropriate role for action in poetry that I have been looking at here—how "inward revolution," as George Eliot and Henry James would term it, gained legitimacy as a subject matter for literary work.[90] As a reviewer in the *Dublin University Magazine* argued in 1854: "The present age is a metaphysical and a psychological one, and poetry, as the reflex of the age, must, to be popular, exhibit the inner life of man—mental action, feelings, passions, spiritualities."[91]

Amours de Voyage

We can register the shift toward the inner workings of the mind in the way that inaction becomes both subject and method of Clough's poem. As we have seen, concerns about action and about marriage were intimately related for Clough. The link between them also manifests itself in the plotting of *Amours,* where the hero's early unwillingness and later inability to commit to marriage stand for his unwillingness and inability to act: the "I do" of marriage seems impossible to him. And a letter to Blanche written in December 1851 (one can only wonder how she felt upon reading it) again demonstrates the connection:

> Fortified by bread and cheese I return and rise to the sublime . . . here in this dim deceitful misty moonshiny night-time of existence we grope about and run up against each other, and peer blindly but enquiringly into strange faces, and sooner or later (for comfort's sake for the night is cold you see and dreary) clasp hands and make vows and choose to keep together and withdraw again sometimes and wrench away hands and seize others and do we know not what.[92]

Here is another Epipolie: the same confusions, the same blindness, the same longing for a lost plan. The situation resembles that described in Arnold's "Dover Beach," only now, rather than providing a sanctuary from the surrounding night-battle, love participates in it. "*Il doutait de tout, même de l'amour,*" states the second epigraph to *Amours de Voyage.* Like Clough, Claude worries that acts of love are no more genuine than—or, in the language of *Amours,* are as "factitious" as (II.xi.271)—any other kinds of action; they are as much as everything else the result of circumstance and demonstrate neither real choice nor Providential planning. So Arnold's plea, "Ah, love, let us be true / To one another!" represents merely another prayer to a false god.[93]

Amours de Voyage, as its title suggests, plays itself out primarily on the field of Venus rather than Mars, but the great chase across Italy represents a version of the battle by night. So when Clough transfers the language of laissez-faire from the political realm to that of the novelistic courtship plot, it is actually fitting. Thinking of his "conquest" of the Trevellyns—and of Mary in particular—Claude reflects on the mechanics of social life:

> I am glad to be liked, and like in return very kindly.
> So it proceeds; *Laissez faire, laissez aller,*—such is the watchword.
> Well, I know there are thousands as pretty and hundreds as pleasant,
> Girls by the dozen as good, and girls in abundance with polish
> Higher and manners more perfect than Susan or Mary Trevellyn.
> Well, I know after all, it is only juxtaposition,—
> Juxtaposition, in short; and what is juxtaposition? (I.xi.220–26)

The tone of this passage is interrogative, but Claude's question leads him in circles; the at first drawling and then almost desperate repetitiveness of these lines, emphasized by their frequent central caesuras, parallels the endless and meaningless repetitions of the social—and the economic—cycle. Such questions and repetitions are common features of Clough's verse, and they lend to it the quality of immediacy that makes it so attractive, the sense of our overhearing a man's thoughts, as they lead one into the next. And the hexameters give Clough room to mimic the somewhat halting flexibility of ordinary speech, with its interjections, hesitations, and qualifications; they provide an example of Clough's tendency toward what I have called generic hybridity, incorporating the skeleton of the epic, the immediacy and inwardness of the lyric, and the colloquialism of the novel. But because of these features, Clough's epic hexameters rarely invigorate; rather, their constant rise and fall focuses attention on the difficulties of escape from metrical—and, by association, from social—conventions. The action of the meter is improgressive, anticlimactic, and self-reflexive—again, an *in*action.

Clough's emphasis in this passage on the concept of juxtaposition seems to represent a grab for some notion that will lead him out of the maze of his own verse, but the concept proves to be so ungrounded in any kind of positive knowledge that it only bewilders him further, as the move from a statement of cause ("it is only") to one of question ("and what is") indicates. Why, Claude wonders, should he fall for Mary rather than some other girl who would be equally suitable and equally attractive? Is love just the chance collision of two people who are, as the saying goes, in the right place at the right time—a kind of lucky hit in the dark? "Juxtaposition," within the framework of *Amours,* fits into two sets of metaphors. The first of these is chemical and has to do with the concept of elective affinities: the idea that elements have varying inherent tendencies to form combinations and that they will combine and recombine according to these tendencies when placed in solution with each other. Goethe had explored the social and sexual implications of the concept in his novel *Die Wahlverwandtschaften* (1809), a work that obviously influenced Clough's reflections on the subject in *Amours*.[94] Goethe's novel is really more of a thought experiment about Enlightenment than anything else. In it, a hyperrational couple invite into their home a pair of outsiders, only to discover that the foreign elements bring with them dangerous forces of elective affinity. The four main characters find themselves reshuffling their relations according to these affinities, and the results are devastating.

The point that Goethe made—and that Clough worries about—is that there is nothing genuinely elective about elective affinities: we have no choice in these matters, other than the choice to oppose our inherent passions. This restriction proves to be severe. In the jottings of his "1849 (Roma) Notebook" Clough describes how "Mechanical Ethics" ("training of bodies of men") is taught by Aristotelian habituation: "You get soldiers into the way of marching to music—boys and girls of dancing—schoolboys of taking places—learning off by heart." But such ethics must be distinguished from what he calls a "Spiritual Ethics," which is taught not by action but by inaction: "its virtue is negative; to check or suppress inferior vital effluxes—and coalescences—combinations / to withdraw oneself / to decline solicitations." We can see by the context that the term "Spiritual Ethics" refers specifically to control of sensual attractions; his examples are sexual and gustatory. Clough seems to want to argue that while we can teach a boy to recite his lines by making him say them over a hundred times, we cannot teach a man to love a woman by what we call "going through the motions" of lovemaking: this is not true love (nor true action—again, the connection) but rather something else, "to sham-to-act."[95] So "doing" in the sexual sense poses a threat to action.

Unfortunately, we have a greater "affinity" for "lower kinds of juxtaposition" (that is, the sexual kind) than for the higher, spiritual ones. Such attraction must be resisted if we ever wish to engage in genuine acts of love. In "Sa Majesté Très Chrétienne," a Browningesque dramatic monologue composed during the same period as *Amours*, Clough imagines the French king Louis XV's horror of action, and of sexual action in particular, as so great that he considers castration: "With one short act, decisive for all time / By sharp excision sever the seed of ill."[96] Clough hardly condones the king's attitude—in fact, it comes across as pathological—but he seems also to feel some sympathy for his protagonist's position: "Poor Kings, must forth to

action, as you say; / Action, that slaves us, drives us, fretted, worn, / To pleasure, which anon enslaves us too" (lines 42–44). And Clough's notebooks
show that he shared in the king's sense that routine inaction provides the
only solution to the problem:

> If ought there be for sinful souls below
> To do, 'tis rather to forbear to do;
> If ought there be of action that contains
> · The sense of sweet identity with God,
> It is, methinks, it is inaction only. (lines 59–63)

In part, "Sa Majesté" must be read as a critique of Christian quietism, a
revelation of its morbidity, and another push forward in Clough's campaign
for action. And yet the disease, as we can see with Claude, has spread to
the secular limbs of the nineteenth century.

Clough located his only hope of genuine acts of love in his belief that
the lower, sexual affinities, though strong, were also temporary. Any mix-
tures formed on the basis of the lower attractions would prove themselves
unstable and would, like oil and water, rapidly dissolve into their component elements.[97] Claude uses the language of elective affinity to describe the
distinction between genuine love (that which forms a stable molecule from
its elements) and mere sexual attraction (a short-lived emulsion):

> There are two different kinds, I believe, of human attraction;
> One which simply disturbs, unsettles, and makes you uneasy,
> And another that poises, retains, and fixes, and holds you. (II.xi.264–66)

But how then do we know that what we are feeling is love rather than mere
sexual attraction? The difficulty of distinguishing between the two kinds
of attraction leads Claude to follow upon this distinction with the reflection that "action / is a most dangerous thing" (II.xi.270–71). "To act commits us," as Clough declares in the Roma notebook,[98] and Claude
expresses the same worry:

> *Action will furnish belief,*—but will that belief be the true one?
> This is the point, you know. However, it doesn't much matter.
> What one wants, I suppose, is to predetermine the action,
> So as to make it entail, not a chance-belief, but the true one.
> (V.ii.20–23; original emphasis)

Clough, like Aristotle, thought that we are habituated to the good by doing good deeds. Our society trains us in virtue by teaching us to do—at first by rote or under duress, with neither understanding nor belief—what it deems to be right. Eventually we learn to believe in what we are doing; only at this stage can our deeds be said to be truly virtuous. Aristotle's faith in his system of ethics was predicated on a faith in his society's system of beliefs. Claude, though, has lost such faith: how do we know that those conventions we are raised with uphold the "true" beliefs? And what kind of action is conventional action, anyway? As Florence Nightingale remarked: "What is conventional life? *Passivity* when we want to be active."[99]

The concept of convention, the link between costume and custom, and the parallel double meaning of "habit" (both a costume and a customary act) all show the blurring of the distinction between action and acting, as in these canceled lines from *Amours,* I.v.83–86:

> Curious work, meantime, this re-entering society: how one
> Sits and perceiving no meaning, consents to converse without meaning
> Suffers the gesture and speech to adopt the costume of convention.
> Then of a sudden one loses the limit; true Nature immingles,
> Lives in the false; the hard seed develops and grows in convention.
> Make-belief changes to fact; and acting converts into action.[100]

Again note the repetition in the verse, here heightened by Clough's adroit use of alliteration and assonance. The slurring of words through repeated syllables, like the slurring of a dandy's voice, suggests the deep connection between matters of form and of content, and even, perhaps, the subsuming of the content into the form. Each step along the way seems so insignificant: from consenting to converse, we suddenly find ourselves costumed in convention. Each "act" is rendered impure by the slip of a letter or the addition of a suffix that follows quite naturally and almost necessarily from the lost root: from fact (and its corresponding vocabulary of the "factitious") to acting to action. With so little to separate the words, how can there be much to separate the concepts? The regularity of the dactyls in the second and third lines quoted pulls the reader along in the process of conversion. The two spondaic phrases, "true Nature" and "hard seed," present a temporary break in the flow of the meter, testifying to an almost elegiac longing for an innate core of self that could swim against the river of costume, custom, conversation, and convention down which Claude is being dragged. But the dactyls pick up again in the final line, as the course of conventionalization is completed.

One can see here how deep the Aristotelian tendency of Clough's thought ran: "acting converts into action" is as succinct and accurate a description of Aristotelian habituation as one is likely to find. But because of his lack of faith in conventional action, Clough's description of Aristotle's lesson comes across as a nightmarish reflection on the impossibility of genuine action—or genuine love. "I am in love, you say; I do not think so exactly," Claude remarks. And the sad thing is that he really cannot be sure; all he can do is let things progress as they will—*laissez faire, laissez aller.* Actively to pursue any course is to implicate himself in a possible falsehood; only by abrogating responsibility can Claude maintain his sense of integrity. (Mary seems to understand Claude's worries: this is precisely what he likes in her. As her sister says—again reflecting the language of laissez-faire—she "Lets him go on as he likes, and neither will help nor dismiss him" [II.viii.234]). Again, Carlyle highlights how Clough's dilemma is representative of his age; with skepticism, "Genuine Acting ceases in all departments of the world's work; dexterous Similitude of Acting begins. . . . Heroes have gone-out; quacks have come-in."[101] Action threatens to become acting in its dramatic sense, tainted by falsehood; as Clough's hero Claude puts it in another canceled passage of *Amours de Voyage,* "What is all Action and Life but a series of affectations? / Parts we assume; tinsel drapes we wear and are fain to act up to?"[102]

The alternative to acting, as Clough had noted, is abstinence, willed inaction, and for a while Claude attempts this: he avoids any declaration of his intentions; he does not leave Rome with the Trevellyns. "I do not like being moved," Claude declares,

> for the will is excited; and action
> Is a most dangerous thing; I tremble for something factitious,
> Some malpractice of heart and illegitimate process. (II.xi.270–72)

The dilemma is one Claude, who shares his author's uncompromising honesty and his capacity for self-scrutiny, will repeatedly confront in the *Amours* under the name of the "factitious." Claude hesitates acknowledging his feelings because he distrusts the relationship between emotion and motion. The former leads to the latter, but any falseness in feeling will corrupt the action it generates, so rendering the entire process false and leading to an unforeseeable and uncontrollable chain of events, all subject to the taint of the original act. Yet no matter how much he dislikes it, Claude finds himself moving:

But I am in for it now,—*laissez faire,* of a truth, *laissez aller.*
Yes, I am going,—I feel it, I feel and cannot recall it,—
Fusing with this thing and that, entering into all sorts of relations,
Tying I know not what ties, which, whatever they are, I know one thing,
Will, and must, woe is me, be one day painfully broken,—
Broken with painful remorses, with shrinkings of soul, and relentings,
Foolish delays, more foolish evasions, most foolish renewals.
(I.xii.231–37)

Again the verse progresses relentlessly: repeated words and sounds cause phrase to follow phrase with the appearance of inevitability. Claude's description of love presages Clough's nightmarish letter to Blanche of 31 December 1851. And Claude's vision of the affair turns out to be prophetic of the voyage of love upon which he is about to embark.

That voyage provides the second metaphoric framework in *Amours* for the concept of juxtaposition. Indeed, a version of the travel theme extends through all three of Clough's major works: *The Bothie* is an escapist "vacation pastoral" located in the Scottish Highlands, the voyage of *Amours* constitutes a leg of the Grand Tour, and *Dipsychus* is set in the tourist's Venice. Clough's characters' status as tourists reflects their sense of homelessness in the world, their alienation from society, and also their restlessness. His travelers are the descendants of the Romantic wanderers: the Cains, the Ancient Mariners, the Don Juans. As the title of the work indicates, *Amours de Voyage* is as much a rumination on the love of—or perhaps, more accurately, the need for—travel, as on the romance that develops between the hero and heroine. In fact, it suggests that these two forms of love actually reflect the same underlying search: a quest for authenticity, a desire to escape the "factitious" elements of modern life. But the move from Romantic traveler to Victorian tourist should be noted. As James Buzard has shown in *The Beaten Track,* the claim "that 'the tourist' is one of the best models available for 'modern-man-in-general' derives from . . . an image of the tourist as a figure estranged from the authentic."[103]

Amours de Voyage begins with a reflection on travel as a search for authenticity: "Come, let us go,—to a land wherein gods of the old time wandered, / Where every breath even now changes to ether divine" (I, opening elegiacs, lines 3–4). But from the very first, Claude expresses a sense of alienation from his cultural past that renders the quest itself suspect: "'Tis but to prove limitation, and measure a cord, that we travel"; "'Tis but to change idle fancies for memories willfully false" (I, opening elegiacs, lines 7, 9).[104] The tourism of *Amours* acts as a metaphor for broader cultural alienation.

Where the epic hero once stood, the tourist now gawks. In fact, Clough's heroes sightsee at Revolution, as though it were one more of the cultural attractions to take in. Clough himself recorded with irony how on the trip to Rome that formed the basis for *Amours,* he found it necessary to disturb the revolutionary hero Mazzini from his political pursuits in order to get a letter of permission to study some rare collections of sculpture (presumably, those very sculptures Claude uses as an excuse for staying behind in Rome).[105] War becomes something that can be appreciated only from the tourist's perspective. In one remarkable scene in *Amours,* Claude stands amidst a group of fellow tourists atop the Pincian Hill and looks down upon the battle, enjoying the view and pointing out its peculiarities:

> Twelve o'clock, on the Pincian Hill, with lots of English,
> Germans, Americans, French,—the Frenchmen, too, are protected,—
> So we stand in the sun, but afraid of a probable shower;
> So we stand and stare, and see, to the left of St. Peter's,
> Smoke, from the cannon, white,—but that is at intervals only,—
> Black, from a burning house, we suppose, by the Cavalleggieri.
> (II.v.113–18)

Recall Clough's letters home during his stay in Paris in 1848, where he talked of "potter[ing] about under the Tuileries' chestnuts, and here and there about bridges and streets, *pour savourer la république.*"

Claude describes how he gets his first "sign of the battle" one morning when he is sitting in a café, "*Murray,* as usual, in hand"—sensing a change in the weather, "but thinking mostly of Murray"—when the waiter tells him that there is no milk (II.v.101, 96, 98). The passage perfectly describes the tourist's strange dialectic of nearness to and distance from the visited culture: even as Claude considers the cultural artifacts of the city, he demonstrates his ignorance of its current political truths. In another shocking scene in *Amours,* already mentioned, Claude writes home about seeing a priest attacked by a mob. On the way back from St. Peter's, "Murray, as usual, / Under [his] arm," he notices a disturbance. As he tells his friend, "So I have seen a man killed! An experience that, among others! / Yes, I suppose I have; although I can hardly be certain" (II.vii.167–68, 162–63).[106] Witnessing a murder is not so different from looking at St. Peter's, and *Murray* serves as a guidebook to both "experiences." After all, everything Claude sees comes to him at the tourist's distance, through gaps in the crowd, in a language he can't quite comprehend: "History, Rumour of Rumours," he continues, quoting Carlyle.

The search for authenticity also occurs on the literary level. The movements of Mary and Claude over the crossed and scarred soil of the Italy of the *Amours* seem to reflect the palimpsest-like cultural markings of the terrain on which History and Culture have left so many confusing traces. As Buzard would put it, they are on a "beaten track." But the traces of ancient greatness appear to Claude as the waste products of a dead civilization:

> Rome disappoints me much; I hardly as yet understand, but
> *Rubbishy* seems the word that most exactly would suit it.
> All the foolish destructions, and all the sillier savings,
> All the incongruous things of past incomprehensible ages,
> Seem to be treasured up here to make fools of present and future.
> (I.i.19–23)

The form of waste, though, most evident in the poem is not that of the actual crumbling structures with which Claude is surrounded (although the opening canto in particular includes several descriptions of the local sights, relayed in a rather jaded guidebook manner). Rather, the cultural detritus that most pervades the poem is that of previous writers who have engaged with Rome.

Clough creates in *Amours* a web of allusions that replicates Rome's infamous architectural jumble (the same "stupendous fragmentariness" that would so disturb George Eliot's Dorothea during her honeymoon there[107]). He often does this by quotation. A characteristic example of the process is his revision of Brutus's declaration, "There is a tide in the affairs of men, / Which, taken at the flood, leads on to fortune."[108] Claude's take on the lines of the famous Roman (as written by the most famous of Englishmen) adds only a few words but produces a dramatic shift in meaning: "There is a tide, at least in the *love* affairs of mortals, / Which, when taken at flood, leads on to the happiest fortune" (IV.iii.33–34). The alteration typifies the paradigm shift in *Amours* from a primary concern for the fortunes of war to the fortunes of the heart. But as modern buildings in the Eternal City stand on Renaissance foundations covering Roman ruins, so the layering here contains many levels: the allusion is also a direct one to the interim text of Byron's *Don Juan,* a poem that like *Amours* can be thought of as a "novel-in-verse," a quest-romance travelogue led by a famously passive (although bodily active) hero, who refuses to end his tale with a wedding. (Byron's narrator quips: "There is a tide in the affairs of women / 'Which taken at the flood leads'— God knows where."[109]) "Should I incarnadine ever this inky pacifical finger [?]" (II.iv.72), Claude wonders. But Clough's sense of loss is as much

about literature as about heroism, about the authenticity of the inky finger
as that of the bloody one, about the ability to say something in a modern
voice rather than through the words of the dead.

From France, Clough had alluded to Wordsworth's Intimations Ode to
describe his own sense of revolutionary disappointment; comparing the Paris
he walked through to that of '89, he noted that "the glory and the freshness of the dream is departed."[110] Claude also expresses his sense of
Romantic belatedness by invoking the famous Ode, the iconic poem of a
lost golden age, and it is telling that for him the golden age is one of natural action. He explains why he must discontinue his pursuit of Mary:

> There was a time, methought it was but lately departed,
> When, if a thing was denied me, I felt I was bound to attempt it; . . .
> It is over, all that! I am a coward and know it.
> Courage in me could be only factitious, unnatural, useless.
> (V.v.77–78, 84–85)

Clough's quest for a poetic voice through which to express himself authen-
tically has become inextricably tied to the genuine revolutionary experiences of the poets of the past. Wordsworth's France and Byron's Italy peep
through the cracks of Clough's Rome. But the connection to these places
has altered dramatically: absent "genuine" experience, the only kind of
poetry that seems possible is the poetry of tourism.

So travel allows Clough to express his hero's sense of cultural alienation.
But Clough also makes travel represent the almost inevitable failure of plotting in a complicated world. No matter how carefully plans are laid, no matter how often timetables are poured over, something always disrupts one's
intended course. *Amours* makes particularly adroit use of the phenomenon
that the Victorian critic John Addington Symonds, himself a great traveler,
called "a natural accident of travelling": "when once missed," a sought-after
party (here the Trevellyns) "cannot be caught up again."[111] What results is
a parody of the Grand Tour. Take, for example, letter ii of canto IV:

> Gone to Como, they said; and I have posted to Como.
> There was a letter left, but the *camariere* had lost it.
> Could it have been for me? They came, however, to Como,
> And from Como went by boat,—perhaps to the Splügen,—
> Or to the Stelvio, say, and the Tyrol; also it might be
> By Porlezza across to Lugano, and so to the Simplon
> Possibly, or the St Gothard,—or possibly, too, to Baveno,

Orta, Turin, and elsewhere. Indeed, I am greatly bewildered.
(IV.ii.19–26)

So is the reader.

Yet the uncertainty generated by travel functions in two directions: while it is difficult when traveling to find someone we are searching for, we inevitably meet random people. Dickens, a Victorian writer who unlike Clough preserved a firm faith in action, as his carefully plotted novels demonstrate, took advantage of such random collisions, the famous "coincidences" that propel his stories.[112] In a statement to John Forster about the plan for *Little Dorrit* (1857), he described his methods:

> It struck me that it would be a new thing to show people coming together, in a chance way, as fellow-travellers, and being in the same place, ignorant of one another, as happens in life; and to connect them afterwards, and to make the waiting for that connection a part of the interest.[113]

Dickens may have made the original meetings seem accidental, but he ensured (by "connect[ing]" his characters "afterwards") that our sense of providential planning would be preserved. Clough, though, never reconnects the dots. Claude calls such chance crossings of paths "juxtapositions," and unlike Dickens, he is very much troubled by them:

> Juxtaposition, in fine; and what is juxtaposition?
> Look you, we travel along in the railway-carriage, or steamer,
> And, *pour passer le temps*, till the tedious journey be ended,
> Lay aside paper or book, to talk with the girl that is next one;
> And, *pour passer le temps,* with the terminus all but in prospect,
> Talk of eternal ties and marriages made in heaven. (III.vi.107–12)

Love, then, the idea that two people are "meant" for each other, is merely an "illusion" (III.vi.113), and Claude, unlike most of us, cannot pretend it is anything more. "Where does Circumstance end, and Providence where begins it?" Philip asked in the battle-by-night passage from *The Bothie* (IX.49). Both Claude and Clough find it impossible to hide from this question; inevitably—especially once the idea of Providence is abandoned—the act of falling in love contains an element of chance. You get married to a girl because she happened to be seated next to you on the train.

Of course you can also think of such juxtaposition, more positively, as a matter of destiny. In his extraordinary poem "Natura Naturans" (1846–47), Clough's narrator imagines the entire process of evolution as he stares across a railway carriage at a young woman sitting opposite him. The poem is unusual in that in it Clough celebrates those same sexual instincts—elective affinities, here figured as "elections"—that he fears elsewhere:

> Yet owned we, fused in one,
> The Power which e'en in stones and earths
> By blind elections felt, in forms
> Organic breeds to myriad births. (lines 41–44)

The narrator continues by ascending a kind of biblically inflected evolutionary ladder: from lichen to lily to cedar to bee to bird to gazelle, and finally, to man and woman. The prime mover in this proto-Darwinian process is the "primal prime embrace" (line 76). But as the poem makes clear by its ending, the "genial heat" (line 77) of sexual energy can be preserved only in an atmosphere where "young Desire" is never "told the mystic name of Love" (lines 87–88). The incident can represent evolutionary destiny rather than random juxtaposition precisely because the encounter in the train is between perfect strangers who never enter the realm of social intercourse: they do not even speak to each other, much less begin talking of "eternal ties and marriages made in heaven." The man and woman never become individuated; they remain male and female representatives of the human species. Any imagined act between them bears no mark of the individual will; it is essentially collective.

In contrast, *Amours de Voyage* is plotted like a courtship novel, so love and marriage cannot be avoided. Moreover, individuation (that is, a sense of characters rather than of mere types) stands at its center. This is appropriate to a love story. We like to believe, after all, that we fall in love with people for their peculiarities, for the things that make them different from everyone else we have met. We call the resultant distinct entities their essential selves. But evolutionarily, the essential self is the very opposite of such individuality: it is what we all have in common, the human genome. What can seem like destiny when you think in terms of an entire race appears random when you bring things down to the level of the individual; acts that are meaningful collectively—the workings of the market, the social conventions—can lose their meaning viewed from the perspective of one pair of eyes. Hence Claude's crisis in action: from where he stands things just don't make much sense.

As elsewhere in *Amours,* the marriage referred to in the "strangers on a train" passage represents a larger commitment to action. A little later on in the same letter, while musing on the fact of death, Claude comments that "But for the steady fore-sense of a freer and larger existence, / Think you that man could consent to be circumscribed here into action?" (III.vi.123–24). Men can stand to marry, to do the deed that will tie them to one person for the rest of their lives, only because they know there will be an escape in death. Claude's speech weirdly rewrites Hamlet's famous "To be, or not to be" soliloquy. Only here, marriage replaces suicide, and the "something after death"—"The undiscover'd country," so dreaded by Hamlet, "from whose bourn / No traveller returns"—is positively embraced by Claude, and instead of making him "lose the name of action" would give him the courage to take it.[114] But it is not enough. When Claude gives up the search for Mary, he also forsakes any lingering impulse toward a life of directed action. To believe in action is to look toward to a future in which one's deeds bear fruit; the move from Italy to Egypt takes Claude into a yet-more-distant past.

Hamlet stands at the center of the debate about action and character in nineteenth-century literature.[115] Emerson wrote that the "speculative genius" of the age was "a sort of living Hamlet."[116] I suggested in the previous chapter that *The Borderers* owed something to Shakespeare's great drama of inaction; one can see how both play and character also resonate with my discussion of Clough and *Amours de Voyage.* A. S. McDowall indicates the source of the connection in his belief that "no other English poet has so anatomized the idea of duty, or the possibilities of acting truly, or even (*Hamlet* always excepted) the possibility of acting at all [than Clough]."[117] Furthermore, the resonance was not lost on contemporary critics, scarcely one of whom missed the chance of bringing it up, frequently in the service of describing Claude as a spirit of his age. In his treatment of *Amours de Voyage* in the *Fortnightly Review,* J. A. Symonds (probably with Arnold's Preface in mind[118]) compared Claude to both Hamlet and Faust, those two "princes of metaphysical perplexity. However exceptional, his skepticism is natural to himself, and to the temper of his century."[119] W. Y. Sellars criticized the poem as a debased version of Shakespeare's play, featuring "a very modern Hamlet [who] is seen playing a weak and common-place part in the very common-place drama of modern English society in Rome."[120] Today's critics seem to prefer comparing

Amours to "The Love Song of J. Alfred Prufrock," thus emphasizing its modernity. But of course, this comes to much the same thing, as *Prufrock* is itself a belated Victorian offspring of *Hamlet,* its hero a man who cannot muster the grandeur of the Prince, but, in the form of "an attendant lord," shares his inability to act.

Claude himself seems to recognize the justice of the comparison. At one point, he declares his Hamlet-like aversion to being "the observed of such observers" (III.13.279).[121] And when making his excuses for his abandonment of politics in the midst of the revolutionary fervor that surrounds him, he alludes to the Prince's response to the speech of the Player King: "And what's the / Roman Republic to me, or I to the Roman Republic?" (III.3.66–67).[122] Moreover, Hamlet also stands at the center of the myth of Clough's life. Stopford A. Brook was by no means the first or last to compare the poet to Hamlet, but he was unusually astute in his recognition of the double-sidedness of the allusion: "Thus moving, like a Hamlet, through the strifes of theology and religion, he resembles Hamlet in another way. When the Prince is suddenly flung into the storm of action, he takes momentarily a fierce part in it, and enjoys it, till overthinking again seizes on him. Clough repeats this with his life and his poetry is touched with it."[123]

But as the Romantic predilection for conferring upon it the status of closet drama suggests, *Hamlet* also featured in a generic argument of the period. The work is Shakespeare's greatest expression of the art of the monologue (or soliloquy), and a correspondingly problematic example of the dramatic form. Tennyson highlights this oddity by designating his own "little *Hamlet,*" *Maud,* a "monodrama."[124] The debate in the period about the term *dramatic* (discussed above) often seems to be a debate about the relative importance of action and character in Shakespeare's plays in general and *Hamlet* in particular. (As suggested in the previous chapter, *Hamlet* is particularly relevant to the dispute over the importance of character and action in literature because of the degree to which the Prince's superbly rendered consciousness relates to his inaction.) Drawing on the Romantic tradition of Shakespeare criticism exemplified by Hazlitt, Victorian critics took it for granted that what made Shakespeare great was the realism of his characters.[125] William Roscoe's argument against Arnold's Aristotelianism took precisely this tack: "In Sophocles, the action is predominant, and the characters are interesting as they elucidate it. In Shakspere [*sic*], the characters are predominant, and the events gain their main interest from the insight which, by their aid, the poet contrives to give us into some human heart."[126] So Shakespeare himself became a keyword indicating the importance of character in literary works. Henry Sidgwick turned to Shakespeare in his praise of the "individuality" of Clough's "personages": "It becomes as impossible for us to attribute a remembered remark to the wrong person as it would be in a play of Shakespeare."[127]

But in *Wilhelm Meister's Lehrjahre* (1795–96), Goethe suggested how to take the debate over genre one step farther. Wilhelm argues that *Hamlet* actually bears a strong structural resemblance to the form of the novel:

> The hero of a novel must be passive [*leidend*], or at least not active to a high degree; from the hero of a play we demand effective action and deeds. . . . [Hamlet] really only has sentiment, and it is only external events that work on him, so that this play has something of the breadth of a novel.[128]

And Sidgwick seems to have been following a similar train of thought when he introduced his comments comparing Clough's character presentation to that of Shakespeare with a different comparison: "There is not one of the personages [of *The Bothie* or *Amours*] whose individuality is not as thoroughly impressed upon us as if they had been delineated in a three-volume novel by Mr. Trollope."[129] So Claude's Hamletism could also reflect Clough's more novelistic concerns in *Amours*.

Walter Bagehot advised the heads of constitutional monarchies to follow a policy of "well-considered inaction"[130]—a phrase that reads like a plot summary of *Hamlet*. He again reveals the connection between the political and literary realms by having used the same word in his review of the posthumous edition of Clough's works to describe the plot of *Amours de Voyage*. Bagehot remarked that while "Mr. Arnold teaches that a great poem must be founded on a great action, . . . this one is founded on a long inaction." But, he added, "Art has many mansions."[131] And perhaps Claude's Hamlet-like propensity for inaction *does* make him more properly the hero of a novel. Barbara Hardy has argued against the novelistic approach to *Amours de Voyage:* "[Clough] is very unlike a novelist, and especially unlike a Victorian novelist. His motion is very erratic, his fluidity and foreshortening and shuttling are all products of an essentially lyrical form, where history is cut down so that feeling is prominent."[132] My point is of course that precisely this close connection to the lyrical, this emphasis on feeling—that is, this following of Wordsworth's prescriptions in the Preface to *Lyrical Ballads* rather than Aristotle's in the *Poetics*—makes the poem like a certain kind of novel that is very much Victorian: the novel of character, as distinguished from the novel of plot.

And as Sidgwick's review suggests, Victorian critics registered the connection (no doubt motivated in part by pressure from the increasing predominance of the novel in the literary marketplace). J. M. Robertson wrote of *The Bothie* and *Amours* as "in essence works of narrative, analytical, psychological fiction" and stressed "the relation that such works bear to the contemporary novel."[133] Rather conveniently for me, he drew explicit links between Clough's characters and those of George Eliot and Henry James, the very writers to whom I now wish to turn.[134] Such readers testify to the contemporary sense of the novel as a genre of character. They also testify to a broader shift from the genre of the epic, with its concern for the great deeds of heroes, to the novel, with its concern for consciousness and belief in the "incalculably diffusive" influence of "unhistoric acts," as George Eliot would memorably phrase it. *Amours de Voyage* stands on the edge of this shift, at the place where the novel, the lyric, the drama, and the epic—and their different attitudes toward action—collide. The generic explosion it represents manifests the disturbance to be found at fault lines.

⇥3⇤

"That girl has some drama in her":
George Eliot's Problem with Action

If I am not for myself, then who will be for me? And if I am only for
myself, then what am I? And if not now, when?

—Rabbi Hillel, *Pirkei Avot*

THE DEBATE CONCERNING the proper role for action in poetry also manifests itself in the Victorian novel, where it is transformed into the division
between novels of plot and novels of character. Etymologically, *prose*
means *sequence,* and plot, the sequence of events out of which a story is
constructed, would seem to be an inherent element of prose narrative. As
Wilkie Collins, one of the fathers of that most pure form of the novel of
plot, the detective story, noted in his Preface to the 1861 edition of *The
Woman in White* (1860), "I have always held to the old-fashioned opinion
that the primary object of a work of fiction should be to tell a story; and
I have never believed that the novelist who properly performed this first
condition of his art, was in danger, on that account, of neglecting the
delineation of character."[1] Nevertheless, with *The Moonstone* (1868), he
also succumbed to the trend for reversing the Aristotelian priority of plot
over character: "In some of my former novels the object proposed has been
to trace the influence of circumstances upon character. In the present story
I have reversed the process. The attempt made here is to trace the influence of character on circumstances."[2]

The pressures on Collins to focus on character were strong. In 1863, a

87

reviewer in *Blackwood's* was driven to protest the increasing tendency to say "the plot is nothing, the character is all."[3] But in general, psychologically driven novels garnered critical approval more readily than the contemporary poetry discussed in the previous chapter. In part, the cultural stakes were lower for the relatively arriviste genre, and comparisons to classical texts could be more easily avoided. In fact, reviewers looked at the novel with increasing seriousness in the light of its ability to delve into the depths of characters' minds. This new approach made the novel a form of art worthy of adult contemplation, while a corresponding impulse relegated the more plot-driven branch of the genre to a lower rung on the ladder of culture. As a critic in *Fraser's* put it in 1851: "Few men feel interest in plot after nineteen. . . . [F]rom that time forward, they look only to the development of character"; although some action may be necessary to display the psychologies of the characters involved, the burden of interest should fall squarely on character.[4] Plot-driven novels were dismissed as boys' adventure tales or, even worse, sensation fiction.

The approval of the tendency to focus on character was not universal, and some critics looked upon it with almost Arnoldian foreboding, as the manifestation of hidden cultural disease. R. H. Hutton's disparaging remarks in 1855 on the modern trend toward devaluing plot hint at an underlying cause of the shift in focus from plot to character:

> The best modern writers of fiction seem to be falling into the error of neglecting the tale in delineating the characters. You feel constantly inclined to say of them, as the grateful layman said of the long-winded divine, "it is very good of him to stop at all; for there was no reason why he should." . . . It is getting quite unusual to conclude with the wedding. . . . The reason is, that the strict experience school of fiction is on the increase, and is carrying out its realism to a faulty extreme. . . . The consequence has been the springing up of a sort of *accidental* school of fiction.[5]

Hutton suggested that realism and plot are incompatible in the real world, where action commonly takes the form of accident and where the story rarely concludes with the wedding.[6] His formula fits perfectly the course of *Amours de Voyage*, as we saw. But for a deeper understanding of the threat to action posed by realism, we must turn to the greatest realist novelist of the Victorian period: George Eliot. In his analysis of Eliot's troubled relationship to plot, Robert Caserio argues that "in Eliot there is an arbitrary relation between what is done and narrative reasoning about what is done that always threatens to return action to the form of accident. And this constant threat to the significance of action . . . is also offered by Eliot as most plausibly representing 'the real.'" [7] In what follows, I wish to explore Caserio's statement in light of the fact that for Eliot (as Caserio seems to be hinting), *accident* was not an "arbitrary" category: rather, it carried all those negative connotations with which the word has been invested by common usage. If action "threatens" to return to accident, then it should come as no surprise that George Eliot's attitude toward it tended to risk aversion.

One way to avoid risk was to internalize the action. D. H. Lawrence remarked that of the novelists, "it was [George Eliot] who started putting all the action inside." [8] So, for example, in *Felix Holt* ("The Radical," 1866), she shifts the focus from the political revolution implied by the title of the novel to Esther Lyon's "inward revolution." [9] When Eliot "puts things inside," willing, judging, desiring, and feeling gain the same ontological status as acting. And yet properly speaking, as I have been arguing, action is set apart by its externality: it is by our actions, by our words and deeds, that we insert ourselves into the world. Community is as much the condition of action as of language; this is why the end of Aristotle's *Nicomachean Ethics*—his treatment of individual action—launches directly into his *Politics*. [10] Moreover, it is only by doing, Aristotle tells us, that we become just or unjust. Eliot knew Aristotle's writings well, especially the *Poetics*. In a journal entry of May 1873, she wrote of "finishing again Aristotle's *Poetics,* which I first read in 1856." [11] And she acknowledged the Aristotelian connection between action and ethics: as the narrator of *Daniel Deronda* (1876) insists, "the fuller nature desires to be an agent, to create, and not merely to look on." [12] In fact, Eliot's shifting inward of action created for her a series of ethical problems with which she wrestled increasingly in her novels. The struggle culminated in *Daniel Deronda,* in which the nature and potential of action become the dominant subject, and it is to this work that I will eventually turn. But first I want to explore some of the causes that lay behind George Eliot's problem with action.

The Problem with Action

Ironically, given (as we shall see in chapter 4) that he is an author frequently accused of writing novels in which nothing occurs, Henry James had a speaker (Pulcheria) complain in his conversational review of *Daniel Deronda:* "I never read a story with less current. It is not a river; it is a series of lakes." [13] But it is not enough to note that relatively little happens in most of Eliot's stories, where even the "murders" are usually and conspicuously (in a manner that recalls the central crime in *The Borderers*) crimes of inaction: Hetty's abandoning her child, Bulstrode's not telling his housekeeper to refrain from administering the liquor, Gwendolen's hesitating to throw Grandcourt the rope. Eliot, as Caserio has deftly shown, is very different from an author like Dickens to whom narrative activity—the external working of plot—functions as a kind of meaningful agency.[14] Yet, *pace* Lawrence, Jane Austen resolutely pulled her plots inside without encountering the problems Eliot faced. For while Austen is primarily a novelist interested in epistemology, Eliot's first concern is always with the ethical. V. S. Pritchett has brilliantly recognized that Eliot has a mind "that has grown by making judgments,"[15] but these judgments are rarely allowed to find outward expression in positive action. Her optimism, her sense of progress, seems to have been much more about the human potential to will the right things than about the human potential to do the right things.

Even Aristotle appreciated that both goodwill and good deed are essential to virtue.[16] But Eliot seems more troubled than Aristotle by the gap between internally driven will and externally conditioned action. As the narrator of *Felix Holt* notes, we must learn to discern between will and destiny (FH 11): because our ability to act is hindered in part by forces outside our control, by the actions of others as well as ourselves, morality involves an element of what could be called luck. Sorrow can be inherited, we are told in Eliot's Introduction to *Felix Holt;* this is the great lesson Harold Transome comes to recognize: "It was the most serious moment in Harold Transome's life: for the first time the iron had entered into his soul, and he felt the hard pressure of our common lot, the yoke of that mighty resistless destiny laid upon us by the acts of other men as well as our own" (FH 385). The yoke of resistless destiny forms a leitmotiv throughout Eliot's writing. In the first motto she ever originated for a chapter, one gentleman declares to another, "Our deeds are fetters that we forge ourselves," only to be reminded, "Ay, truly: but I think it is the world that brings the iron."[17] In her favorite metaphor for this scenario, free will is constrained in the web of human interaction.

Hannah Arendt, Aristotle's greatest modern interpreter and disciple, uses the same figure to describe, in terms remarkably close to Eliot's, the role of action in linking character to community:

> The disclosure of the "who" through speech, and the setting of a new beginning through action, always fall into an already existing web where their immediate consequences can be felt. Together they start a new process which eventually emerges as the unique life story of the newcom-

er, affecting uniquely the life stories of all those with whom he comes into contact. It is because of this already existing web of human relationships, with its innumerable, conflicting wills and intentions, that action almost never achieves its purpose; but it is also because of this medium, in which action alone is real, that it "produces" stories.[18]

In fact, what Arendt describes is the narrative of an Eliot novel. The positive aspect of this scenario is the creation of community; as both Arendt and Eliot recognize, the acknowledgment of our essential interrelatedness that allows for the working of sympathy depends on the web woven of our collective deeds. Yet because of the web, individual action (especially action conceived on a grand scale; as we shall see, this distinction was important to Eliot) rarely achieves its purpose. Think of the way in which Felix's desire to stop the riot is constrained by the "tangled business" of the "small selfish ends" of the other rioters (FH 266), or the way in which the deed that is Casaubon's will actually works to bring about the very event (Dorothea's marriage to Ladislaw) it was written to hinder.

So Eliot's trouble with action rested partly in her sense of the impossibility of controlling consequences in the world. Through the voice of Felix, she warns each person to take care how his "tugging will act on the fine widespread network of society in which he is fast meshed."[19] Eliot's stories are produced by the ricochet of a few cue deeds on a table where the other balls are already moving in a determined fashion. Or, to use her own metaphor in *Felix Holt,* her characters are trying to play chess with pieces that have passions and intellects of their own (FH 236). Of course Eliot herself has control, but she is the only real author. This distinction points to the crucial difference between the production of art and the living of life. Arendt interestingly continues the passage quoted above by disparaging the conceit of being the author of one's own life: "although everybody started his life by inserting himself into the human world through action and speech, nobody is the author or producer of his own life story. In other words, the stories, the results of action and speech, reveal an agent, but this agent is not author or producer."[20] Autobiography can happen only after the fact.

But the problem Eliot wrestled with is twofold: not only are we constrained by the deeds of others, our own past acts also limit present and future choices. Mrs. Transome, who "felt the fatal threads about her" (FH 94), has learned the hard way that activity can entangle the struggler in the meshes of her own deeds. In *Adam Bede* (1859), the narrator comments of Arthur Donnithorne, "Our deeds determine us, as much as we determine our deeds. . . . There is a terrible coercion in our deeds which may first turn the honest man into a deceiver, and then reconcile him to the change; for this reason—that the second wrong presents itself to him as the only practicable right."[21] Again and again, Eliot reminds us of this lesson: Tito Melema's decision to sell Baldassarre's ring occasions the narrator's comment that "he had chosen his color in the game, and had given an inevitable bent to his wishes."[22] And Eliot's fear was compounded by her awareness of the irreversibility of acts, the worst kind of "woeful progeny" (FH 11). There is a "dreadful vitality of deeds"—"children may be strangled, but deeds never" (R 156). One can sense her terror in this analogy. Eliot would have been fascinated by chaos theory's butterfly effect. In her novels, the smallest actions can bring about vast and unimaginable consequences. So when Eliot declared that we are "struggling, erring human creatures,"[23] she wished to imply a connection between sin and activity that is only partly within the control of the agent. Her awareness of the incredible power of action lies behind that search for safe forms of action by which her novels are driven.

Yet while she was troubled by the force of destiny, her sense of the "inexorable law of consequences," Eliot also believed firmly in free will.[24] Her position resembles that which John Stuart Mill explored in his *Autobiography* (1873):

> I perceived, that the word Necessity, as a name for the doctrine of Cause and Effect applied to human action, carried with it a misleading association; and that this association was the operative force in the depressing and paralyzing influence which I had experienced. I saw that though our character is formed by circumstances, our own desires can do much to shape those circumstances; and that what is really enspiriting and ennobling in the doctrine of free will, is the conviction that we have real power over the formation of our character; that our will, by influencing some of our circumstances, can modify our future habits or capabilities of willing.[25]

Like Eliot, Mill was disturbed by the degree to which circumstances can limit one's ability to act. But what is particularly interesting in his description of free will is the way in which after the difficulty is defined as one of human action, action itself drops out of the account, to be replaced by character, will, and habit. Such substitution typifies how Eliot treated action. She wanted to preserve a sphere for action, in which the will could find free outward expression, but the only sphere she could envision, given her determinism, was tremendously limited. As Eliot declared in a letter to her friend Mrs. Ponsonby, "I shall not be satisfied with your philosophy till you have reconciled necessitarianism—I hate the ugly word—with the practice of willing strongly, willing to will strongly, and so on, that being what you certainly can do and have done about a great many things in life."[26] Yet no matter on how many levels the activity of the will can recur—and Eliot seems to have attributed some magical force to that "and so on"—it will never break through into a real "doing," an action.

When it comes to forming habits, though, the repetitions of "and so on" can attain an almost magical force. Eliot was obsessed with habits. Because of its incremental force, habit allows for a greater element of control over action; habitual deeds are less subject to chance than other, more radical forms of activity. Habit also provides protection against self-interested behavior, which might otherwise dominate in a moment of crisis; if one has been habituated to do the good, then the virtuous deed is simultaneously the instinctive deed. In a fascinating earlier letter to the same friend, Eliot attempted to respond to determinism's tendency to lead to the loss of "all sense of quality in actions" by distinguishing between it and "hideous fatalism." Her proof of effective action rested in Mrs. Ponsonby's habits of cleanliness: "And if they [i.e., necessary combinations of cause and effect] don't hinder you from taking measures for a bath, without which you know you cannot secure the delicate cleanliness which is your second nature, why should they hinder you from a line of resolve in a higher strain of duty to your ideal . . . ?"[27] Happiness, which to Aristotle was activity, was to Eliot a kind of habit: "there is naught less capable of magical production than a mortal's happiness, which is mainly a complex of habitual relations and dispositions" (FH 311). Eliot's safety-seeking tendencies are perfectly captured in this rather extraordinary claim. To be sure of happiness, she wished to take away from it that element of chance under which she felt we all labor. Yet while habit may act as a kind of harness on action, a harness can strangle as well as control. Habits can be good or bad, as Eliot recognized. In its negative manifestation, she called habit "the purgatory in which we suffer for our past sins."[28] As Carlyle put it, "Habit is the deepest law of human nature. It is our supreme strength; if also, in certain circumstances, our miserablest weakness."[29] In *Romola*, Romola's virtue and Tito's evil are both emphatically the product of habituation.

Nevertheless, the force of habit is essentially conservative, as Burke understood. In fact, *Romola* stresses the very Burkean (or Wordsworthian) concept of moral tradition: "Our lives make a moral tradition for our individual selves, as the life of mankind at large makes a moral tradition for the race; and to have once acted nobly seems a reason why we should always be noble" (R 331). Habit is its own reason for action: when Romola comes upon the ailing Baldassarre, "Her hands trembled, but their habit of soothing helpfulness would have served to guide them without the direction of her thought"

(R 353). J. S. Mill actually went as far as to define purpose as "a habit of will-ing."[30] Given that all voluntary action must have an end toward which it can be directed, we see another reason why habit was so important to Eliot. Her stake in it can be related to the famous comment to Frederic Myers concerning the relative natures of "God, Immortality, Duty."[31] Something must fill the void left by the death of God, and duty does not really mean much in the abstract. But duty can become purpose when defined by a habitual inclina-tion (whereas a lack of "sufficient ducts of habit" can turn our nature, as it does Grandcourt's, into "mere ooze and mud" [DD 132], taking us back to the primordial slime out of which we have evolved). The relationship between habit and a secular concept of duty that can stand in for Christian charity helps explain the remarkable transition between the end of chapter 68 and the beginning of chapter 69 of *Romola*. The shift is one from a nos-talgia for belief—"Many legends were afterwards told in that valley about the blessed Lady who came over the sea"—to a description of the strange habit-ual nature of Romola's activity in the valley: "she had not even reflected, as she used to do in Florence, that she was glad to live because she could lighten sorrow—she had simply lived with so energetic an impulse to share the life around her, to answer the call of need and do the work which cried aloud to be done, that the reasons for living, enduring, laboring, never took the form of argument" (R 527). Habit has become its own purpose.

Yet habitual action is in some sense a contradiction in terms, precisely because habit acts as a substitute for will. If our habits are good, we need no longer choose what we do: our wills can sit back and relax, so to speak. "Habit is activity without opposition," Hegel wrote,[32] but the laws of dynam-ics teach that each action is defined by its reaction. William Godwin described how habits form:

> In proportion as our experience enlarges, the subjects of voluntary action become more numerous. In this state of the human being, he soon comes to perceive a considerable similarity between situation and situation. In consequence he feels inclined to abridge the process of deliberation, and to act today conformably to the determination of yesterday. Thus the understanding fixes for itself resting places.[33]

That search for the similarity between situation and situation resembles closely Eliot's narrative technique, her forced exercise of our "power[s] of comparison" (M 164). Yet Eliot would never wish to "abridge the process of deliberation." So habit works both ways; it curtails some of the dangers of action, but it also hampers some freedom of thought.

The emphasis on habit also vastly limits the possibilities for progress. Aristotle, the supreme political thinker, believed that one is habituated into a state of virtue: virtue provides the backbone needed to do great deeds. But whereas good habits can clearly go far in establishing cleanliness, are they to be our only potential source of effective action? Moreover, can we really expect political reform to spring from the near impossible universal reform of individual habits? This seems to have been the starting point of Eliot's political agenda. George Levine has stated her position as logical necessity: "Since real change can only come about through the slow increment of myriad causes working through history, revolution is doomed to failure."[34] But I wish to stress that as much fear as logic motivated Eliot's beliefs: the risks accompanying any action were tremendous; those of political revolution unthinkable. In an 1856 review of *Antigone*, Eliot noted that "we shall never be able to attain a great right without doing a wrong. Reformers, martyrs, revolutionists, are never fighting against evil only; they are also placing themselves in opposition to a good."[35] When Felix involves himself in the riot, he kills a man. Revolution requires wrongdoing, and since any wrongdoing breeds "woeful progeny," Eliot favored caution. In a letter to John Blackwood, written while she was working on *Felix Holt*, Eliot mentioned "one passage of prophecy which I longed to quote, but I thought it wiser to abstain. 'Now, the beauty of the Reform Bill is, that under its mature operation, the people must and will become free agents'—a prophecy which I hope is true, only the maturity of the operation has not arrived yet."[36] The letter captures perfectly both Eliot's longing for and fear of such "free-agency."

Eliot's sensitivity to the force of consequences must have come in part from the fact that her life's story, like those of both Wordsworth and Clough, was crucially determined by a few dramatic acts: her crisis of religious doubt as a young woman, marked by a refusal to attend church with her father in 1842, her entrance into a nonlegalized marriage with G. H. Lewes in 1854, and her legal marriage to John Cross in 1880. Most of us live lives where our decisions are so many and so slight in and of themselves, their effect so generally cumulative rather than independent, that it would be hard to see how we ended up where we are. But Eliot's three major acts stood at visible crossroads on the map of her existence, making her particularly self-conscious of their influence on her life.

They also effected a dramatic breach between Eliot's sense of external action and her sense of will or internal choice. As Rosemarie Bodenheimer has shown, her three crucial deeds caused Eliot to think of a "woman's life as a rich and strenuous process of choice, invisible to a world in which she is defined by requirements about conduct." Bodenheimer demonstrates that

"George Eliot's representation of choice is about the essence of her experience, about how it was internally structured and how it was externally read and misread by others."[37] The most objective descriptions of her acts—not going to church, a sexual relationship with a married man, marriage (shortly after his death) to another, one much younger than herself—could reveal little on their own about Eliot's moral qualities. So her acts and their aftereffects forced her to relocate the moment of heroism from its usual external manifestation in action to the internal process of decision that precedes action. Such internalized heroism can occur as easily on the domestic front as on the battlefront, as can be seen in her use of the term "holy war" to designate what amounted on the surface to a domestic conflict between a father and his daughter about her conduct. As she told a friend: "Oh, if I could transport myself to your dining-room, where I guess you and Mr. Pears are sitting in anticipation of tea, carrying on no 'Holy War,' but at peace with the world and its opinions."[38] While the term is used somewhat ironically, it anticipates the domestication and internalization of heroism that we see so frequently in Eliot's writings.

From an early age, Eliot took the idea of consequences very seriously. Her conduct toward her father during the Holy War was something she would later live to regret, in spite of her assurance to Dr. Allbutt of the careful consideration she had given the subject: "the bent of my mind is conservative rather than destructive, and that denial has been wrought from me by hard experience—not pleasant rebellion."[39] *Rebellion* almost never figures positively in her lexicon. So Eliot transformed what could be thought of anachronistically as a moment of "teenage rebellion" (and the unbridled activity we associate with the term) into something very different; instead, her fall into adult consciousness was marked by what she later would call "the labour of choice."[40] It is an interesting construction, one that asserts a parallel between strenuous bodily work and a mental effort characteristic of Eliot. Eliot's religious doubt was actually described by a contemporary as "modern atheistic pietism"[41]—a phrase that nicely captures the sacred attention she gives to her own uncertainty. Profound deliberation also marked what John Cross, and virtually every other commentator on the subject, called "the most important event in George Eliot's life—her union with Mr. George Henry Lewes."[42] As Eliot told Mrs. Bray in 1855, "If there is any one action or relation of my life which is and always has been profoundly serious, it is my relation to Mr. Lewes."[43] Seriousness—and the intense internal scrutiny it entails—can help to legitimate otherwise rash-seeming action. As Henry James noted, "The union Miss Evans formed with [Lewes] was a deliberate step, of which she accepted all the consequences."[44]

One of those consequences was an effect on her writing, a tendency to treat action with a seriousness that dramatically retards its progress. James's observation continues: "The fault of most of her work is in the absence of spontaneity, the excess of reflection; and by her action in 1854 (which seemed, superficially, to be the sort usually termed reckless) she committed herself to being nothing if not reflective, to cultivating a kind of compensatory earnestness."[45] While she never regretted it, Eliot maintained a painfully vivid awareness of what could be called the ethical cost-benefit analysis of her choice. Soon after her elopement with Lewes, she wrote to John Chapman, "I have counted the cost of the step that I have taken and am prepared to bear, without irritation or bitterness, renunciation by all my friends."[46] But almost three years later, she was still making calculations: "If I live five years longer, the positive result of my existence will outweigh the small negative good that would have consisted in my not doing anything to shock others, and I can conceive no consequences that will make me repent the past. Do not misunderstand me, and suppose that I think myself heroic or great in any way."[47] One senses her racing against the clock in an effort to make up her moral balance.

What will allow her to get into the black is the social good that will accrue from her work as a novelist, to which she has come only as a result of her union with Lewes. Lewes frequently appears in her letters as high priest to the religion of her novel writing. Eliot seems to have greeted her vocational "annunciation"—the discovery of her talent for writing fiction over which he presided—with relief as well as joy: "I have at last found my true vocation, after which my nature had always been feeling and striving uneasily without finding it," she wrote to her friend D'Albert Durade.[48] Moments of vocation are essential to Eliot's conception of a successful life, as her novels demonstrate.[49] In fact, such moments frequently represent the greatest "event" of her heroes' and heroines' lives, as we shall see. Perhaps *Middlemarch* provides Eliot's most extensive analysis of the concept. Almost every character in the novel can be looked at in terms of vocation: from Dorothea, who is always searching after one, to Lydgate, who has found his but must forsake it, to Farebrother, whose job and vocation (clergyman and entomologist) are distinct in troubling ways, to Fred Vincy, whom Mary wants to preserve from Farebrother's fate. Eliot's fondness for using the term *vocation* in a secular context shows her desire to reinvest work with the potency that had been lost with the demise of the providential order. It also represents an attempt to seek out a new realm for heroism, for all her denial of a "heroic" element to her work. All action that occurs under the auspices of vocation is sanctified. So authorship-as-vocation became, like habit, a form of safe action for Eliot, one that could stand in the place of riskier endeavors such as rebellions.

But even the less elevated form of vocation, work (itself a form of habitual action), garners Eliot's attention in her quest for safe substitutes for large-scale action. In fact, she implies that any distinction between a job and a vocation lies exclusively in the attitude of the worker. Adam Bede's carpentry provides a clear example of how Eliot constructs her argument of the heroic worker. The opening two chapters of *Adam Bede* are titled "The Workshop" and "The Preaching," but before we hear Dinah, we listen to Adam expound his "gospel" of work:

> And there's such a thing as being over-speritial; we must have something beside Gospel i' this world. Look at the canals, an' th' aqueducs, an' th' coal-pit engines, and Arkwright's mills there at Cromford; a man must learn sommut beside Gospel to make them things, I reckon. But t'hear some o' them preachers, you'd think as man must be doing nothing all his life but shutting's eyes and looking what's a-going on inside him. . . . [W]hat does the bible say? Why, it says as God put his sperrit into the workman as built the tabernacle. (AB 11)

Walter E. Houghton has noted that "Except for 'God,' the most popular word in the Victorian vocabulary must have been 'work.'"[50] But as we saw in the case of Clough, when one does "except" God, work becomes even more important. As Adam declares, "there's nothing but what's bearable as long as a man can work" (AB 115).

Carlyle discussed the nobility of work in relation to his observation that sorrow (which he linked to Jesus' suffering) and not happiness (as Aristotle believed) is the end of man: "All work, even cotton spinning, is noble; work alone is noble." For him, the modern epic was not of arms and the man but of "*Tools and the Man.*"[51] Arendt, though, limits nobility to the sphere of action, which she defines as "the only activity that goes on between men. . . . [It] corresponds to the human condition of plurality, to the fact that men, not Man, live on the earth. . . . [T]his plurality is the specifically *the* condition of political life." Work, on the other hand, has a limited range: "Within its borders each individual life is housed." Arendt argues that "to have a definite beginning and a definite, predictable end is the mark of [work]. . . . This great reliability of work is reflected in that the fabrication process, unlike action, is not irreversible; everything produced by human hands can be destroyed by them."[52] One can see why such limitation would be attractive to the risk-averse Eliot, with her sense that "children may be strangled, but deeds never" (R 156).

As Carlyle's beliefs about work and sorrow anticipate, Eliot's emphasis on habitual forms of action also connects to a corresponding emphasis on passive endurance and on suffering as a form of activity. In the letter to Mrs. Ponsonby in which she tried to persuade her friend of the possibility for action, Eliot followed her allusion to habit by recommending "that stoical resignation which is often a hidden heroism."[53] In the same manner, Felix suggests the model of those who "have endured much with patient heroism" to his working men.[54] The passage from *Romola* quoted above, about Romola's activity in the valley, concludes with her recognition that "if the glory of the cross is an illusion, the sorrow is only the truer" (R 527). Eliot is sounding an old note here: Romola's "new baptism" (R 527) through suffering looks back to Adam Bede's "deep, unspeakable suffering [that] may well be called a baptism" (AB 425). Adam's baptism comes about precisely because "this brave, active man, who would have hastened towards any danger or toil to rescue Hetty" (AB 425) is unable to act. "Doubtless a great anguish may do the work of years," the narrator tells us (AB 426).

When Arendt describes the frustration inherent in action, she also links it to suffering: "All this is reason enough to turn away with despair from the realm of human affairs and to hold in contempt the human capacity for freedom, which, by producing the web of human relationships, seems to entangle its producer to such an extent that he appears much more the victim and sufferer than the author and doer of what he has done." "To do and to suffer," she writes elsewhere, "are like opposite sides of the same coin."[55] The radical Felix Holt, whose "excess" used to lie in "being too practical" (FH 308), has turned passive after his misbegotten attempt at action in the riot. He now advises his listeners that "it is constantly the task of practical wisdom not to say, 'This is good, and I will have it,' but to say, 'This is the less of two unavoidable evils, and I will bear it,'" although he tries to dignify such behavior by calling it "activity."[56] "I am a man of this generation," Felix declares (FH 223), and the present is not the proper time for action. As Eliot told her friend Mrs. Congreve, "Mr. Congreve's suffering during the journey and your suffering in watching him saddens me as I think of it. For a long while to come I suppose human energy will be greatly taken up with resignation rather than action."[57]

The correlative of suffering is of course sympathy, and the work of sympathy occupies the very center of Eliot's moral and artistic program. Eliot's ability to make us realize the effort that stands behind a successful operation of sympathy is perhaps the most remarkable aspect of her ethical vigor. "If Art does not enlarge men's sympathies," she wrote to Charles Bray, "it does nothing morally." Eliot considered her vocation to be the expansion of human sympathies through her writing: the "only effect I ardently long to produce in my writings, is that those who read them should be better able to *imagine* and to *feel* the pains and joys of those who differ from themselves in everything but the broad fact of being struggling erring human creatures."[58] In other words, the only effect is an internal effect. This makes it relatively safe—her works will not lead the masses to revolt—but it also dramatically reduces the sphere of her influence. "I wish my feelings for you could travel by some helpful vibrations good for pains," she added to Mrs. Congreve. But they can't; sympathy has its limits.

Eliot's focus on sympathy as a form of work links her writing to that of the Romantic poets, for whom the work of poetry was the work of sympathy. Her connection to Wordsworth is especially strong.[59] Both writers developed their interests in consciousness (and in particular, the consciousness of suffering) and habit as alternatives to action in response to fears surrounding revolutionary forms of activity. As I hope will become clear, though, I believe that Wordsworth achieved by the end of the composition of *The White Doe of Rylstone* a far more secure resolution to his commitment to inaction than Eliot ever managed. In part, the complacency with which he seems to have regarded his attempt to elevate the moral status of consciousness may well have owed something to the fact that his position was arrived at in a much less self-conscious fashion than Eliot's.

Eliot's Romanticism comes from her sense of the power of feeling, and also of the intimate connection between feeling and other forms of knowledge. Poetry, as Wordsworth defined it, is "the first and last of all knowledge," but it appears in the form of "the spontaneous overflow of powerful feelings."[60] Or as Eliot herself puts it, through the voice of Adam Bede, "It isn't notions sets people doing the right thing, it's feelings" (AB 181), but "feeling's a sort o' knowledge" (AB 510). "The great secret of morals is Love," Shelley declared, therewith pronouncing the poets legislators of the world.[61] As Eliot remarked in 1857, "My own experience and development deepen every day my conviction that our moral progress may be measured by the degree in which we sympathize with individual suffering and individual Joy."[62] Keats described the "camelion" poet's capacity to sympathize—to be "continually in for— and filling some other Body." This capacity allowed him to assume any character on which he focused his attentions: "It has as much delight in conceiving an Imogen as an Iago."[63] Similarly, Eliot would attempt, by conceiving Casaubon's feelings with as much sensitivity as Dorothea's, to exercise her readers' sympathetic imaginations. Given her fear of the consequences of action, Romanticism allowed Eliot to envision an alternative form of morality in which the essential activity could be mental rather than physical, internal rather than external.

Eliot's focus on sympathy also corresponded to increasing the attention paid to character at the expense of plot. This led some contemporary critics to question the generic status of her works: "Her materials for excitement and interest are not the excitements of adventure, with their varieties of surface incident; her materials for tragedy are not murders or escapes from murder, with the maneuvers of criminals and detectives: but they are the inner spiritual events that take place beneath the surface. . . . Her works partake thus of the quality that separates the poetry of a great drama from the prose of a great novel. The essential difference, for instance, between 'Hamlet' and 'Pendennis.'"[64] Yet sympathy works via a process of identification with the other, a process that stands as much at the heart of the novelist's enterprise as of the dramatist's. E. S. Dallas noted that while Eliot had not attained "ease of story telling," "the secret of her power is to be found in the depth and range of her sympathies. She gets to the heart of her characters, and makes us feel with them, care for them, like to know about them. . . . When we come to care for people . . . it really does not matter what their story is: it fixes our attention."[65] Eliot herself complained about Dickens that his lack of interest in depicting round characters limited the moral effects of his writing: "We have a great novelist who is gifted with the utmost power of rendering the external traits of our town population; and if he could give us their psychological character . . . his books would be the greatest contribution art has ever made to the awakening of social sympathies."[66] Her own work cannot be charged with the same flaw.

So Eliot believed that as a writer she could act in a safe and secure fashion, without undue risk of accident and with widespread positive effect. As she wrote encouragingly to a fellow author, "Whether the circulation of a book be large or small there is always this supreme satisfaction about solid honest work, that as far as it goes its effects must be good, and as all effects spread immeasurably what we have to care for is *kind* and not quantity."[67] Of course, a writer loses some control as soon as she sends her book out into the world; as Eliot ponders in *Middlemarch,* "Who shall tell what may be the effect of writing?" (M 406). But in general, she seems to have felt that the level of control available to the author exceeded that of other forms of agency.

Curiously, Dorothea's "unhistoric acts" at the conclusion of *Middlemarch* provide a parallel to Eliot's work of authorship. Eliot's modern-day Saint Theresa may indeed be a "foundress of nothing," but although they clearly do not center "in some long-recognizable deed," "her loving heart-beats and sobs after an unattained goodness" are not "dispersed among hindrances" (M 4). Rather, they form the centerpiece of a "home-epic" (M 815) and are, Eliot insists, "incalculably diffusive" in their effects (M 822)—as she hopes her own "home-epics" will be. Both novel writing and domestic activity allow for private deeds to have public benefits. In fact, Eliot frequently emphasizes such connections between public and private life: in *Romola,* "the fortunes of Tito and Romola were dependent on certain grand political and social conditions which made an epoch in the history of Italy" (R 195); and in *Felix Holt,* "there is no private life which has not been determined by a wider public life" (FH 43). But it is notable that Eliot almost always puts the equation thus, in terms of the effects of the political world on domestic life; it is much harder to prove the converse. Even Eliot's comments concerning the diffusive nature of Dorothea's activity are made only at the end of the novel, when they need no longer be detailed. Nevertheless, within the scope of her works, public acts generally prove ineffective in comparison with private activity: Romola serves as the ministering angel to both the poor citizens of Florence and the people in the plague-stricken village, while Savonarola burns at the stake; in *Felix Holt,* as Rosemarie Bodenheimer notes, "Public business makes nothing happen except for unanticipated airings of private secrets,"[68] and the most effective "action" (FH 373) in the novel turns out to be Esther's testimony of love in the courtroom.

Eliot's focus on domestic action suits the genre through which she has chosen to express her beliefs. The novel is the literary manifestation of the private realm. As we have seen, E. S. Dallas attributed the rise of the novel, which he considered to be "gossip etherialized, family talk generalized," to the general decline of heroes—the fact that in a society driven by commerce, while "great deeds are achieved as yore . . . they are not to be accredited to one man so much as they used to be." As a result, "the little men and the private men and all the little incidents of privacy" came "into repute."[69] Yet more often than not, these "little men" turned out to be little women: "Now all the more important characters seem to be women," Dallas noted, though this was "all the more natural, seeing that most of our novelists just now seem to belong to the fair sex." And especially "natural" since "woman peculiarly represents the private life of the race. Her ascendancy in literature must mean the ascendancy of domestic ideas, and the assertion of the individual, not as a hero, but as a family man—not as a heroine, but as an angel in the house."[70]

The focus on women had particular consequences in the battle between plot and character that was being fought in the journals. Women had traditionally been defined by what they were rather than what they did: recall Wordsworth's use of this distinction in creating Emily's character in *The White*

Doe of Rylstone. As Eliot puts it in the motto to chapter 45 of *Daniel Deronda,* a woman's "arduous function" was "solely 'to be there'" (DD 475); who she was could not be determined on the basis of any outward deeds. So, Dallas recognized, the female focus of Victorian literature tended to privilege character over action, being over doing:

> The first object of the novelist is to get personages in whom we can be interested; the next is to put them in action. But when women are the chief characters, how are you to set them in motion? The life of women cannot well be described as a life of action. When women are thus put forward to lead the action of a plot, they must be urged into a false position. . . . This is what is called sensation. It is not wrong to make a sensation; but if the novelist depends for his sensation upon the action of a woman, the chances are that he will attain his end by unnatural means.[71]

As a realist (that is, not a sensation novelist), Eliot stressed the limits placed on female activity throughout her writing. The Victorian understanding of female *accomplishments*—music, painting, languages, needlework—demonstrates beautifully the accepted range of feminine activity. The irony of the term would not have been lost on Eliot. Dorothea's attempt to help those around her through her wealth are hampered by her subjection to men: "Since I can do no good because a woman, / Reach constantly at something that is near it," states the epigraph to chapter 1 of *Middlemarch.* And Eliot's unusually isolated social position, her status as a woman living out of wedlock with a man she considered to be her "husband," would have made her particularly sensitive to women's limited sphere of action. In *The Mill on the Floss,* she openly acknowledges the connection between gender and action, and also, implicitly, genre:

> While Maggie's life-struggles had lain almost entirely within her own soul, one shadowy army fighting another, and the slain shadows for ever rising again, Tom was engaged in a dustier, noisier warfare, grappling with more substantial obstacles, and gaining more definite conquests. So it has been since the days of Hecuba, and of Hector, Tamer of horses: inside the gates, the women with streaming hair and uplifted hands offering prayers, watching the world's combat from afar, filling their long, empty days with memories and fears: outside, the men, in fierce struggle with things divine and human, quenching memory in the stronger light of purpose, losing the sight of dread and even of wounds in the hurrying ardor of action. (MF 309)

Eliot tried to sympathize equally with her Hecuba-Maggie and her Hector-Tom. Her attempt highlights her ambivalence with regard to action, her combined desire for and fear of it. But most readers sense that Eliot's instinctive feelings tended toward the suffering girl rather than the struggling boy.[72] Hecuba, after all, is the proper heroine of a home-epic, or novel.

So when Eliot championed the moral effectiveness of private forms of action—both internal and small scale—she was simultaneously making an argument about women's ability to effect positive moral change. Eliot's tendency to link domestic action with public benefits is typical of conservative discourses about the role of women in Victorian society. For example, in *The Women of England, their Social Duties, and Domestic Habits* (1839), Sarah Stickney Ellis argued "how intimate is the connexion which exists between the *women* of England, and the moral character maintained by their country in the scale of nations." But Ellis based her assertion on her belief that "so entirely do human actions derive their dignity or their meanness from the *motives* by which they are prompted, that it is no violation to say, the most servile drudgery may be ennobled by the self-sacrifice, the patience, the cheerful submission to duty, with which it is performed."[73] Sound familiar? For Eliot, "as a fact of mere zoological evolution," woman had "the worse share in existence." But, she insisted, "for that very reason I would the more contend that in the moral evolution we have 'an art which does mend nature.' It is the function of love in the largest sense, to mitigate the harshness of all fatalities"—those fatalities being the external strictures placed on women's condition and action.[74] In *A Woman's Thoughts about Women* (1858), Dinah Craik described the "natural" difference between "man's vocation and woman's": "one is abroad, the other at home: one external, the other internal: one active, the other passive."[75] Eliot often seems to prefer the female form of vocation, even for the male. Because of her preference for unhistoric acts, the limitation to the domestic sphere, once accepted, could really be appreciated as a form of liberation. Women may have been cut off from grand-scale heroism, but they were surrounded with opportunities for the commission of incalculably diffusive smaller deeds. In *The Mill on the Floss,* Eliot repeats the famous observation that the happiest women, like the happiest nations, have no history (MF 385)—that is, that their biographies are devoid of recognizable acts, of deeds done on the epic scale. But one senses that she might wish to extend this remark to men, as well. After all, grander masculine activity hardly fares well in her works: Tom dies along with Maggie, and Lydgate's great ambitions are strangled in the bonds of his marriage to Rosamond.

Yet some late reflections in *Impressions of Theophrastus Such* (1879) indicate that Eliot must have felt a degree of ambivalence about her championing of domestic action:

> Seeing that Morality and Morals under their *alias* of Ethics are the subject of voluminous discussion and their true basis a pressing matter of dispute—seeing that the most famous book ever written on Ethics [i.e., Aristotle's], and forming a chief study in our colleges, allies ethical with political science or that which treats of the constitution and prosperity of states, one might expect that educated men would find reason to avoid a perversion of language which lends itself to no wider view of life than that of our own village gossips. . . . [W]hen a man whose business hours, the solid part of every day, are spent in an unscrupulous course of public or private action which has every calculable chance of causing wide-spread injury and misery, can be called moral because he comes home to dine with his wife and children and cherishes the happiness of his own hearth, the augury is not good for the use of high ethical and theological disputation.[76]

While Eliot notes the connection between ethics and the political, she seems nervous of the divisions between public and private spheres that can open up when morality becomes a category of purely domestic behavior. She wishes *Morality* (a term that carries with it connotations of the domestic and social realms) to be considered a synonym for *Ethics* (a term that cannot be divorced from Aristotle's political conception of virtue, as Eliot's reference to his great treatise indicates): to be a man of "pure moral character," she insists, one must be as publicly virtuous as one is domestically so.[77] That is, to be moral, one must be ethical; Eliot seems to wish to reinvigorate the more political, Aristotelian category.

And while Eliot's women tend to showcase her conception of heroism, bringing out its peculiarities, her least heroic character, Rosamond Vincy, demonstrates again that she may well have felt uncomfortable with some of her own conclusions. Rosamond is arguably the most effective agent— almost daemonically so—in all Eliot's writing. Her passive-aggressive purposiveness represents a nightmarish realization of the kind of novelistic activity Eliot appears to be advocating: it is habitual and petit bourgeois in the extreme. In a single paragraph, Eliot actually compares her efficacy to both the unstoppable force of nature and also, implicitly, the force of the people in a laissez-faire state:

> Mrs. Vincy's belief that Rosamond could manage her papa was well founded. Apart from his dinners and his coursing, Mr. Vincy, blustering as he was, had as little of his own way as if he had been a prime minister: the force of circumstances was easily too much for him. . . . [A]nd the circumstance called Rosamond was particularly forcible by means of that mild persistence which, as we know, enables a white soft living substance to make its way in opposing rock. (M 341)[78]

Perhaps Rosamond Vincy's successful co-opting of the very forces of modernity that had so constrained notions of the heroic helps explain the intensity of Eliot's hatred of her. Eliot's sympathies, otherwise so diffusive, discovered their limits; Cross remarked that "Of all the characters she had attempted she found Rosamond's the most difficult to sustain with [a] sense of 'possession.'"[79]

R. H. Hutton used Eliot's "dead set" against Rosamond to describe the impression of roundness Eliot generates with her characters: "Her characters are so real that they have a life and body of their own quite distinct from her criticisms of them; and one is conscious at times of taking part with her characters against the author."[80] Of course Rosamond's selfishness is the antithesis of Dorothea's benevolence, but it also anticipates Gwendolen Harleth's selfish willfulness at the start of *Daniel Deronda*.[81] Eliot seems to have created Gwendolen partially in an attempt to remedy her failure of sympathy with regard to Rosamond, although it is interesting that in order to allow her sympathetic identification with Gwendolen to proceed, she had to make Gwendolen fail in precisely those ways Rosamond had succeeded. It is as though the act of sympathy depends in some measure on the frustration of action inherent in suffering. Yet Gwendolen's position with regard to action is far more complex than Rosamond's had been, as I shall show. Of all Eliot's characters, she finds it hardest to accept restrictions on her activity, and her struggle must in part be seen to represent Eliot's struggle with the conclusions of her own beliefs. This is one of the forces behind Gwendolen's own, even more striking, roundness of character, which will be the subject of the final section of this chapter.

Eliot's "revision" of Rosamond in Gwendolen suggests her tendency to refine from novel to novel her position with regard to action. This tendency appears in a subtle shift that takes place in her approach to habit and to the related categories—all substitutes for traditional, epic, forms of action—of work, suffering, and sympathy. The shift occurs around the point Eliot wrote *Romola,* and in fact, one can think of the entire "second half" of Eliot's oeuvre—from *Romola* on out—as consisting of "political" novels.[82] *Romola* questions Romola's right to "rebellion" (R 442) during a period of civil rebellion in republican Florence, just as *Felix Holt* sets Esther's "revolution" against the backdrop of a potentially revolutionary England at the time of the First Reform Bill; in both novels, as we saw, Eliot emphasizes the connection between public and private life. *Middlemarch* continues the political trend with its similar backdrop of the Reform Bill and with Ladislaw's (and Mr. Brooke's) political ambitions. Finally, in *Daniel Deronda,* the politics of Daniel's mission come into the foreground. Eliot's increasing concern for the political arena must be seen as a reflection of the ambivalence she felt toward her own risk aversion with regard to action, toward her tendency to internalize and restrict it.

Moreover, it is important to register a gradual change in the novels from an emphasis on suffering toward one on habit and to see this as a result of developing interest in the political sphere; although Eliot's interest in habit is present from the outset of her literary career—*habitual* is ever a favorite word—the sharp focus on habit as a substitute for action sets in with *Romola.* In the earlier works, it seems that to know sorrow is to know virtue: *Adam Bede*'s narrator tells us, "Let us . . . be thankful that our sorrow lives in us as an indestructible force, only changing its form, as forces do, and passing from pain into sympathy" (AB 487). The indestructible force of sorrow serves as a substitute for the indelible consequences of action. Eliot even suggests in these novels that our capacity to suffer is the defining quality of humanity—"that superior power of misery which distinguishes the human being, and places him at a proud distance from the most melancholy chimpanzee" (MF 46–47). *Adam Bede* and *The Mill on the Floss* are both infused with a somewhat sentimentalized version of Wordsworth's pastoral atmosphere, and they clearly share in the belief examined in chapter 1 that literature should emphasize feelings, not action, that "a common tale / By moving accident uncharactered / A tale of silent suffering" is the most interesting kind of story.[83] Part of their Wordsworthian emphasis has to do with a glorification of the past via the exercise of memory; in these works, the past creates the sole law. Maggie Tulliver's "final rescue" comes only after she accepts this: "If the past is not to bind us, where can duty lie?" (MF 475). Memory is her "clue of life" (MF 471), her Ariadne's thread that will lead her through the labyrinthine confusions of the web of action.[84]

Through the introduction of habit as a bridge from endurance to action, *Romola* marks a change. When Romola turns back to Florence for the first time, she declares her intention "to thread life by a fresh clue" (R 348); rather than Maggie's backward glance of memory, the cautious force of habit will lead her forward. But why write a political novel as a historical novel? Why put the action so far back? The book is still conservative, and political activity ends in disaster: Tito slips irredeemably into sin; the impressive Savonarola, in many respects a precursor to Mordecai (another man for whom political vision and religious vision are one and the same) succumbs to the need for a "doubleness" (R 539) that seems perilously close to falseness; and the virtuous Bernardo is executed as a traitor. Ultimately Romola, like Maggie, must return to her past. Yet the very presence of her second flight, the difference between it and the first, aborted attempt at escape, from which Romola is sent back by Savonarola as one who has forgotten both wifely and civic duty, indicates a new willingness in Eliot at least to toy with the idea of a "sacred" rebellion (R 442). In *Felix Holt,* Eliot again scrutinizes the concept of revolution, and the results lead her to try for the limited efficacy of action in Dorothea's "unhistoric acts" in *Middlemarch.*[85] And although these novels, set in the period of the First Reform Bill, still look backward in time, they also look, Janus faced, to the present times of the Second Reform Bill. Finally, in *Daniel Deronda,* George Eliot attempts to gaze into the future.

Daniel Deronda: Gwendolen Harleth

Daniel Deronda's virtual contemporaneity marks its willingness to look forward, to try activity.[86] Hannah Arendt defines action as "the capacity of beginning something anew";[87] the finale of *Middlemarch* had declared every limit to be "a beginning as well as an ending" (M 815). But George Eliot opens her final novel with the wise observation that "men can do nothing without the make-believe of a beginning" (DD 3). Still, although *Daniel Deronda* firmly asserts the connection between doing and beginning, its author depends upon an element of make-believe to get the narrative dough to rise. I wish to suggest that the heroine and hero of the story actually represent not only two kinds of plot—those of realism and romance[88]—but also two kinds of activity. When Henry James's Theodora wonders what Daniel accomplished in the East, Pulcheria's response— they had tea parties, Daniel talked, and Mirah sang a little—indicates her refusal to leave Gwendolen's realistic mode.[89] Eliot sacrifices any potential for realistic progress when she scapegoats Gwendolen, leaving her behind to suffer in an outdated England while Deronda departs for Palestine and the future. But Pulcheria is unable to consider seriously the possibilities of romantic political idealism, of make-believe as a leaven for doing. Ultimately, one's feelings about the success of the novel as an instrument for progress will depend in part on one's willingness to see beyond realism. Politics cannot be divorced from plotting.

Eliot had tried out the plot of *Daniel Deronda* in an earlier work in a different mode: *The Spanish Gypsy* (published in 1868 but originating in 1864, roughly the same period as *Felix Holt*). Like Deronda, Fedalma (the heroine of *The Spanish Gypsy*) is a foundling who has been raised by nobility. On the eve of what Eliot calls "the great event" of her life as a woman—her marriage to Don Silva, the duke of Bedmar—Fedalma experiences a moment of vocation.[90] The moment corresponds, as in *Daniel Deronda,* with a discovery of her birth (and membership in a hated and scorned tribe): she is the daughter of the imprisoned Zarca, chief of the Zincali. And as in the novel, the discovery of birth affects marriage choices. So instead of marrying Don Silva and becoming an angel in the house, Fedalma accepts her lot: "To be the angel of a homeless tribe."[91] But first she must free her father: "A work as pregnant as the act of men / Who set their ships aflame and spring to land, / A fatal deed" (SG 112).

While the escape is successful, Zarca's plans to get his people a homeland run afoul when Don Silva refuses to accept his lot with that "grand submission" that, Eliot tells us in her "Notes" to the poem, characterizes Fedalma's response to fate.[92] Instead, he exhibits what Eliot calls "the tragedy of entire rebellion": "I will elect my deeds, and be the liege / Not of my birth, but of that good alone / I have discerned and chosen" (SG 213). Don Silva, his "nature over-endowed with opposites" (SG 151), resembles a Byronic hero: his mixed essence renders him unsuited to life in the world. He follows Fedalma to the Gypsies' camp and pledges his support for their cause in order to stay with her. "I'll face the progeny of all my deeds," he blusters ominously (SG 155); we recall that for Eliot, deeds themselves represent "woeful progeny" (FH 11). When Zarca leads an attack against Bedmar, though, Silva finds that his divided loyalties (which resemble both Francis's in *The White Doe of Rylstone* and Daniel Deronda's*)* prove too much for him: he kills Zarca to revenge the Zincali's slaughter of his people. The conclusion of the drama lacks the hope of the ending of *Daniel Deronda.* Fedalma leads her people to their promised land in northern Africa, but the prognosis is poor without her father's presence: "His image gone, there were no wholeness left / To make a world of for the Zincali's thought" (SG 247). "She saw the end begun" (SG 255), Eliot remarks, and we have no sense here that the ending will also prove to be a new beginning.

Clearly, *The Spanish Gypsy* shares with *Daniel Deronda* a deep concern about the efficacy of political action. Zarca insists that "No great deed is done / By falterers who ask for certainty"—a certainty Eliot had often seemed to require before venturing forth into action. Yet the new approval of action does not rely on a belief that deeds are necessarily efficacious, but rather on the faith that

> The greatest gift the hero leaves his race
> Is to have been a hero. Say we fail!—
> We feed the high tradition of the world
> And leave our spirit in our children's breasts. (SG 120)

That is, it relies on a sense of the force of character to prevail. And Zarca's optimism about the moral efficacy of heroic character seems strangely out of step with the dismal conclusion to the poem. As Eliot's "Notes" to the poem tell, Zarca represents "the struggle for a great end, rendered vain by the surrounding conditions of life."[93]

Eliot obviously worried about the message she was delivering. Curiously, in her "Notes" she used Clough's poetry as a foil to her own enterprise. Eliot's comments were aimed at what she saw as Clough's dispiriting notion of "duty," a concept that she herself linked to "piety," or an "Inward impulse"—"i.e., loving, willing submission, and heroic Promethean efforts toward high possibilities which may result from our individual life"—a conglomerate of those substitutes for external action discussed in the previous section. (Eliot's "piety" also marks a distinct shift from the *pietas* of Aeneas, an inward feeling indivisible from its outward manifestation as the motive behind the quest to found Rome.) Ostensibly, Eliot objected to Clough because she viewed him as wishing to divorce, in the manner of Kant, the concept of duty from any perceived ends we see as goods. This, she felt, was counterproductive: "That favorite view, expressed so often in Clough's poems, of doing duty, in blindness as to the result, is likely to deepen the substitution of egoistic yearnings for really moral impulses."[94]

But the context of the reference to Clough makes clear that her real worry was about the representation of action in art produced by a skeptical world (that is, a world motivated by duty rather than by God), as the next paragraph indicates:

> The art which leaves the soul in despair is laming to the soul, and is denounced by the healthy sentiment of an active community. The consolatory elements in "The Spanish Gypsy" are derived from two convictions or sentiments which so conspicuously pervade it that they may be said to

be its very warp on which the whole action is woven. These are—(1) The importance of individual deeds; (2) The all-sufficiency of the soul's passions in determining sympathetic action.[95]

Yet the very adamancy of the protest should raise the warning flags. Eliot's own poem seems, like most of her work, to depend on her second statement to mitigate her failure to demonstrate the truth of her first claim. Sympathetic action takes over from individual deeds. Indeed, the dispiriting conclusion to her drama causes it to suffer from the same enervating sins as Clough's poetry. Not coincidentally, *The Spanish Gypsy* also shares in the generic hybridity of Clough's *Amours de Voyage*. Eliot's "drama" contains both narrative interludes and lyric songs (performed by a minstrel, Juan—perhaps with subtle allusion to Byron's hero of another generic hybrid, the epic-novel-in-verse, *Don Juan*). Moreover, like the romantic closet dramas, it is (according to Eliot) "eminently unsuited for an acting play."[96] Again, we see the link between genre and attitudes toward action; the epic intent (the founding of a new nation, as in the *Aeneid*) flounders amidst the confusions of competing modes.

Daniel Deronda, in its combination of the realistic "Gwendolen-plot" with the romance "Deronda-plot," also presents something of a generic mix. Yet the genre withheld from the blend is epic, and the trouble is that rightly speaking, Gwendolen belongs in epic—or at least in an adventure story. From the first sentence of novel, Eliot associates Gwendolen with activity; her glance, we are told, has a "dynamic" quality (DD 3). Henry James's Pulcheria is not the only one to accuse Eliot of a want of tact in using so unfamiliar a word—Eliot's publisher, Blackwood, also objected—but the choice is deliberate, and Eliot wants us to notice it.[97] Comte, in his *Introduction to Positive Philosophy,* divided the study of humanity into two categories, "the static and the dynamic; that is, as fitted to act and as actually acting."[98] Again and again, Eliot affiliates Gwendolen with the love of action; "she was never fearful in action," we learn early (DD 58). A modern-day Camilla, she thrives on movement: she enjoys sports, both archery and riding. For Eliot gambling usually represents a will-not-to-will, a relinquishment of the principle of choice, a "narrow monotony of action" (DD 5) the numbness of which is the obverse of real action (although a little like habit; not a resemblance Eliot would wish to stress). Of the *Kursaal* where Eliot had the well-documented encounter with Byron's niece that formed the germ for the beginning of her novel, Eliot complained that "there is very little dramatic 'Stoff' to be picked up."[99] But Gwendolen, at least at first, goes to the roulette table in search of passion rather than to escape it (DD 12). Being "bored to death," her response is: "I must make something happen" (DD 9). Eliot notes the general sense that it would have been "folly" to expect her to "wear a gown as shabby as Griselda's" (DD 30); patience is presumably not to be expected of such a character. "I mean to do something" rings as her clarion call (DD 200).

Although Gwendolen desires to be an effective agent, she fails. Her strength of will may be remarkable (DD 18, 32, 43), but the events of the novel systematically crush it out of her, destroying her "belief in her own power of dominating" (DD 363) and slowly transforming it into a Griselda-like self-suppression, "an almost miraculous power of self control" (DD 503). Gwendolen must be taught to submit. When her first plan, "to do what pleases me" (DD 56), can no longer be carried out due to the financial losses of the family (a typical blow of destiny), Gwendolen's initial impulse is characteristically "to do something" (DD 195): "I don't resign myself. I shall do what I can against it. What is the good of calling people's wickedness Providence? . . . [I]t was his improvidence with our money. . . . My uncle ought to take measures" (DD 198). Her impotence, as Eliot describes it, owes much to the vagueness of the "something" Gwendolen wishes to accomplish. She herself announces, "I would rather emigrate than be a governess," therewith suggesting her recognition of the limited number of paths open to her and her desire to take the most adventurous one available (DD 199). But as a young lady, she cannot escape so easily—unlike Deronda at the end of the novel or any of the other figures we have encountered who have sought to clear themselves of the entanglements of their past actions by emigration.[100]

So Gwendolen attempts, rather tellingly, to be an actress. But she is told she lacks the talent for it—she does not have the vocation. Gwendolen's flirtation with the stage shows how the theatrical theme in the novel connects with the theme of action.[101] Acting is acceptable to Eliot only when it takes the form of vocation, as it does for the Princess, when it is "sincere acting" (DD 539). Even then, it is dangerous. On the stage, actors deny responsibility for their actions; people commit deeds of which their real characters would be ashamed. Yet the ground between such acting and the truth is slippery, as Laure's "murder" of her husband by a "slip" of the foot shows in *Middlemarch* (M 151). In *Romola,* Tito tries to "strip himself of the past, as of rehearsal clothing, to robe himself for the real scene" (R 450). The fact of a practical life, however, is that there is no "practice time"—what is done cannot be undone. Notably, Mirah can act only "when it was not really acting, but the part was one I could be myself in" (DD 185). Like Fanny Price, the passive heroine of Austen's *Mansfield Park* (1814), another novel that exploits the connection between acting and action in a conservative cause,

Mirah hates acting and desires only to be. She is inherently passive; think of the crossed feet that Henry James registered as her characteristic pose.[102] Her suicide attempt represents a supreme act of will: "And a new strength came into me to will what I would do. You know what I did" (DD 190). Yet though her will is strong, what Mirah *does* is renounce action completely by "lying down to sleep" (DD 189) in a manner that recalls Mortimer's frequent yearnings after sleep in *The Borderers*.[103] It is Mirah's nature "to submit" (DD 190), Mrs. Meyrick tells Daniel: "The force of her nature had long found its chief action in resolute endurance" (DD 626). Mirah's message is Eliot's: "Acting is slow and poor to what we go through *within*" (DD 557; emphasis added).

After Gwendolen's disappointment at her failure to become an actress, she attempts to resign herself: "it makes no difference to anyone else what we do. . . . Help me to be quiet" (DD 225). She wants to be more like her rival, Mirah, to have her self-possession, and she sees that such composure is incompatible with a thirst for activity. But her principle of action is too strong; in her, resignation takes the form of "world nausea" (DD 231), a "sick motivelessness," a "numbness" (DD 232). "I can't do anything better," she laments, feeling herself akin to a man whose profession is too narrow for his powers (DD 234). Yet her problem really belongs to her own gender—and class—as Eliot's friend Barbara Bodichon, the women's rights activist, recognized: "The want of stimulus to energetic action is much felt by women of the higher classes. It is agreed that they ought not to be idle, but what they ought to do is not so clear."[104] Eliot describes Gwendolen in the same language that she had used for Maggie and Romola: "Surely a young creature is pitiable who has the labyrinth of life before her and no clue" (DD 232). And although we can accept that her desire for pleasure was an inadequate vocation—she herself accepts this by the conclusion of the novel—the only proffered substitute, sympathy toward those closest to her, leaves little scope for her activity. As a woman, Gwendolen is expected (in the words of the epigraph to chapter 51) to sit and spin like Erinna, "In insect-labor, while the throng / Of gods and men wrought deeds that poets wrought in song" (DD 535). Gwendolen realizes the truth in what she tells Grandcourt: "We women can't go in search of adventures—to find out the North-West Passage or the source of the Nile, or to hunt tigers in the East." Grandcourt's reply suggests the range of female doing: "But a woman can be married" (DD 113).

Within the frame of *Daniel Deronda,* marriage can represent meaningful activity. Catherine Arrowpoint's "decisive effort" to wed Klesmer is compared to "the leap of a woman from the deck into the lifeboat" (DD 208–9), a deed markedly opposed to the leap Gwendolen makes to follow her drowning husband into the water.[105] But it is worth noting that once Catherine marries, her story is more or less over; she drops from sight in the narrative. Gwendolen, unlike Catherine or Dorothea, both potential heroines of the home-epic, does not see in marriage "the fulfillment of her ambition; the dramas in which she imagined herself a heroine were not wrought up to that close" (DD 30). In her resistance to the marriage plot, she resembles the Florence Nightingale of Lytton Strachey's *Eminent Victorians:* "There was nothing in the world to prevent her from making a really brilliant match. But no! She would think of nothing but how to satisfy that singular craving of hers to be doing something. As if there was not plenty to do in any case, in the ordinary way, at home."[106] Nevertheless, while initially, like Nightingale, Gwendolen feels untempted by marriage, the resemblance ends there. For in contrast to Nightingale's purposeful pursuit of her nursing career, "what [Gwendolen] was not clear upon was, how she should set about leading any other [life], and what were the particular acts which she would assert her freedom by doing" (DD 43). To Eliot, as I have suggested, the idea of asserting freedom through action is necessarily troubling. Gwendolen may think she will be able to regain her freedom after the act of marriage ("she was going to do just as she liked" [DD 111]; "she would know how to act" [DD 265]), but she soon discovers that marriage, like all other forms of action, enslaves.

Of course, the most compelling courtship plot—that is, the possible romance between Gwendolen and Deronda—remains what Gillian Beer has called "a willful and conscious form of negation: its power comes from not telling the stories we anticipate hearing."[107] By the time the novel opens, Deronda has already met and rescued Mirah; the most he can ever say is, "I should have loved her, if—" (DD 532). In fact, the disruption in *Daniel Deronda* between chronological and narrative sequence *(story* and *plot,* to use the Russian formalist terms), causes a general devaluation of the events as we encounter them as readers; options that had seemed to be real possibilities are frequently revealed to be dead ends because of the prior occurrence of events of which we had no knowledge. So the "ifs" in *Daniel Deronda* remain curiously sterile. Henry James complained of the same phenomenon that Beer describes as "thickening, barely provisional counter-plots of possibility" when he lamented in his review of *Middlemarch* the "wealth of dramatic possibility" given up by not allowing more interaction between Dorothea and Lydgate. Such potentially satisfying courtship plots haunt the two novels, casting ghostly shadows of doubt over the very concept of purposeful action represented by the "I do" of the marriage plot.

Ironically, in *Daniel Deronda* both the proposal scene and the "murder" are properly scenes of inaction rather than of action. Gwendolen never does do anything other than suffer. The proposal scene is perhaps the greatest example in all of Eliot's writings, rife with such examples, of a slip into sin that is unaccompanied by any real activity. Instead, Gwendolen's act is characterized by the same "hurry [that] would save her from deliberate choice" with which she replies to Grandcourt's note naming his intended visit (DD 248). Gwendolen never actually makes the *choice* to accept him; at each step along the way, she relinquishes her will, for all her belief on going in to the encounter that it will afford her the opportunity to "exercise her power" (DD 254). Her "drift[ing]" (DD 257) recalls Maggie's voyage downstream with Stephen in *The Mill on the Floss,* but the narrator, hinting at the degree to which past acts determine present choices, reminds us that "the sails have been set beforehand" (257). (Eliot thereby aligns the proposal scene with Grandcourt's death—at sea, so emphasizing the manner in which the marriage not only resembles but also determines the "murder.") All Gwendolen's evasions to Grandcourt's questions lead her irrevocably into that corner in which "Yes" seems the only possible response; although suggestively, her crucial move toward agreement comes when she replies to Grandcourt's "Do you command me to go?" with a "No." "[T]hat negative was a clutch," Eliot informs us (DD 257).

Grandcourt's method of proposal suits a man consistently represented in the negative. The first thing we hear of him is that "whatever Grandcourt had done, he had not ruined himself" (DD 77). Gwendolen's attraction to him is defined by what he is not: "he is not ridiculous" (DD 92); he is "free from absurdities" (DD 115); there is "less to dislike" in him than in other men (DD 117). Graham Handly describes how the "pauses in his conversation with Gwendolen are proleptic of the long 'do-nothing' voids which are the words *and* punctuation of Gwendolen's married life" (DD xxi). Grandcourt's nature is one of "refined negatives" (DD 574), of "dreamy do-nothing absolutism" (DD 573), like the yachting that he enjoys.[108] Eliot has created the worst possible husband for the active Gwendolen, and, for a while, the "benumbing effect" of his torpedolike will (DD 363)—the same force, incidentally, possessed by Rosamond Vincy, whose "torpedo-contact" so stuns Lydgate (M 621)—seems to suck the life out of her.

Ironically, Gwendolen becomes a good actress only when she ceases to be an actor: "I think I am making a very good Mrs. Grandcourt," she remarks (DD 473). But unlike her mother's, Gwendolen's unhappy marriage does not lead her to succumb to a life of passive suffering. The real tragedy of Gwendolen's story lies in the replacement of a bold intention, "I mean to do something," with a desperate plea to which no adequate reply is given: "What should I do?" (DD 382). This is the question that, again and again, Gwendolen asks of Deronda. Eliot's heroines have asked it before: Dorothea does repeatedly, both in a general sense, throughout *Middlemarch* (M 27, 272), and specifically of Lydgate with regard to Casaubon's illness (M 286); Rosamond also asks it of Lydgate, but in a damningly different register (M 558). Yet by the end of the book, Dorothea's question is answered, apparently to the (realistically limited) satisfaction of all concerned.

Deronda never comes up with a reply that can satisfy the dynamic Gwendolen. He tells her that her deed, the marriage to Grandcourt that deprived Mrs. Glasher and her children of what should have been theirs, is "not to be amended by doing one thing only—but many." But when Gwendolen eagerly asks "What?" Daniel responds by informing her that "there are many thoughts and habits that may help us to bear inevitable sorrow" (DD 382). We have heard this answer before from Eliot, yet by the time she came to write *Daniel Deronda,* it must have been as unsatisfactory a description of doing to her as it is to Gwendolen, who can only repeat her question. "I must get up in the morning and do what everyone else does," Gwendolen cries, "It is all like a dance set beforehand" (DD 386). This was precisely Mrs. Ponsonby's worry, and it indicates that Gwendolen's frustration is not specific; it is a version of that inherent in human agency. Deronda tells her that "nothing is feebler than the indolent rebellion of complaint; and to be roused into self-judgment is comparative activity" (DD 388). "Self-judgment" represents just that form of inward contemplation of which Eliot was herself such a great practitioner. But when Gwendolen informs Daniel of her intentions— "I will try . . . I will think" (DD 388)—we know her well enough to suspect her struggles are not over. She is still looking for a way to do.

In fact, Eliot repeats such a scene between Deronda and Gwendolen, in which Gwendolen makes a heart-wrenching appeal for some outlet in action, twice more: once before and once after the "murder" (DD 521ff., 657ff.). Unfortunately, Gwendolen can now, like her author, imagine action only as something awful, something to be avoided: "The vision of her past wrong-doing, and what it had brought on her, came with a pale ghastly illumination over every imagined deed that was a rash effort at freedom, such as she had made in her marriage" (DD 576). Bereft of all faith in action, she is left to dwell on "the benignity of accident" (DD 576). Eliot, we may recall, is the proponent of what Hutton called an "accidental school of fiction"—that is, she is a realist. But for realists, accident is rarely a "benign" force; at best, it is neutral. To depend upon it is to embrace a chaos over which we must relinquish all control. Of course, "the benignity of accident" hints forward to Grandcourt's "accident" or "murder" at sea (neither term adequately represents what happened). The "accidental status" of this event is highly questionable, not only as regards Gwendolen but also as regards her author. It is the product of a kind of quasi-wishful thinking on both their parts, and it can correspondingly be thought of as half-action and half-accident. It is also only "half-benign." Through the accident, Eliot lets Gwendolen escape her horrible marriage. But she does not give her heroine to the hero of her dreams, and she ensures Gwendolen remains burdened with an inescapable sense of guilt.

Insofar as it represents a desired event, the "murder" can be thought of as a weird externalization of Gwendolen's repressed active principle: "I only know that I saw my wish outside me . . . and my heart said, 'Die'—and he sank; and I felt 'It is done—. . . . That was what happened. That was what I did" (DD 596). But because it was merely a matter of thought (and perhaps a moment of hesitation), it cannot be seen as a real act. If her first crime of inaction—the "I do" of her acceptance of Grandcourt, which was unaccompanied by any real "I will"—locks her into the prison of her marriage, her second crime of inaction, better seen as a will unaccompanied by any doing, makes Gwendolen realize the inescapable prison of past deeds.[109] Curiously, Gwendolen echoes in her account of the event the detached cadences of Mirah's earlier description of her suicide attempt: "And a new strength came into me to will what I would do. You know what I did. I was going to die" (DD 190). But unlike Mirah's, Gwendolen's "half" of *Daniel Deronda* offers no opportunities for new beginnings, even in make-believe. As the motto of chapter 22 declares, we may "please our fancy with ideal webs / Of innovation, but our life meanwhile / Is in the loom" (DD 202).

Gwendolen is in fact stuck fast in a web, but it is a web of inaction rather than of action. Although she struggles valiantly, she cannot free herself. After Grandcourt's death, Eliot compares Gwendolen to a "lost, weary, storm-beaten white doe, unable to rise and pursue its unguided way" (DD 597). As Shifra Hochberg has recognized, the allusion is to Wordsworth's *The White Doe of Rylstone*. Hochberg suggests that the reference to the doe indicates the Wordsworthian element to Gwendolen's moral education in sympathy. Yet she notes a difference: "While in Wordsworth's poem, the Doe becomes Emily's constant companion until the heroine's death, in *Daniel Deronda* physical presence as overt symbol is ultimately replaced by the internalization of moral principle after Daniel's departure for the East."[110] I am arguing that the process of internalization proves more costly to Gwendolen than Hochberg's statement intimates; Eliot's struggle with action lacks Wordsworthian assurance. Deronda asks Gwendolen, "What sort of earth or heaven would hold any spiritual wealth in it for souls pauperized by inaction?" (DD 387). But at the end of the novel, while Gwendolen may have learned sympathy, crucially, she does "not yet see how" she can translate that knowledge into acts that better the lives of others (DD 694). Daniel's final advice to her, that a motive will be formed from the repetition of small, inconsequential acts (DD 658), follows Mill's observation on the relationship between habit and purpose. Yet the strongest sense of purpose Gwendolen possesses comes from her love for Daniel (DD 481, 653), and he deserts her. After hearing of Deronda's plans to go to the East, "Gwendolen had sat like a statue with her wrists lying over each other and her eyes fixed—the intensity of her mental action arresting all other excitation" (DD 689). The stance resembles Mirah's characteristic crossed feet, but the posture is neither natural nor comfortable for the energetic Gwendolen.

Sir Hugo, on first seeing Gwendolen, makes the acute observation that "that girl has some drama in her" (DD 137). The drama, though, for all the melodrama of the "murder," stays *in,* remains internalized. Early on, Eliot stakes a novelist's claim for the importance of such inner activity in terms similar to those she used in *Middlemarch:*

> Could there be a slenderer, more insignificant thread in human history than this consciousness of a girl . . . ?—in a time, too, when ideas were with fresh vigor making armies of themselves . . . : when women on the other side of the world would not mourn for the husbands and sons who die bravely in a common cause. . . .
>
> What in the midst of that mighty drama are girls and their blind visions? They are the Yea or Nay of that good for which men are enduring and fighting. (DD 102–3)

But by the end of the novel, although she has still not made clear what Gwendolen is to do, Eliot uses the image of the American Civil War to chastise her for the former narrowness of her vision: "Life looks out from the scene of human struggle with the awful face of duty, and a religion shows itself which is something else than a private consolation" (DD 689). Nevertheless, "wide vision, narrow action" is an inherently frustrating motto to live by, for both Gwendolen and her creator.

Daniel Deronda: DANIEL DERONDA

Daniel Deronda's Judaism represents just the kind of religion Gwendolen lacks, and Eliot wants to show how Daniel becomes, through the course of the novel, an effective agent of large-scale political change. Precisely how this change will come about remains something of a mystery. Henry James (as Constantius) put it thus: "There is something very fascinating in the mission that Deronda takes upon himself. I don't quite know what it means, I don't understand more than half of Mordecai's rhapsodies, and I don't perceive exactly what practical steps could be taken."[111] But such difficulty has long been associated with idealism, as Eliot knows, and as the conversation of the Philosophers at the Hand and Banner makes clear. The very name of the pub demonstrates the conflict: can a banner bring about change, or are active hands required?[112] From our perspective, fifty years after the foundation of the Jewish State, the problem seems less severe. But when Eliot was writing her novel, the Zionist movement had not been given the clarity even of a name, and Deronda's mission as presented in the text really is remarkably undefined; James was right to wonder about practical steps.[113] Moreover, as Graham Martin has noted, even if one accepts the force of ideas to occasion real political change, "The choice of Zionism has the effect of removing the ideal aspirations associated with Deronda from any effective engagement with the English scene."[114] The power of make-believe can extend only so far; it is impossible for Eliot to imagine a new beginning at home. Like Coleridge and Southey in their "Pantisocratic" phase, she has to go to what is for her virgin territory—a place where the web of past deeds has not yet formed to entangle newcomers—to envision useful wide-scale activism.

We can compare Eliot's novel to an earlier work in which an aristocratic English hero sets out for the holy land on a "new crusade": Disraeli's *Tancred* (1847), the concluding part of his Coningsby trilogy. In that novel Tancred, the thoughtful only son of an ancient and magnificent family, embarks on his travels to discover the true source of religion and so restore meaning to an increasingly trivial world. "Ah! there is nothing like action," one character declares, voicing Disraeli's own beliefs; and Tancred replies, "But what action is there in this world? . . . The most energetic men in Europe are mere busybodies. . . . [U]nless we bring man nearer to heaven, unless government become again divine, the insignificance of the human scheme must paralyse all effort." Hence the need for a crusade. Yet although Disraeli's novel, unlike Eliot's, concentrates on the hero's adventures in the East, Tancred himself admits that while "it is very easy now to get to Jerusalem," the "great difficulty . . . is to know what to do when you are there."[115] And for all Disraeli's desire to show that modern life, too, can be "full of adventure," the terms of that adventure have shifted: "There may be no longer fiery dragons, magic rings, or fairy wands, to interfere in its course and to influence our career;

but the relations of men are far more complicated and numerous than of yore; and in the play of the passions, and in the devices of creative spirits, that have thus a proportionally greater sphere for their action, there are spells of social sorcery more potent than all the necromancy of Merlin or Friar Bacon." Again, note the move inward, into the arena of feelings and the social passions. The conclusion of Disraeli's story reflects this fact: even on holy soil, Tancred discovers that he becomes "mixed up with intrigue, and politics, and management, and baffled schemes, and cunning arts of men." The East is not such a blank slate after all, and the intrigues Tancred becomes ensnared by are as old as its soil and ruins. When Tancred declares his love for Eva, the Jewish heroine of the tale, in the opaque and open-ended final pages of the book, she laments, "You no longer believe in Arabia." To which Disraeli's hero replies, "Why thou to me art Arabia."[116] As in *Felix Holt,* the courtship plot has subsumed the political plot.

But while the success of Eliot's visionary politics in *Daniel Deronda* depends on her avoidance of a direct description of what happens in the East, I do think it is a success—at least insofar as it concerns Daniel's mission.[117] We believe Deronda when he tells us that "if we look back to the history of efforts which have made great changes, it is astonishing how many of them seemed hopeless to those who looked on in the beginning" (DD 457). Men can do nothing without make-believe for a beginning, and the leap of faith Eliot requires of us seems worth the effort. Her achievement owes something to her use of Shelley and the Prometheus legend. When Mordecai and Deronda enter the Hand and Banner, the idealistic Miller is reading from *Prometheus Unbound* (DD 445). He has chosen the passage containing the great simile of the avalanche:

> Hark! The rushing show!
> The sun-awakened avalanche! Whose mass,
> Thrice sifted by the storm, had gathered there
> Flake after flake, in heaven-defying minds
> As thought by thought is piled, till some great truth
> Is loosened, and the nations echo round
> Shaken to their roots: as do the mountains now.[118]

Obviously, the simile represents the possibilities of a revolutionary idealism—of the changes to the world that can be brought on by incremental, practically invisible (snow-flake-sized) shifts of thought in the minds of individuals. These are just the kind of gradual shifts that the cautious Eliot would advocate, although one might have expected the idea of an avalanche to put her off. But perhaps the most surprising—and character-istic—thing about this simile is not what it describes, but the way in which it describes. Shelley has reversed the ordinary relationship between tenor and vehicle. Usually, metaphor is used to compare the insubstantial world to the substantial, the less palpable to the external and everyday. So, for example, we might say: "Her mind raced like a locomotive," thereby offer-ing an objective equivalent to a subjective experience. But here Asia sees the avalanche and compares it to a revolution in thought in order to clar-ify her experience. The implication is that the world of the mind is in some sense more real than the physical world for Shelley—or at least should be more real. The simile itself enacts one of those revolutions (literally, a turn-ing around) of thought that he wishes to bring about via his drama.

Shelley is the supreme poet of what Miller calls "the transforming power of ideas" (DD 447). Klesmer refers to his *Defense of Poetry* when he states his claim for the political power of artists to the heavy, pedestrian Mr. Bult: "We count ourselves on level benches with the legislators" (DD 206). Early on, the narrator associates Daniel with "the author of Queen Mab" (DD 152), the political Shelley. Eliot's new interest in the work of artists comes from her desire to find a safe kind of political activity in *Daniel Deronda*. The novel closely affiliates action with creativity (DD 407). In the work of another novelist, say, Henry James, Daniel would have been a writer, or a sculptor like Roderick Hudson. His less effective precursor Ladislaw (also associated with Shelley, by Mr. Brooke [M 355]) actually toys with the arts before turning to the more directly ethically useful activity of politics. Deronda never becomes, or even wants to be, an artist. In fact, when Sir Hugo sug-gests the profession of singer to him, he is mortified (DD 143), and he tells his tutor he would rather like to be "a greater leader, like Pericles or Washington" (DD 147). But the chapter in which he announces his vocation is headed by an epigraph in which Heine declares that in spite of his aversion to art, Moses was a great artist, the creator of Israel (DD 637).

"Genius," states the narrator of *Middlemarch,* consists in "a power to make or do, not anything in general, but something in particular" (M 82). Initially, Daniel's problem with action arises from his "many-sided [general] sym-pathy, which threaten[s] to hinder any persistent [particular] course of action" (DD 307). His negative capability is so great as to be a burden, bringing on a "meditative numbness" oddly reminiscent of Grandcourt's numbness (DD 308). What he needs, according to Eliot, is "either some external event or some inward light, that would urge him into a definite line of action, and compress his wandering energy" (DD 308). Indeed, more troubling than the vagueness of his idealism is the manner in which Deronda receives even his *sense* of a mission. As it turns out, his particular quest comes to him much as Kant says genius comes to the poet, as a gift from the gods.[119]

In *Daniel Deronda,* revelation takes the place of revolution. To act safely and effectively, one must experience a call. But vocations are not to be had on demand, as Savonarola implies to Romola (R 343), and without the call, Eliot cannot condone acting (the Princess suffers even with a vocation). Moreover, while *Daniel Deronda* works to suppress Gwendolen's activity, it argues for Daniel's passivity as an effective instrument of progress. Daniel does not choose to do; he is Chosen. As Zarca tells Fedalma in *The Spanish Gypsy,* "being of the blood you are—my blood— / You have no right to choose" (SG 115). Daniel's moment of "choice" has as little to do with genuine choice as Gwendolen's actions had to do with genuine activity, for all that it supposedly will enable him to act purposefully:

> His mother had *compelled* him to a decisive acknowledgment of his love, as Joseph Kalonymos had *compelled* him to a definite expression of his resolve. This new state of decision *wrought* on Deronda with a force which surprised even himself . . .—his judgment no longer wandering in the mazes of impartial sympathy, but *choosing* with that noble partiality which is man's best strength, the closer fellowship which makes sympathy practical. (DD 638; emphasis added)

Daniel Deronda can be thought of, like many of Eliot's works, as an exercise in how to make "sympathy practical." But the solution Eliot offers here would be difficult to replicate in the real world. "What my birth was does not lie in my will," Deronda had told Mordecai (DD 430). Happily for the cause, it does lie in Eliot's will. This is the providential plotting of romance. Throughout the course of the novel, Deronda is the agent of "rescue" (DD 655): of Hans, of Mirah, of Gwendolen, and finally of the Jews. But he never really does anything. His characteristic gesture, as James notes, is a clutching of the coat collar, as though to hold himself back.[120] Daniel appears to become the "new executive self" (DD 435) Mordecai—and Eliot—need him to be: "It seemed as if Mordecai were hardly overrating his own power to determine the action of the friend whom he had mysteriously chosen" (DD 435). Yet we always sense that the force that occasions the rescues lies outside of Deronda; he is, to return to Arendt's terms, agent but not author.

The narrator may say that Deronda's "entailed disadvantage" has not rendered him an "Ishmaelite" (DD 148), but the novel makes his tendency to wander very clear (DD 638). Yet for all his wandering, we are told that Daniel has "a wonderful power of standing perfectly still" (DD 381); as with Byron's Don Juan, wandering and stillness are manifestations of the same essentially passive nature. In a particularly revealing allusion, Sir Hugo actually compares Deronda to an English Don Juan figure: "You are always looking tenderly at women, and talking to them in a Jesuitical way. You are a dangerous young fellow—a kind of Lovelace who will make the Clarissas run after you instead of running after them" (DD 304). Richardson's *Clarissa*, considered by many to be the first novel of consciousness, carefully allies action with its villain Lovelace's "plotting genius," just as it allies character with Clarissa's virtuous unwillingness to act.[121] As Jay Clayton puts it, "her virtue lies in the power that makes it so difficult for her to act at all, her heightened sense of consciousness."[122] Clarissa's passivity stands in stark contrast to Gwendolen's desire for action, including her desire to run after Deronda. But Gwendolen's inability to act on this desire generates its own "heightened sense of consciousness," as we shall see. Similarly, Sir Hugo's comment demonstrates how dangerous a force Deronda can be, in spite of a passivity that seems very different from Lovelace's attitude in pursuit of Clarissa.

Deronda is rightly affiliated with the world of "romance" (DD 159). Sir Hugo jokes about his "Quixotic enthusiasm" (DD 311), and Hans calls him a "knight-errant" (DD 237). R. E. Francillon, in his 1876 review of the novel as a romance, picks up on the same concept, referring to Deronda as a "nineteenth century knight errant."[123] The knight-errant, notes Caserio in relation to Eliot's hero, is "perpetually rescuing others in distress" but "finds his activity only the mask of an essential passivity, indeed of a suffering passion."[124] When Daniel comes upon Mirah, he is indulging himself in "that solemn passivity . . . [when] what in other hours may have seemed argument takes the quality of passionate vision" (DD 160). Deronda exhibits the Romantic conflation of thought and feeling that Wordsworth described in the Preface to *Lyrical Ballads*. When he later asks himself why he should continue helping Mirah after the original rescue, Eliot informs us that while "he gave himself several good reasons," "whatever one does with a strong unhesitating outflow of will has a store of motives that it would be hard to put into words. Some deeds seem little more than interjections which give vent to the long passion of a life" (DD 192). Again, the passion (with its connotations of both passivity and feeling) gives meaning, the deed serves merely as an escape valve for that meaning; and again, habit provides the moral apparatus for action.

The epigraph with which Eliot heads the chapter in which she goes back to narrate Deronda's "exceptional" childhood declares the importance of "those moments of intense suffering which take the quality of action—like the cry of Prometheus" (DD 139). We have returned to the world of *Adam Bede,* where suffering can substitute for action. But the shift in model from Christ to Prometheus, the iconic hero of revolutionary idealism, indicates Eliot's new political concerns: in 1862 she had written that "surely the acme of poetry hitherto is the conception of the suffering Messiah and the final triumph, 'He shall reign for ever and ever.' The Prometheus is a very imperfect foreshadowing of that symbol wrought out in the long history of the Jewish and Christian ages."[125] Still, there is also something Christ-like about Deronda and his passionate passivity. He appears for Mordecai like the long-awaited Messiah.

Sir Hugo still believes in an Old England in which "Reform [is] not likely to make any serious difference in English habits of feeling" (DD 680). In *Daniel Deronda,* Eliot criticizes this traditional stance, one close to that which she implicitly endorses in her earlier work. When Sir Hugo states his opinion that "there is no action possible without a little acting" (DD 324), he is expressing a truth that Eliot has acknowledged in the past and accepted as good reason to doubt the beneficence of political action. And we can recognize in Daniel Deronda's idealism and passivity a model for a kind of political progress devoid of theatricality. Savonarola's gradual decline into "doubleness"—a version of acting—led to his death. Felix Holt slipped into "acting" when he involved himself in the riot, and the results demonstrated to him how dangerous and ultimately useless such action is. *Daniel Deronda* attempts to show that there can be such a thing as pure political action, but it achieves this goal only by sacrificing any more realistic forms of action along with acting. Eliot wishes to allow Daniel agency without forcing him "to draw strongly at any thread in the hopelessly-entangled scheme of things" (DD 160)—that is, without ensnaring him in the web of action. Of course, the attempt is futile: for all his efforts, when Deronda leaves England, he makes Gwendolen "the victim of his happiness" (DD 690). Eliot is too honest with herself to indulge fully in make-believe. Like Gwendolen's, her struggle with action does not end.

The Question of Consciousness

Reviewing *Daniel Deronda,* R. R. Bowker noted that "Tito Melema . . . we know through his deeds, but neither Deronda nor Grandcourt do anything." Bowker recognized that we respond to Deronda's inaction very differently from the way we respond to Gwendolen's anxiety and frustrations: "The reader looks on him more as a force than as a person. On the other

hand, the reader's attention is concentrated upon Gwendolen, this throb-
bing, bleeding heart, torn by the circumstances we all know to our pain,
herself the product of circumstance and the battle-field of opposing character—because this is human and near to us."[126] We sympathize with
Gwendolen because she is caught between will and destiny—because she
is unable to do exactly as she likes. Gwendolen's vast and "wonderfully
mixed consciousness" (DD 595), that awareness we have of "unmapped
country within" her (DD 235), owes its power of presence to the fact that
it is within, and must remain so. Dorrit Cohn has argued that "the most
real, the 'roundest' characters of fiction are those we know most intimately, precisely in ways we could never know people in real life."[127] But one
could also argue that the roundest characters, those who possess what
Bakhtin has called a "surplus of humanness,"[128] are rather those we both
know and don't know, precisely as we know and don't know people in real
life. Such characters allow us room for speculation, as with the notorious
debate about Lady Macbeth's children. They leave us with a sense of the
hidden that is felt as a presence, like the ghostly plots that hover over
Eliot's novels, like the unmapped country of Gwendolen's internal empire.

Eliot's most-quoted remark on the nature of character hints at a complicated dialectic between things hidden and things revealed: "Character
. . . is a process and an unfolding," the narrator of *Middlemarch* declares
(M 140). "Process" suggests the making of a self out of one's acts, an effort
of will; "unfolding" implies the unveiling of an essential self, an effect of
destiny. Nevertheless, Henry James used Eliot's word "process" to describe
Gwendolen's specifically *internal* maturation: her mind was made to "ache
with the pain of the process."[129] A comment in *Felix Holt* shows that Eliot
firmly believes in a core of character, whether that character has been formed
over time or was there from the start: "A man can never do anything at vari-
ance with his own nature. He carries within him the germ of his most exceptional action" (AB 171). But while a man's actions may represent a part of
his character, there will be many "germs" that never bear outer fruit. Eliot
actually attributes the "iridescence of [Gwendolen's] character—the play of
various, nay, contrary tendencies" in her, to the degree to which her desires
are *not* allowed outward expression in deeds: "For Macbeth's rhetoric about
the impossibility of being many opposite things in the same moment, referred
to the clumsy necessities of action and not the subtler possibilities of feeling. We cannot speak a loyal word and be silent, we cannot kill and not
kill in the same moment; but a moment is room wide enough for the loyal
and mean desire, for the outward and murderous thought and the backward stroke of repentance" (DD 33). "Action is transitory," as Wordsworth

wrote; it lacks the layers that mark feeling, and those layers are what provide the sense of depth necessary to make a character seem round. Yet the
strangely liminal nature of the "act" that is Gwendolen's "murder" of
Grandcourt seems to be Eliot's attempt to show what it would be to "kill
and not kill in the same moment."

Eliot frequently attributes "consciousness" to Gwendolen, and the
growth of her "conscience," her "struggle of mind attending a conscious error"
(DD 280), seems simultaneously to be the growth of her "consciousness"
(DD 262, 368). The process closely resembles that which I described in
relation to Wordsworth in chapter 1. For Hannah Arendt, the etymological links between the two terms imply a deep connection between the kind
of thinking attributed to consciousness or self-knowledge (and vitally distinct from action) and the morality associated with conscience.[130] Arendt
was of course driven to this conviction by the awareness the Holocaust left
her with of the terrible and coercive force of action. Eliot's desperate search
for a secure form of action took her down a similar path.

Gwendolen's roundness, however, comes not only from our active sense
of her consciousness, but also from the glimpses Eliot gives us into her "underconsciousness" (DD 300). In particular, her complex relationship to action
functions on a number of levels: at times, Gwendolen appears to be aware
of her feelings; sometimes she seems to sense but wishes to avoid them. Some
of Gwendolen's responses are obscure to her, and some are perhaps hidden
even from Eliot herself, and from the most discerning readers. Her strange
reaction to the panel painting of the dead face and fleeing figure—"How
dare you open things up which were meant to be shut up" (DD 20)—suggests, for all Gwendolen's love of action, her subconscious desire to keep
things locked up inside, self-suppressed. Curiously, the one "act" she
admits to when she makes her contorted "confession" to Deronda following Grandcourt's death is the stealing of a knife that she has also kept "locked
in the drawer" of her dressing case (DD 592–93). The accomplished deed
parallels the closeted act represented by her desire to kill her husband.

Gwendolen's tendency to "lock away" her dread can in part be attributed to a more general trait: "I think I dislike what I don't like more than
I like what I like," she recognizes (DD 258). It is her own form of nega-
tivity, and lies behind her decision to marry the "negative" Grandcourt. Combine
Gwendolen's remark with Eliot's description of her greatest fear, in which
she recurs to the nightmarish panel: "her vision of what she had to dread
took more decidedly than ever the form of some fiercely impulsive deed,
committed as in a dream that she would instantaneously wake from to find
the effects real though the images had been false: . . .—a white dead face

from which she was for ever trying to flee and forever held back" (DD 577). Together, these statements of Gwendolen's situation recall Wordsworth's nightmare interjection in "Tintern Abbey," where he describes himself as "more like a man / Fleeing from something that he dreads, than one / Who sought the thing he loved."[131] Wordsworth's dread is Gwendolen's—and Eliot's. This is why "Tintern Abbey" makes its way with such frequency into Eliot's writing in the context of attempts to ease a hazy sense of responsibility concerning action. In *Middlemarch,* Eliot describes a more positive form of her ghostly guilt: "The idea of some active good within [Dorothea's] reach 'haunted her like a passion'" (M 749). For both Wordsworth and Eliot, crises of action generated a concern for the diffusive influence of "unhistoric" or "little nameless unremembered acts." But these crises also lay behind a truly revolutionary interest in portraying psychologies of depth, in which guilt can be felt but not understood.

Yet what makes Eliot so remarkable, as I have tried to show, is the degree to which she was self-conscious about her own struggle with action. She seems to have recognized the immense moral cost of her aversion to risk—the limitations it set on progress—and her novels were written to compensate (at least in part) for both her inability and her unwillingness to participate in or advocate larger revolutions. Her self-consciousness is responsible for the continued, indeed the increasing, forcefulness of her work. Wordsworth generated his most interesting poetry in the years in which he was actively struggling with his beliefs. This *struggle,* rather than (as is so often thought) the liberal or conservative bent of his work—its specific ideological position—accounts for its power. The stand he takes on the question of action in *The Excursion* is every bit as interesting philosophically as that in his earlier works (and is, in fact, as close to Eliot's position as he comes), but to the degree to which he has achieved a *stand,* the poetry itself has ceased to be groundbreaking. Because Eliot continued to explore the consequences of her positions, because although she could not avoid them, she was unable to rest with her conclusions, her work never ceases to be compelling and, in its own way, revolutionary. In her last completed book, *Impressions of Theophrastus Such,* she experimented further with our need for action by removing plot altogether and replacing it with a series of essays that, under the rubric of "character-studies," attempted to characterize her age.

And as an experiment, the character of Deronda is every bit as interesting as anything Eliot ever did. That the greatest of the English realistic novelists was able to envision him in all his idealism—and to envision him envisioning a new nation—represents a feat of remarkable daring and shows Eliot to possess a courage in her moral vision that she may have lacked in regard to action. But in portraying Gwendolen's consciousness, she reached the apex of her achievement. In February of 1857, Eliot informed Blackwood, "my stories always grow out of my psychological conception of the dramatis personae."[132] According to James's Constantius (and I must agree), Gwendolen's is the best portrait Eliot ever produced: "see how the girl is known, inside out, how thoroughly she is felt and understood! It is the most *intelligent* thing in all George Eliot's writing, and that is saying much. It is so deep, so true, so complete, it holds such a wealth of psychological detail, it is more than masterly."[133] It also stands behind James's conception of Isabel Archer, the young lady at the heart of his own *Portrait of a Lady*.[134] Like Eliot, James began his novel with a psychological conception of his heroine, but he then asked: "Well, what will she *do?*"[135] As we shall see in the next chapter, his answer to his own question would have further consequences for the relationship between plot and character in the novel.

⊰4⊱

Henry James's Nefarious Plot:
Form and Freedom in the Hands of the Master

Since one was dealing with an Action one might borrow a scrap of the Dramatist's all-in-all, his intensity—which the novelist so often rue-fully envies him as a fortune in itself.

—Henry James, Preface to *Roderick Hudson*

"What is character but the determination of incident? What is incident but the illustration of character?"[1] Henry James's most famous statement about the interplay of action and character in literature is usually quoted out of context. The passage continues,

What is either a picture or a novel that is *not* of character? What else do we seek in it and find in it? It is an incident for a woman to stand up with her hand resting on a table and look out at you in a certain way; or if it be not an incident I think it will be hard to say what it is. At the same time, it is an expression of character.

No doubt James was correct, but his choice of "incident" shows his colors: character is not identified with the doing of great deeds; it may be revealed by the smallest of gestures. In 1888, in a letter to Mrs. Humphry Ward (Matthew Arnold's niece) praising her religious novel, *Robert Elsmere*

(1888), James stated his position even more boldly: "The interesting thing to me in your book (& its great success) . . . is that you have seen a personal history in the richest and most interesting way—the way that yields most fruit—seen the adventures of the real being, the intensely living inner nature & seen them (rendering them too) so vividly that they become exciting, thrilling, strongly attaching as a 'story.'"[2] Once again, "story," or plot, is internalized to the point of disappearance.

In the Preface to the New York edition of *The Portrait of a Lady,* Henry James demonstrates his commitment to internalized action by acknowledging his debt to two of the writers on whom I have concentrated. He first glances at Wordsworth's achievement in *The Prelude* by speculating that true vividness of character could best be reached "if one could do so subtle, if not so monstrous, a thing as to write the history of the growth of one's imagination." Then he moves on to a more important precursor for him, George Eliot. In *Daniel Deronda,* Eliot had defended her choice of centering on a female consciousness during the upheavals of the American Civil War: "What in the midst of that mighty drama are girls and their blind visions? They are the Yea or Nay of that good for which men are enduring and fighting. In these delicate vessels is borne onward through the ages the treasure of human affections."[3] James, who (as Leon Edel has argued) carried his own burden of guilt about his inability to participate in the conflict that so devastated the lives of two of his brothers, recalls Eliot's defense in the context of his own attempt to make his readers see how one can make an "ado" about a subject so slight as the picture of "a certain young woman affronting her destiny."[4]

James's use of "ado" in this context invokes the most famous instance of the word in the language, in Shakespeare's *Much Ado about Nothing.* "The novel," James insists, is in contrast "of its very nature an 'ado,' an ado about something, and the larger the form it takes the greater of course the ado."[5] James definitely made his novel a "large" one. Almost all contemporary critics complained of the length of *The Portrait of a Lady,* and almost all related this complaint to the want of external incident—or "doing"—in the story. As the critic in the *Nation* put it (more sympathetically than many) in by-now familiar terms, "his true distinction—that is to say, his strength and weakness also—consists in his attempt to dispense with all the ordinary machinery of the novelist except the study of subtle shades of character." The result is "the elaborate placidity of these 519 pages."[6] Yet perhaps the "ordinary machinery" of the novelist does not consist of the kind of incident and action implied by the *Nation*'s critic. When James takes "ado," a word that carries with it dramatic associations, and places it within the context of the novel, he suggests that in fact it is the strength of the genre to make "something" out of what had been previously deemed "nothing." And as the *Nation's* critic recognized, that something turns out to be a form of portraiture.

The "ado" I make over James's use of the word strikes me as merited by the degree to which forms of "doing" lie at the heart not only of the Preface to *The Portrait* but also of the novel itself.[7] James seems to be ringing the changes of the verb, and in the process, he alters its meaning. What James elsewhere referred to as "the whole question of the novelist's 'doing'" becomes strangely implicated in the kinds of "doing" he can envision for his characters.[8] To say this is to argue that the way in which James is "really 'doing'" Isabel Archer connects to his "primary" question in the Preface to *The Portrait of a Lady,* "Well, what will she *do?*"—a question so central that he asks it again a few pages later.[9] The question seems to grow right out of those repeated demands of "What should I do?" made by Eliot's heroines,[10] and James's acknowledgment of Eliot in the Preface stems from his recognition of how influential this question was for him. Of all the possible readings one might give to Eliot's works, James chose to read her as one who was involved in the crisis of action. But there is a difference. When James replaces Eliot's "should" with his own "will," he indicates that his ethical concerns will be more about freedom than about duty. In addition, James's version of Eliot's struggle with free agency takes place on a much more self-consciously formal level than do Eliot's ethical dilemmas. Together, these shifts show the move from the Victorian to the modernist frame of mind.

James's intention to make his characters "true agents"[11] has been summed up by Yvor Winters: "James displays in all his more serious works an unmistakable desire to allow his characters unrestricted freedom of choice and to develop his plots out of such choice and out of the consequent acts of choice to which the initial acts may lead."[12] It was also recognized immediately by critics as a revolutionary gesture, and one that was influenced by the tendency away from action or plot and toward character. As William Dean Howells wrote in the *Century Magazine,*

> The new school [of fiction] derives from Hawthorne and George Eliot rather than any others. . . . The moving accident is certainly not its trade, and it prefers to avoid all manner of dire catastrophes. . . . Will the reader be content to accept a novel which is an analytic study rather than a story, which is apt to leave him arbiter of the author's creations? . . .
>
> [James] has finally made his public in his own way of story-telling—or call it character-painting if you prefer.[13]

An emphasis on readerly participation comes out of the emphasis on the priority of character over plot. As the critic of the *Quarterly Review* noted in response to Howells, "The novelist provides the characters, and everybody is left free to dispose of them according to his own taste."[14] So the freedom of the Jamesian reader parallels the freedom of the Jamesian character.

As a result of this conflation, though, James's characters seem incapable of escaping from a readerly—that is, an internalized and imaginative—conception of action. In "The Dilemma of Determinism," William James argued that "our first act of freedom, if we are free, ought in all inward propriety to be to affirm that we are free."[15] His brother Henry seems to have felt the need to place the emphasis on the "inward" nature of this act.[16] Isabel's "adventures" are to be "mild," they are to be independent of "flood and field, of the moving accident, of battle and murder and sudden death," because as James puts it, "Without her sense of them, her sense for them, as one may say, they are next to nothing."[17] Isabel must read her own story. In other words, for any adventure to be interesting, it must be translated in the mind of its protagonist: "Place the center of the subject in the young woman's own consciousness," James says to himself.[18]

Consciousness—the quality Eliot had attributed with such frequency to Gwendolen Harleth—is a word James makes his own, and its distinction from the more Aristotelian or deed-derived *character* speaks volumes about James's attitudes toward action. Writing of his favorite scene in the novel, Isabel's fireside vigil in chapter 42, James himself draws the connection between the kind of activity he envisions as adapted to displaying consciousness and the kind of activity we associate with the critical enterprise of reading. He rings the final change on "doing" when he purports to "show what an 'exciting' inward life may do for the person leading it."[19] An odd displacement of agency happens here: as Isabel's actions will be frustrated, some abstract category termed the "inward life" will take over for her. "[R]educed to its essence," James announces of Isabel's dark night of faith,

> it is but the vigil of searching criticism; but it throws the action further forward than twenty "incidents" might have done. . . . It is a representation simply of her motionlessly *seeing*, and an attempt withal to make the mere still lucidity of her act as "interesting" as the surprise of a caravan or the identification of a pirate.[20]

"Criticism," the activity of the reader, replaces a more bodily form of action. James's description of an act as possessing "still lucidity" (the phrase is almost

Wordsworthian) is particularly shocking in the context of a story that was to have shown its heroine in all the glory and freedom of agency.

So what happens to bring about this unexpected change? To put it simply, for all James's attempts to avoid it, plot happens. James's refusal of plot leads him to start with a central character, Isabel Archer. Instead of making her act, he wishes to do justice to what he calls his "pious desire but to place [his] treasure right."[21] In the process, he displaces responsibility for plotting onto "the concrete terms of [his] 'plot'"—his phrase for the characters with whom he surrounds Isabel. He engages in such sophisticated sleights of hand because of a desire to avoid what he terms the "nefarious name" of plot.[22] Peter Brooks has argued that in modern literature the sense of plot as a secret plan to accomplish an evil or unlawful purpose "nearly always attaches itself to the other" sense—that is, the action of a story: "the organizing line of plot is more often than not some scheme or machination, a concerted plan for the accomplishment of some purpose which goes against the ostensible and dominant legalities of the fictional world, the realization of a blocked and resisted desire."[23] As we shall see, James's distrust of action stemmed from his inability to see it as anything other than either intrigue ("plot" as sinister "scheme") or sacrifice.

But for James the problem took on a particular slant connected with his aesthetic interests. We can register this in his replacement of the category of action with that of situation: he will "place" Isabel, "his treasure," right. One is reminded of Gilbert Osmond's treatment of Isabel, whom he reduces to the most precious of his bibelots. Plot has a "nefarious name" because James is unable to escape his sense that plotting is a "doing with" rather than a pure doing and therefore a direct infringement of Kant's categorical imperative, to treat agents as ends rather than means. I want to turn first to *The Portrait of a Lady* to demonstrate James's problem with plotting. My focus, however, will be on the most obvious example of plot in James's fiction: the revolutionary plot at the center of *The Princess Casamassima*. Finally, I will conclude by looking at the apotheosis of the Jamesian plot, in "The Beast in the Jungle." What should become clear along the way is how, over the years, James became increasingly concerned about his own techniques of handling action.

The Portrait of a Lady

Isabel Archer's desire to be a Jamesian reader—to escape the nefarious name of plot—entraps her within the confines of the narrative in which

she finds herself.[24] Isabel begins the novel every bit as entranced by the
sense of her own agency as was Gwendolen Harleth—a resemblance many
critics have noted.[25] Both heroines exhibit a "love of movement" (330). If
Gwendolen liked archery, Isabel is an Archer. In an early scene reminiscent
of Eliot's use of rowing as a symbol of agency, we hear that Isabel has just
been "handling the oars" (65). "If there's a thing in the world I'm fond of,"
she declares to Caspar Goodwood, "it's my personal independence" (142).
The aura of possibility surrounding Isabel makes her the subject of much
suspense, both for readers and for the characters in the text. In fact, the
characters surrounding Isabel seem, like readers, intent on finding out
what she will do. But in their curiosity they also resemble their own
author; James's question in the Preface makes its first appearance in the
mouth of Ralph when he asks his mother: "What do you mean to do with
her?" (46). The question strikes Ralph as so pressing that he repeats it
shortly thereafter, only to be reprimanded by Mrs. Touchett: "Do with
her? You talk as if she were a yard of calico. I shall do absolutely nothing
with her, and she herself will do everything she chooses" (49). Already, the
distinction between "doing" and "doing with," between subject (Isabel)
and object (the calico), has been introduced. But it is much harder to dispense with than Mrs. Touchett's quick retort suggests.

   "A character like that," Ralph remarks to himself, "a real little passionate force to see at play is the finest thing in nature" (63). James would agree.
Ralph's comment sounds like that of an author admiring his subject. But
while "play" connotes the freedom of Schiller's *Spieltrieb,* it also carries a
suggestion of the chessboard deity, hovering over his pieces, determining
the next move. Both Ralph and James wish to avoid such manipulative plotting. The freedom from plot that they envision is also a freedom from that
most conventional—and therefore restrictive—of female plots: the
courtship plot.[26] When Ralph asks himself once again, "what was she going
to do with herself?" (even here, with regard to Isabel herself, "doing" becomes
"doing with"), he recognizes that in Isabel's case the realm of possible answers
far exceeds the usual: "This question was irregular, for with most women
one had no occasion to ask it. Most women did with themselves nothing
at all; they waited, in attitudes more or less gracefully passive, for a man to
come that way and furnish them with a destiny. Isabel's originality was that
she gave one an impression of having intentions of her own" (64). It is also
James's originality—as well as his primary goal in the construction of *The
Portrait.*

   At first, Isabel seems likely to escape from the marriage plot. "I don't want
to begin life by marrying," she declares to Ralph, "There are other things

a woman can do" (133). As I argued in relation to *Daniel Deronda,* the capacity for new beginnings is central to a belief in action: when James's novel moves from America to England, to begin, as it were, again, Isabel's stated desire to "begin afresh" (39) bodes well for her story. We are told that she had already experienced "beginning afresh a great many times" (39), and the repeated refusals of would-be lovers with which the novel opens suggests continued capacity in this regard. It also, though, calls into question the very idea of starting anew by intimating that a story that is always beginning is unlikely to go anywhere. Nevertheless, when Isabel sends away Caspar Goodwood, she does so in part because his capacity for action limits hers: in spite of his being "a man of high, bold action" (92), he seems "to deprive her of the sense of freedom" (104–5). His activity would ensnare her as surely as any nefarious plot. Her dismissal of Lord Warburton leaves Isabel with the sense that "if she wouldn't do such a thing" as marry such a man, "then she must do great things, she must do something greater" (102).

Like Gwendolen, Isabel never seems sure what "greater" thing she will do. Saying "no" to Caspar stands as her greatest "victory" thus far: "it appeared to her she had done something; . . . she had done what was truest to her plan" (145). But saying no comes closer to renunciation than to positive action, and her "plan" remains remarkably indistinct. The vagueness hints at a strange ambivalence in Isabel's character: this most active of heroines is also marked by a deep passivity. Henrietta Stackpole asks Isabel, "Do you know where you're drifting?" (146).[27] Her question brings to mind Maggie Tulliver's drifting downriver into sin in *The Mill on the Floss* and also contrasts sharply with our earlier vision of Isabel holding the oars. "You're drifting to some great mistake," Henrietta warns. Like George Eliot, Henry James was possessed of what he himself called "the imagination of disaster."[28] His heroine shares in it but insists on her agency nonetheless. Yet action brings with it the possibility of catastrophe: this, in large measure, is the recognition lying behind Isabel's often commented upon "certain fear" (78). When Goodwood remarks, "One would think you were going to commit some atrocity," Isabel's reply is telling: "Perhaps I am. I wish to be free even to do that if the fancy takes me" (143).

Ralph negotiates his father's bequest to Isabel precisely in order to stop her drifting by putting "a little wind in her sails" (160). Isabel recognizes that the virtue of wealth lies in its ability to aid action, but she soon sees, like Dorothea, that the translation of money into acts is not easy: "the girl presently made up her mind that to be rich was a virtue because it was to be able to *do,* and that to do could only be sweet. . . . Just now, it is true, there was not much to do—" (182; James's emphasis). "The world lay all before her—she could do whatever she chose," James tells us, setting up, like Wordsworth, the inevitable comparison to Miltonic epic. But James's next sentence is typically deflating: "There was a deep thrill in it all, but for the present her choice was tolerably discreet; she chose simply to walk back from Euston Square to her hotel" (273). Any action to which her riches leads occurs offstage in James's novel. He happily skips over "several months; an interval sufficiently replete with incident" (270) in order to return Isabel to Osmond's Florence. Travel affects her, but Isabel's response to Rome (which had so bewildered poor Dorothea on her honeymoon) is notably nostalgic: "She had always been fond of history, and here was history in the stones of the street and the atoms of the sunshine. She had an imagination that kindled at the mention of great deeds, and wherever she turned some great deed had been acted. These things strongly moved her, but moved her all inwardly."[29] All the actions, all the great deeds of the past, are internalized. Like Ralph, she reacts to Rome so strongly because she sees it as "confess[ing] to the psychological moment" (245). Isabel's greatest "exploring expedition" (235), her traveling adventure to the East with Madame Merle as companion, occurs, like most of the overt action in the book, entirely between the acts.[30]

The one great deed of Isabel's life is her marriage to Gilbert Osmond, which she will later think of as "the most serious act—the single sacred act—of her life" (386). Appropriately, though, even the engagement scene happens outside of the narrative; we hear about Isabel's decision only afterward, in conversation. James had earlier related how Lily Ludlow was perplexed by how little effect the Touchett legacy seemed to have had on her sister. "But," he tells us, "Lily knew nothing of these discriminations [that is, Isabel's various romantic opportunities and her decisions concerning them] and could only pronounce her sister's career a strange anticlimax" (272). Her inability to penetrate Isabel's consciousness brands Lily as a poor Jamesian reader—one who could see little more than "strange anticlimax" in such a novel as her sister inhabits. But Isabel marries Osmond precisely because he represents everything that the discriminating Jamesian reader should admire. Consider how Madame Merle tells Isabel that Osmond has "no career, no name, no position, no fortune, no past, no future, no anything" (172). Like Eliot's Grandcourt, he is a man defined by the "negative" (227). Gwendolen's choice was determined by her need for money and the belief that Grandcourt's passivity would allow her greater license to pursue her own ends. Isabel's selection has far more to recommend it, especially given James's own literary positions.[31]

Gilbert admits to Isabel that his own plan has been "to be as quiet as possible. . . . Not to worry, not to strive nor struggle. To resign myself" (227). He speaks of a "willful renunciation" in terms that bring to mind Wordsworth's "choice" of "submissiveness" in the "Ode to Duty." In other words, he seems to stand outside of the constraints of plotting, and this is precisely what Isabel admires in him. As Madame Merle puts it to the Countess, "What has he done? He has done nothing that has had to be undone. And he has known how to wait" (233). Among the ambiguous and ominous suggestions in her comment is a possible intimation that just such inaction defines the successful life. When Osmond tells Isabel, "The events of my life have been absolutely unperceived by anyone save myself" (228), he is opening the door for her to be the discriminating reader who can recognize, in James's words to Mrs. Ward, "the truth of view of the interesting novel, that it's a history of our moral life & not simply of our physical accidents."[32] Isabel, James informs us, "was fond, ever, of the question of character and quality, of sounding, as who should say, the deep personal mystery" (267), and Gilbert Osmond strikes her as being every bit as interesting a subject as Isabel herself is for us. When Caspar Goodwood asks her, "What has [Osmond] ever done," Isabel's response indicates how closely her reasoning follows that of the ideal Jamesian reader: "That I should marry him? Nothing at all. . . . If he had done great things would you forgive me any better? Give me up, Mr. Goodwood; I'm marrying a perfect nonentity. Don't try to take an interest in him. You can't." But Goodwood's reply proves that he understands better than she thought: "I can't appreciate him; that's what you mean. And you don't mind in the least that he's a perfect nonentity. You think he's grand, you think he's great" (279). And so she does. What she sees in him is a form of character free of the contamination of action. Again, choices serve as substitutes for deeds: when Isabel looks at Osmond's home, "it spoke of the kind of personal issue that touched her most nearly; of the choice between objects, subjects, contacts—what might she call them?—of a thin and those of a rich association" (237).

What, indeed, might she—or rather, might Osmond himself—call them: objects, subjects, or contacts? Gilbert Osmond's unwillingness to distinguish among these categories proves to be one major cause of Isabel's tragedy. Gilbert is defined by his things, by his ability to choose them, by what Madame Merle calls his "adorable taste" (208), and this is a form of discrimination. Troublingly, though, he wishes to acquire Isabel, whom he (also rightly) recognizes as a worthwhile possession, a portrait of a lady fine enough to "figure in his collection of choice objects" (258). The phrase "choice objects" hints at how Gilbert Osmond directs his faculty of choice. It accords with his belief, as he tells Isabel, that "a woman's natural mission is to be where she is most appreciated" (226)—"to be" and not "to do." Madame Merle complains of Gilbert's activities as a connoisseur, "But as the only thing you do—well, it's so little. I should have liked you to do so many other things" (208). Nevertheless, Osmond's inability to differentiate between Isabel as an object and as a subject makes his seemingly passive role in her fate (which he himself regards as an "altogether exceptional effort" [260]) morally equivalent to Madame Merle's active role. They are equally culpable.

Madame Merle serves as James's scapegoat in *The Portrait of a Lady:* she carries the very burden of plot with which James himself was so unwilling to dirty his hands. James twice invokes the "nefarious name" of "plot" in describing her manipulations of Isabel (453, 455). Appropriately, as with so many other active heroines in novels, Madame Merle has something of the stage actress about her (212, 275, 283). And explicitly, her form of "doing" is a "doing with." When Osmond asks Madame Merle, "What do you want to do with [Miss Archer]," her reply shows the limits of action in James's world: "I don't pretend to know what people are meant for. . . . I only know what I can do with them" (207). At least she is honest. Gilbert Osmond's inactive stance hides his very potent abilities to do things with other people, as Isabel soon learns. Moreover, James himself can be accused of a similar irresponsibility for his inaction; in the end, it is his plot that leaves Isabel caged in her marriage. Yet the deeper implication is that to focus on situation can be as dangerous as to focus on action. Like James, Osmond merely "places" Isabel,[33] but such placement can be as nefarious as outright plotting, as the events of the novel prove. On the other hand, Serena Merle's "doing with" significantly also represents a "doing for," as the Countess explains: "She worked for [Osmond], plotted for him, suffered for him" (455). It is a distinction worth keeping in mind while constructing a moral calculus of the novel.

The great question raised by commentators on James's novel concerns the "anti-climax" of Isabel's "career" (to use Lily's earlier phrase): why does Isabel return to her marriage at the end? Soon after she weds Osmond, Isabel learns her mistake: "she had not read him right" (357). Like Dorothea after her marriage to Casaubon, who felt "that the large vistas and wide fresh air which she had dreamed of finding in her husband's mind were replaced by anterooms and winding passages which seemed to lead nowhither," Isabel sees the expanses of thought and experience that she had envisioned her marriage would open before her instead close off: "She had taken all the first steps in the purest confidence, and then she had suddenly found the infinite vista of a multiplied life to be a dark, narrow alley with a dead wall at the end" (356).[34] Like Gwendolen, though, Isabel learns from her mistaken marriage to internalize her active principle; "she had more and more of the air of being able to wait" (310). Her belief that "unhappiness was a state of disease—of suffering as opposed to doing," and that "to 'do'—it hardly mattered what—would therefore be an escape, perhaps in some degree a remedy" (348), slowly changes into a recognition of "suffering" as "an active condition; it was not a chill, a stupor, a despair; it was a passion of thought, of speculation, of response to every pressure" (356). Recall Ralph's description of Isabel as "a real little passionate force to set at play" (63). If one stresses the relationship between passion and passivity, then "passionate force" becomes an almost oxymoronic concept that sheds real light on the paradox inherent in Isabel. Isabel's "passion" is indeed a suppressed force, an inaction rather than an action, but no less strong for that.

Isabel asks the same question Eliot's heroines asked in response to their unhappy marriages: "what ought *she* to do?" (363; James's emphasis). Yet Isabel's very commitment to action keeps her in the cage of her stifling marriage. Staying with Osmond validates her deed: "almost anything seemed preferable to repudiating the most serious act—the single sacred act—of her life" (386). "One must accept one's deeds," she insists: "I married him before all the world; I was perfectly free; it was impossible to do anything more deliberate" (407). Of course she was not free, as James's language makes sure we recognize: "It was impossible to pretend that she had not acted with her eyes open; if ever a girl was a free agent she had been. . . . [T]he sole source of her mistake was in herself. There had been no plot, no snare; she had looked and considered and chosen" (340). James lays the dramatic irony on thickly. Isabel will learn that Madame Merle has been "a powerful agent in her destiny." Her "sense of accident" will be replaced by recognition of Madame Merle's nefarious plot (428).

Why then does this recognition not free her from the plot in which she has been ensnared and allow her to resume her course of action, to continue on her adventures? In part, she is now aware, like so many of Eliot's heroines, of a sense of "duty" beyond herself. Pansy has become her "article of religion," the clue to lead her through the labyrinth of life (341). But James goes a step beyond Eliot. After the plot has been revealed, Osmond appropriates Isabel's own argument: "I think we should accept the consequences of our actions," he announces to her (446). And not only does Isabel's respect for action keep her bound to Osmond, her newly experienced but always appreciated awareness of the force of inaction—and its correlative, internal action—also constrains her. Osmond's statement stuns her: "Ten minutes before she had felt all the joy of irreflective action—a joy to which she had so long been a stranger; but action had been suddenly changed to slow renunciation, transformed by the blight of Osmond's touch" (446).

We hear a resonance of Grandcourt's "torpedo-like touch" in *Daniel Deronda*. Yet James's frightening suggestion is that Isabel may, on some level, be glad of the opportunity "to live only to suffer" (466). She may see her connection to Osmond not as numbing, but as liberating in a way that no other marriage could be, as an "active condition" (356) that must be contrasted to "the joy of irreflective action." After all, Isabel chose Osmond because of his capacity for interior action. And the degree to which the active Caspar Goodwood's "touch," his lightninglike kiss, represents an "act of possession" clearly frightens Isabel; hence her relief "when darkness returned" and she is again "free" (489). The only kinds of acts that remain clear of the taint of "doing with" in this novel are acts of sacrifice and interior acts. Isabel is left "free" to do both. Again, James seems to be hinting at the conclusion of *Paradise Lost:* "She had not known where to turn; but she knew now. There was a very straight path" (490). With the world all before her, what she has "chosen" is precisely her "place of rest."[35] Having "wandered," she decides to take the "straight path" of inaction that now lies before her, a welcome relief from the confusions of action.

Unsurprisingly, contemporary critics balked at James's ending with a fervor reminiscent of the response to the conclusion of Clough's *Amours de Voyage*. In spite of James's reference to the "straight path," R. H. Hutton complained that Isabel was left "without compass and without clue," and he added that he was uncertain whether the novel could even be said to have an "ending."[36] His objection demonstrates the degree to which readers considered formal issues on a moral level. Hutton's outrage stemmed in part from his sense that Henrietta Stackpole's words to Caspar Goodwood at the conclusion of the novel, "just you wait!" (490), accompanied by Goodwood's upward (that is, presumably hopeful) glance at Henrietta, indicated that James intended us to believe Isabel's "straight path" would lead through adultery or divorce to Goodwood. Yet Henrietta's phrase aptly lends itself to both optimistic and pessimistic readings, ones that emphasize either possibility or resignation. As the critic in the *Athenaeum* rightly complained, "this so-called 'portrait of a lady' is left unfinished just at the point where some really decisive and enlightening strokes begin to be possible."[37] It is a typically Jamesian tease, and it must reflect on some level James's desire to leave Isabel a free agent at the end of his narrative; we cannot tell what choices she will eventually make.

In the process, James also, paradoxically, makes Isabel seem more alive. Those critics who single her out as a successfully "round" character tend to do so because, like Gwendolen, she is both known and not known. As one early critic wrote: "It is claimed that the heroine is of all the characters the one least clearly painted, least perfectly understood. But it would not be

difficult to say that we know her and her motives as the author chooses for
us to know, and the interest of the novel comes in great part from the vagueness of our acquaintance with Miss Archer; and after all, when we lay down
the book, we cannot deny, if we are candid, that we know as much of the
motives which induced her . . . as we do of the impulses which lead our sis-
ters and cousins to similar results."[38] F. R. Leavis suggests that Isabel's "peculiar kind of impressiveness . . . is conditioned by her *not* being known inside
out"[39]—that is, much of her remains what could be called "inside in." James,
by virtue of a kind of modest reticence, allows her a privacy that ensures
that whatever constraints she may face in the physical world, her interior
universe remains very much her own space.

But as I have been arguing, Isabel's understanding of free agency has shifted.
Whereas at the beginning of the novel, her sense of action seems to dominate in her, by its conclusion she has succumbed to lure of passionate suffering, of an outer passivity that conceals an "'exciting' inward life." When he
revised *The Portrait,* James made the meaning of Henrietta's advice to
Goodwood clearer, adding a final sentence: "She walked him away with her,
however, as if she had given him now the key to patience" (490). Is patience
to serve as the key to the novel? Consider Henry James's letter to Edith Wharton,
written decades later in regard to her treatment at the hands of her own bru-
tal husband: "Only sit tight yourself *and go through the movements of life.* That
keeps up our connection with life—I mean of the immediate and apparent
life; behind which, all the while, the deeper and darker and the unapparent,
in which things *really* happen to us, learns, under that hygiene, to stay in its
place. . . . Live it all through, every inch of it—out of it something will come—
but live it ever so quietly; and—*je maintiens mon dire*—waitingly!"[40] Again,
patience should rule—even in the face of marital abuse—because what "really
happens" happens internally. But the question still remains: are we to believe
that James sees Isabel's return to the prison of her marriage as an act of moral
heroism (suggesting an internalized conception of the heroic) or as an act of
cowardice and conventionalism (suggesting a more externalized view of
courage)? I think that the very impossibility of fixing on a final reading for
James's novel shows his complex awareness of the relationship of action and
consciousness to the moral life.

REVOLUTIONS IN PLOTTING

Early on in her story, Isabel Archer declares, "I should delight in seeing a
revolution" (71). Her spirit for adventure makes her interest understandable.

Her author, though, expressed a similar desire to his friend T. S. Perry: "If I had nothing else to do I think I should run over to Ireland. . . . The reason is that I should like to see a country in a state of revolution."[41] It seems a strange wish, coming from one so apparently apolitical, and so averse to turbulent action, as Henry James is often considered to be. In another letter to Perry from the early 1880s, he expanded on his political observations: "Nothing *lives* in England today but politics. They are all devouring, and their mental uproar crowds everything out." His comments suggest an almost Wordsworthian objection to the stifling effects of the political fervor: it leaves no mental space for other, perhaps quieter and more discriminating, kinds of thought. Yet James was not wholeheartedly against the invigorating atmosphere. He added that he should "hate it more if I didn't also find it interesting. The air is full of events, of changes, of movement (some people would say of revolution, but I don't think that)."[42]

Whatever he may have thought of the potential for revolution in England, James responded to the current environment. In the latter half of the 1880s he wrote the three novels that combine to form what can be thought of as his "political period": *The Bostonians* (1885–86) (which explores the women's movement of the years following the American Civil War), *The Princess Casamassima* (also 1885–86) (which looks at revolutionary politics in contemporary England), and *The Tragic Muse* (1890) (which forces its protagonist to choose between political and artistic careers). The existence of such a political period indicates James's ongoing exploration of the role of action in the moral life. It also coincides curiously with the era usually thought of as James's "middle phase," following the great early successes and preceding the astonishing formal revelations of the later novels. While all three works display a complicated relationship to the political arena, none so forcefully connects the formal issues of plot with politics as *The Princess,* a novel that revolves around an anarchist plot. So it is to this work that I wish to turn in order to explore how James's stylistic developments relate to his changing sense of action.

One common way of thinking of James's interest in action is to look at his use of melodrama.[43] George Eliot's Sir Hugo had declared to Daniel Deronda, "At this stage of the world, if a man wants to be taken seriously he must keep clear of melodrama"[44]—something James resolutely refused to do. Critics have often remarked on what Leo Bersani calls James's "inferior, corny plots."[45] Dorothea Krook has compared James to Wordsworth by noting that while Wordsworth creates consciousness in his poems by stripping them of the objective, James does so in his novels by overloading them with details of the material world.[46] James's melodramatic flair—another kind of overloading of the objective—parallels this process: he brings the action back into his work, but he changes the way in which his reader comprehends it. In many of his works external melodramas are displaced by what Peter Brooks has termed James's "melodramas of consciousness"[47]—a phrase that describes Isabel's "adventures" in *The Portrait.* Commenting on *The American* (1877), Brooks explains how "what differs [in James] is that the melodrama of external action—the suspenseful menace, pursuit, and combat—are all past by the time" the "ethical conflict" is resolved; "External melodrama has been used to lead to the melodrama of ethical choice."[48]

But James does not limit his melodrama to his characters' consciousnesses. Rather, he includes both versions: internal and external. So his tale "The Story in It" (1903) presents us simultaneously with a "real" (that is, bodily) love affair, between Mrs. Dyott and Colonel Voyt, and the "innocent" love felt by Maud Blessingbourne for the Colonel.[49] The characters argue about the proper role for "drama" and "adventures" in literature—whether they need be of guilty "relations," or whether the inward drama of innocence could also be called a "story."[50] Voyt finally admits that Maud's "consciousness" "was, in the last analysis, a kind of shy romance," although (and these are the final lines of the tale) "who but a duffer—he stuck to his contention—would see the shadow of a 'story' in it?"[51] James is of course the duffer.[52] His point, one he makes again the Preface to *The Princess Casamassima,* is to note "the unreality of the sharp distinction, where the interest of observation is at stake, between doing and feeling."[53] Nevertheless, the paradox presented by "The Story in It" is that James likes to have it both ways. He leaves us to decide which is the more interesting kind of adventure. James keeps titillating us with plot.

Still, he himself seems to have a preference. It appears in his strange inversion of the moral process. As Brooks's comments on *The American* suggest, while we usually think of choice as preceding action, in James, the action often precedes the choice. Because of this reversal, choice becomes the more ethically invigorated category. Action, in contrast, just "happens," as though without prior consideration. Another way of considering this inconsistency is to say that especially in James's earlier works—although *The Ambassadors* (1903) also stands as a great example—the actors are often not the real agents of the drama: those characters who do the most tend not to be the same as those who make the significant moral choices.

But we can identify a shift in James's attitudes toward action over the course of his career—one that suggests his growing awareness of its moral complexities. Brooks has argued that one of the great attractions of melodrama in the nineteenth century was its ability to render conflict visible:

"For melodrama has the distinct value of being about recognition and clarification, about how to be clear what the stakes are and what their representative signs mean, and how to face them."[54] James, though, as critics have long recognized, prefers to avoid the obvious[55]; his use of both external and internal melodrama reflects this fact by increasingly making things opaque rather than clear. And while James's position in *The Portrait* already exhibited significant conflict with regard to the moral status of action, the later novels make it much harder to align plot with evil. One can register the change by comparing *The Portrait*'s love triangle of Isabel-Osmond-Madame Merle to that of Milly Theale-Merton Densher-Kate Croy in *The Wings of the Dove* (1902).[56] Densher's inaction (at least until after Milly's death) represents a far subtler version of complicity in crime than Osmond's (I actually find him a correspondingly more sinister character). But the change in James's sense of the morality of plotting is particularly apparent in his revision of Madame Merle in the character of Kate Croy. James seems to have recognized his unfair treatment of Madame Merle, so he tries to make us sympathize with Kate—and with her desire to plot— in a way he never allowed us to sympathize with his earlier villainess. We begin the novel inside Kate's consciousness, subjected to all the insults and pettinesses that attend her daily life and make her wish to work her way out of it; James lets us feel how hard it is to act with a pure will in such circumstances. And in general, the late novels make it harder to tell the heroes from the victims, the good from the bad.[57]

But if moral judgment of characters can be difficult, in the later novels, even the bare plot becomes the subject of mystery. James achieves this effect not via the ordinary process of suspense (that is, by making us wonder what will happen), but by his extraordinary methods of opacity (we often wonder, like his characters, what *is* happening). He thus forces his readers to contemplate plot with a conscious attention very similar to the inward action that he portrays in his characters. As Arnold Kettle puts it, "With James the question 'What happened?' carries the most subtle, the most exciting ramifications. To no previous novelist had the answer to such a question seemed so difficult, its implication so interminable."[58] Think about the role of the ghost in *The Turn of the Screw* (1898); while we do not really know what is going on in the tale, the center of interest rests squarely in the governess's consciousness. The important issue is *whether she is imagining things or not,* and not *whether the ghost exists or not.* Similarly, while there is plenty of action in almost every story James writes, what the reader is left with is a strong sense of the "in"—as though that should be the highlighted word in the title of the 1903 tale: "The Story *in* It."

James's experiments in the political novel come at a crucial juncture in his career in melodrama and also in his relationship to action. Beginning in 1890, notably on the heels of what I have called his political period, James wrote dramas for the stage that, in their efforts to please the audience, flirted with the melodramatic conventions of the time.[59] Rather tellingly, Hyacinth Robinson meets the Princess Casamassima in the theater, at a melodrama boasting a "terribly complicated" plot in which "someone or other was hurled over a precipice."[60] James means this as a joke, of course, but however one wants to look at the role of action in *The Princess Casamassima,* James's story develops out of Hyacinth's reaction to that meeting. And Hyacinth is prepared for his encounter at the play by his own melodramatic lineage: his aristocratic father was murdered by his seamstress mother, who, like the contemporary melodrama, was a French import to England.

When he wrote the novel, James fully intended to emphasize its action. Among the stranger literary friendships on record is that between the author of *The Portrait of a Lady* and Robert Louis Stevenson, the great adventure novelist. In December of 1884, Stevenson had expressed his wish that James would produce "as it were an episode from one of the (so-called) novels of adventure."[61] Soon after, James began work on *The Princess.* In a letter to his brother William, he indicated his plan to make his new novel more exciting than *The Bostonians,* which had been something of a popular failure. Henry recalled how William had voiced objection to that book's "redundancy . . . in the way of descriptive psychology &c.," a flaw that arose from his desire "to establish his people solidly." Henry admits, "I have overdone it," but reassures William that *The Princess* "will be found less tedious, owing to my having made to myself all the reflections your letter contains, several months ago, & never ceased to make them since."[62]

Still, if this was to be an adventure novel, it was to be a strange one. In his comments in the Preface to *The Princess,* written years later for the New York edition, James remembers that another problem he faced in writing had to do with how properly to combine its elements of "bewilderment" and "intelligence." Readers like bewilderment, so long as it is not accompanied by too much intelligence, because intelligence can "endanger" the action, or "slashing," "the subject-matter of any self-respecting story."[63] James's nervousness about overt action comes out in his use of the word "slashing," which suggests the unattractive and dangerous violence of plot. Unusually, these remarks seem to align "bewilderment" with action rather than with consciousness, as though hinting that "what happens" will be more confusing in the novel than "what is thought." And while (as he indicates in the Preface by comparing Hyacinth's situation to that of the Prince of Denmark) we are indeed once more in the world of the nineteenth-century *Hamlet,* where intelligence threatens to close off the possibility for action, James seems to be just as concerned that action could close off the possibility for consciousness.[64]

Nevertheless, contemporary readers recognized the shift in James's perspective in *The Princess.* The critic for the *Saturday Review* responded with excitement to the new form of Jamesian adventure:

> Hitherto he has been the poet of the Fine Shades, . . . [He] might be compared with that other philosopher whose aim it was to bring his horse to live upon a straw *per diem.* . . . He reduced his readers to a straw (of incident) per volume, and the novel expired—or went near to expiring—in his hands. He is now a changed man. He has taken a nearer view of his art, and has found that the good novelist with decency may comprehend in his scheme such qualities as action, vigorous emotion, brave incident, and even romance.[65]

The *Critic* gushed about the book in a similar fashion. "Who would ever have believed that the author of *Daisy Miller* would ever condescend to make a real story," the reviewer asked. Indicating that he had been put to sleep by *The Portrait,* he noted how different this latest work was: "Here is a genuine romance, with conspirators, and harlots, and stabbings, and jails, and low-lived men and women who drop their h's, and real incidents, and strong emotions, and everything 'in a concatenation accordingly.'"[66] Here is a plot-driven novel. Still, there were many dissenting voices. A critic in the *Graphic* remarked that while James had "evidently done his utmost to write a novel with a story in it" (recall the title of James's late tale), he had, "to put the case as mildly as possible, not succeeded. . . . [N]ot the most scornfully plotless of all his works has ever been so vapid or so dull."[67] *The Times* protested that "the plot is fearfully stationary,"[68] while the reviewer in *Punch* went a little deeper into the source of the problem when he argued that James had "used Socialism mainly as a sort of peg on which to hang certain curiously-conceived and delicately executed character-paintings of his own peculiar genre. Possibly that is all that he wanted it for."[69] Such complaints have persisted. W. J. Harvey explains, "One way of stating the failure of *The Princess Casamassima* would be to say that James is no Dickens, while this is the most Dickensian of his novels."[70] In other words, he was a writer of novels of character ("character-paintings of his own peculiar genre") rather than those of plot, and he should have stuck to what he knew best.

The unusual ambivalence of the response to *The Princess Casamassima* owes much to James's choice of the plot at its center. *The Princess* can be thought of as James's attempt to envision action—an attempt that parallels Eliot's foray into visionary action in *Daniel Deronda*. And like *Daniel Deronda*, *The Princess* has elicited an extraordinary amount of attention from critics concerning either the viability or the historical specificity of the revolutionary movement at its center. As readers of Eliot's novel complain about the details of Daniel's plans in the East, so commentators on *The Princess* have wondered whether James was depicting anarchists or nihilists or socialists.[71] We saw how obscurity was an essential component of Eliot's great proto-Zionist plan in *Daniel Deronda*. James also chose to focus on a plot that is more or less impossible to see; in the Preface to the New York edition, he commented on his hero Hyacinth's "subterraneous politics and occult affiliations."[72] I suggested that behind Eliot's unwillingness to particularize the methods of Deronda's revolution lay her desire for that revolution to signify broadly— to express the possibility for revolutionary idealism in general. James, on the other hand, kept his plot underground not because of a lack of knowledge about revolutionary activity, nor because of any specific understanding of anarchist groups, but because by doing so, he was once again able to keep consciousness at the center of his narrative.

The plot in *The Princess* functions much like the ghost in *The Turn of the Screw:* by keeping it invisible and unknowable, James was able to maintain his focus on Hyacinth's *sense* of the plot, even as he explored the political realm. Irving Howe has written that "there are times when *The Princess Casamassima* seems almost to evade its own theme. Everything is prepared for but little is revealed, doors open upon doors, curtains onto curtains." Yet this process of delving deeper and deeper into our fundamental ignorance of the reality of the situation (an examination of consciousness)—and not "the nature and power of social radicalism" (an examination of action)—represents what I would call, using Howe's phrase, "the central brute fact of the novel."[73] This is not to say that the decision to focus on contemporary radical politics was a random one; rather, James was interested in the relationship between the structure of such plots and action more generally, in both the modern world and the fictional realm. James's claim is a truly startling one: that action is essentially unknowable, that all we can really know about is a mind conscious of a plot.[74] And while, in this novel from his middle phase, James supports his point about action by leaning upon a "real" underground plot, in his later works, he will expand his claim about the inscrutability of deeds and events. Much simpler "happenings" will be presented as impossible to establish. In fact, his extraordinary late style can be thought of in part as a development of his struggle to envision the new forms of action. So underground revolutionary activity can stand in for action-in-general in the Epipolie of our daily lives. Realistic action is inscrutable action, what the Preface to *The Princess* so curiously calls "bewilderment."

Politics also provided James with a particularly convenient venue in which to stage a contest between action and vision. If the shape of action has indeed changed, then the competition between the life of action and the life of the mind is no longer the simple opposition between external and internal that it once seemed to be; recall how the Preface remarks upon "the unreality of the sharp distinction, where the interest of observation is at stake, between doing and feeling."[75] In fact, in James's writing one could argue that the categories have been transposed. We are as far as we could possibly be from the clarity of Homeric epic action. It is the life of the mind, as represented by Hyacinth's typically Jamesian aestheticism, that is visible; the life of action, in contrast, is impossible to see. Indeed, the real "plot" of *The Princess* consists of Hyacinth's *choice* between action and vision, between the invisible plot in which he engages himself and the vision of culture he comes to love: "It made him even rather faint to think that he must choose; that he couldn't (with any respect for his own consistency) work, underground, for the enthronement of democracy, and continue to enjoy, in however platonic a manner, a spectacle which rested on a hideous social inequality" (165). Spectacles, and all forms of the specular, abound in the novel, but they have little to do with politics.[76] James's frequent focus on the visual arts (sculpture, painting, architecture, even bookbinding) as opposed to less material forms of culture such as music and poetry is notable in this regard. His characters sometimes seem to hold on to objects as anchors of knowledge in an unknowable and ever-changing universe.

So by pulling his action underground, James, like Eliot (whom he again invokes in this Preface[77]), succeeds in placing "a lively *inward* revolution" at the center of even his most overtly political novel.[78] He transforms action—what was once an external, objective category—into something that is very much subjective. And once again, this transformation of action results in a novel in which the political becomes subsumed by the personal. In a world "where ignorant armies clash by night," being "true to one another" becomes the most essential form of morality.

The Princess Casamassima

To understand how the contest between action and vision plays out, one must turn to the plot at the center of *The Princess Casamassima*. We first hear of the plot when Muniment asks Hyacinth whether he can "keep a secret"—that is, keep something hidden. Hyacinth replies with excitement, "Is it a plot—a conspiracy?" He expresses a longing for a reason to act: "If you have some plan, something to which one might give oneself, I think you might have told me" (128). "Will you tell me all about your plot?" he implores. But the response could have come from James himself: "Oh, it's no plot. I don't think I care much for plots" (130). What it is instead, Paul tells Hyacinth, is a "little movement"—reminding one of James's comment on the current state of England: "The air is full of events, of changes, of movement (some people would say of revolution, but I don't think that)." The word is intentionally indeterminate: *plot* suggests an organized plan; *movement* can be not only haphazard but even aimless. In fact, Hyacinth's political naiveté is indicated by his asking Muniment, "Don't you belong to the party of action?" Muniment responds scathingly: "Look at the way he has picked up all the silly bits of catchwords! . . . You must have got that precious phrase out of the newspapers, out of some driveling leader. Is that the party you want to belong to?" (151).

The simple answer to this question is "yes." Hyacinth's yearning for membership in the party of action becomes evident in the scene at the Sun and Moon in which he commits himself to the plot. The scene closely parallels the discussion at the Hand and Banner in Eliot's *Daniel Deronda*.[79] But the clubs' names reveal the differences between the political stances of their authors: if Eliot called her club the "Hand and Banner" in an effort to suggest, ultimately, that raising a banner might effect the raising of hands and the forming of nations, James's "Sun and Moon" intimates that the club members might as well be stargazing, for all their discussion is likely to achieve. After all, the real revolutionary threat of the novel is well hidden from such bright lights. And while Eliot respected her club, filling it with intelligent, sincere men, James cannot avert his gaze from the "hideously papered walls" of his "little clubroom" (251).

The difference between the two scenes also comes out in James's distant echo of Eliot's use of Shelley's *Prometheus Unbound*. I argued how important Shelley and his poem were to Eliot's vision of political idealism. As Daniel first enters the room, she has a character quote the avalanche metaphor from the poem, precisely those lines that most reflect idealistic hope: "As thought by thought is piled, till some great truth / Is loosened and the nations echo round."[80] As though he had read Eliot's novel, Hyacinth imagines an answer to the great question (familiar to readers both of Eliot and of James), "Ah, what could he do?":

> If he had a definite wish while he stood there it was that that exalted,
> deluded company should pour itself forth, with Muniment at its head, and
> surge through the sleeping city, gathering the myriad miserable out of
> their slums and burrows, and roll into the selfish squares, and lift a
> tremendous hungry voice, and awaken the gorged indifferent to a terror
> that would bring them down. (293)

In stirring language, James has Hyacinth refigure Shelley's avalanche of
thought as a supremely physical revolutionary riot that will sweep through
the land, a second French Revolution in all its glory. That is to say, he is
imagining the very force from which Eliot backed away with a fear that
led her to replace it with revolutions of thought. What terrified Eliot,
James fantasizes about along with his hero.

But only because he cannot really believe that things would happen this
way. Nothing could be farther from such a conception of heroic revolutionary
action than the plot at the center of *The Princess*. Straightforward revolution belongs to the distant past; it has become the subject of nostalgia. Even
Poupin, who is described as "a Republican of the old-fashioned sort, of the
note of 1848" (114), recalls fondly the "irresistible force" of "'89" (125).
Paul mockingly expresses Hyacinth's naïve views for Lady Aurora by referring to the French Revolution: "The principal conclusion that Mr.
Robinson sees his way to . . . is that your father ought to have his head chopped
off and carried on a pike" (139). Hyacinth, the grandson of a Parisian revolutionary, goes to Paris (like Clough) as a tourist rather than a political
activist. There, far from the field of his own particular battle (and only after
he has lost his revolutionary faith), he experiences his strongest impression
of what he calls "the great legend of the French Revolution, sanguinary and
heroic," which he describes in terms of the language of nostalgia so relevant to the tourist's mode that I explored in chapter 2.

If the French Revolution stands for action, inaction characterizes the modern revolution. Paul carelessly defends his willingness to allow Hyacinth to
join the plot by pointing to his friend's love of action: "You like a lot of things
I don't. You like excitement and emotion and change, . . . whereas I go in
for a holy calm, for sweet repose." Hyacinth counters, "If you object, for
yourself, to change, and are so fond of still waters, why have you associated
yourself with a revolutionary movement?" Paul's response sounds a death
knell for Hyacinth: "Just for that reason! . . . Isn't our revolutionary movement as quiet as the grave?" (442). And it is—precisely because of the way
in which James has buried his plot. When Hyacinth later demands, "in God's
name, why don't we do something? . . . There are plenty of us ready," Paul

replies, "Ready for what? There is nothing to be done here" (295). In his review of the novel, R. H. Hutton made the connection between James's revolutionists and the rest of society explicit in his analysis of Paul Muniment: "Yet so far as Mr. Henry James permits us to judge of his characters, no one of them is more completely adrift, no one of them knows less what he intends to do by way of revolutionizing society, or how it can be done so as to substitute a more tolerable system for the existing system of *laissez faire,* than this same hero of the revolutionary party, Paul Muniment."[81] By invoking the specter of laissez-faire in his discussion of the plot, Hutton shows how James's imagination of revolution resembles Carlylean "Donothingism": his radicals have evolved out of the society against which they are fighting. Paul himself explains, "an *economy* of heroism was an advantage to any cause" (288; emphasis added).

Perhaps the clearest sign of the gap between the new revolutionists and the old comes from James's insistence that the real modern expression of the French Revolution can be found in that working-class Britannia of the Market Place, Millicent Henning.[82] If Paul is indeed the apostle of donothingism, Millicent is a Marianne dressed in the most up-to-date fashions: "Hyacinth could easily see her (if there should ever be barricades in the streets of London), with a red cap of liberty on her head and her white throat bared so she should be able to shout the louder the Marseillaise of that hour, whatever it might be" (161). As a department-store employee, she shows how the river of revolution has been redirected into the less dangerous streams of consumer politics. Nevertheless, Hyacinth recognizes in Millicent a "primitive, half-childish, half-plebeian impulse of destruction, the instinct of pulling down what was above her, the reckless energy that would, precisely, make her so effective in revolutionary scenes" (268). Her undeniable attraction to readers stems from the contrast between her energy and the enervated world in which she moves.

The confusion of heroic roles in James's novel can seen more clearly by comparison with another political work from the period. In Disraeli's *Lothair* (1870), which deals in part with the real role of secret societies in the establishment of an Italian nation, these societies are known as Mary-Anne associations.[83] They are given a visible leadership more important to the cause than even Garibaldi in Theodora, the tragic heroine of the novel. The modern incarnation of Marianne, Theodora leads her troops forward, as in Delacroix's great painting of 1830.[84] But for all his legendary political acuity and his famous restlessness, even Disraeli has trouble envisioning a successful political plot. While his discipleship under Aristotle is evident in the General's motto—"Action may not always be happiness, . . . but there is no happiness without action"[85]—Theodora herself is like Paul an "admirer of repose," acknowledging, "I dislike plots . . . ; they always fail."[86] Indeed the plot does fail, and Theodora dies of wounds received on the battlefield.

The underground revolutionary movement Hyacinth joins has little to do with Marianne-like heroism. Hyacinth longs for the day on which Muniment will reveal all to him, will choose to "exert" his "influence": "it would not be till then, he was sure, that they would all know where they were, and that the good they were striving for, blindly, obstructedly, in a kind of dirty intellectual fog, would pass from the stage of crude discussion and mere sharp, tantalizing desirableness into that of irresistible reality" (281). But that day never comes. Rather, as Paul notes, it is precisely the "very fact of the impunity, the invisibility, of the persons involved in it" that gives the movement its force (288). This force leads the Princess to ask her great question:

> I want to know *à quoi m'en tenir*. Are we on the eve of great changes, or are we not? Is everything that is gathering force underground, in the dark, in the night, in little rooms, out of sight of governments and policemen and idiotic "statesmen"—heaven save them!—is all this going to burst forth some fine morning and set the world on fire? Or is it to sputter out and spend itself in vain conspiracies, be dissipated in sterile heroisms and abortive isolated movements? (200)

The Princess appears as unsure of what is happening as readers of James's late novels tend to be. In fact, such a feeling of not knowing what is going on is the great underlying condition of James's novel.

In this work from his middle period, James repeatedly describes the plot in an opaque, indefinite language that anticipates his late style—as though that style were itself a version of a nostalgia for comprehensible action, incorporating the new sense of action as fundamentally unknowable and invisible. Paul admits, "I quite agree with you that the time has come to settle upon it and to follow it" (290), but what is the "it" to be settled, and how? The conspirators at the Sun and Moon expound similar abstractions: "What they wanted was to put forth their might without any more palaver; to do something, or for someone; to go out somewhere and smash something, on the spot—why not?—that very night" (291). Only the "fat man" voices a (surely understandable) desire for more specifics: "I want to have it all drawn up first; then I'll go in" (289). His words recall by contrast James's own comments on his intention in *The Portrait* not to constrain his heroine in a plot, where his resistance to plot expressed his wish to preserve his characters' free agency. But James is not unlike the fat man; he wrote with some worry in his notebooks for *The Princess,* "I have never yet become engaged in a novel in which, after I had begun to write . . . the details remained so vague."[87] And while Hyacinth also expresses his urge toward action in vague terms ("I am ready to do anything that will do any good; anything, anything—I don't care a rap" [294]), he yearns after something more definite: an embodied leader.

Muniment lures him into the web of plot with the promise of visible leadership: "Should you like to see the genuine article, Robinson?" (295). Hyacinth does eventually see the genuine article, although the reader is not privy to the meeting, hearing about it only afterward. To get to the real thing, Hyacinth must be led through a physical manifestation of the mists in which it is shrouded: by the time the cab taking him to Hoffendahl stops, "Hyacinth had totally lost, in the drizzling gloom, a sense of their whereabouts" (296). Hoffendahl stands in the novel as a surrogate for God, a kind of Prime Mover of the movement.[88] When Hyacinth later describes his encounter with the great man to the Princess, he tells how he has now "been in the innermost sanctuary—I have seen the holy of holies" (330). The revolution is "real" and "solid," he insists, though well hidden. In Hoffendahl, Hyacinth thinks he finds just what he was looking for: "a man who was the very incarnation of a programme" (328). This embodiedness is what makes him "jump at" participation in the plot; "it was just what I was looking for," he tells Paul (447).

Such visibility matters because of the relationship between belief and action. To see is to believe, and Hoffendahl, once seen, represents something Hyacinth can have faith in. After the Princess tells Hyacinth that "You make me believe it"—that is, believe the revolution will happen—Hyacinth replies, "It matters little whether one believes it or not!" (330). Yet it could not matter more. The Princess says of "convictions," "Having them is nothing. It's the acting on them" (451). But (as the case of Arthur Hugh Clough demonstrates) it can be hard to act without them. Questions of belief play a central role in many late-nineteenth-century novels about underground political movements precisely because of their concern for the possibility of political action. In part, anarchist movements were seen as the direct development of the loss of religious conviction. Julia Wedgewood (the niece of Charles Darwin) noted in her review of James's novel that it explored one of the kinds of faith with which religion was replaced: "Princess Casamassima is . . . a picture of the seething revolutionary energy and feverish destructiveness which has, to many in our day, taken the place of the Christianity they have abandoned."[89] In Ivan Turgenev's *Virgin Soil* (1877) the hero

Nezhdanov pledges himself to an underground cause but later commits suicide when he discovers that he has lost faith in it—"I don't believe in it! I
don't believe in it!"[90]—in part because, like Hyacinth, he has a delicate appreciation for culture. Fyodor Dostoevsky's *Demons* (1872), another novel that
explores contemporary radical politics, describes how Pyotr Verkhovensky,
the chief instigator and archplotter of the local underground movement,
looks to the hero Stavrogin to play the lead. As Stavrogin puts it, he is "convinced that I could 'raise their banner.' . . . He's taken it into his head that
I could play the role of Stenka Razin for them."[91] For all his charisma, Stavrogin's
extreme ennui, his passivity, and his inability to commit himself to any cause
or purpose would seem to rule him out for the role of revolutionary hero.
But as Verkhovensky recognizes, all that is really required is a semblance of
leadership—for a few people to be able to say, "We've seen him, we've seen
him"—"The main thing is the legend!"[92] *Demons* finally suggests that the
only solution to social injustice is to be found through a return to native
religion.

James is by far the most secular of the writers I have looked at, yet questions of belief are crucial to him, not least because, as his brother William
also recognized, conviction and action are intrinsically related. In "The Will
to Believe," his best-known treatment of the relationship between faith and
action, William James pointed out that all action depends upon a form of
belief: "The maximum of liveness in a hypothesis means willingness to act
irrevocably. Practically, that means belief; but there is some believing tendency wherever there is willingness to act at all."[93] Appropriately, William
turned repeatedly in the essay to the poetry of Clough to argue his central
premise. Referring to the line "If hopes are dupes, fears may be liars" (from
"Say not the struggle naught availeth"), William commented: "Dupery for
dupery, what proof is there that dupery through hope is so much worse than
dupery through fear?"[94]

"Dupery through hope" would be one way in which to express
Hyacinth's tragedy. Hoffendahl's very name—*hoffen* means "to hope" in German—
indicates the degree to which he figures as the promised redeemer. But like
Christ's, his heroism lies as much in his suffering as in his deeds. When the
members at the Sun and Moon ask, "What the devil has he done then?"
Muniment replies that "he had spent twelve years in a Prussian prison" (287).
James tells us of Hyacinth's "intense desire to stand face-to-face with the
sublime Hoffendahl, to hear his voice, to touch his mutilated hand" (291).
Again, the expressed desire for a visible leader, but Hoffendahl's mutilation
suggests a limited ability to act; Hyacinth calls him "extraordinarily quiet"
during their meeting (331). Hence his own role in the plot. When the Princess,

thinking of Hoffendahl's order, asks Paul, "Wouldn't someone else do his work just as well," Paul pretends to see in her question a reference to Hyacinth's skills as a bookbinder: "His work? Why, I'm told he's a master hand" (453).[95] But Paul knows perfectly well what the Princess meant, and the only kind of "hand" he needs Hyacinth to be is a decidedly servile one to act as a prosthetic for Hoffendahl.

Like Daniel Deronda, Hyacinth feels himself to be chosen: "I struck him [Hoffendahl] as the right person" (331). He speaks in the excited tones of the religious convert, exclaiming that he "had taken a vow of blind obedience, as the Jesuit fathers did to the head of their order" (333). But unlike in Eliot's work, here such sense of a vocation brings no safety for action here. Ominously, Hyacinth himself describes the plot as a theatrical dress rehearsal—hardly the most ennobling of comparisons:

> In silence, in darkness, but under the feet of each one of us, the revolution lives and works. It is a wonderful, immeasurable trap, on the lid of which society performs its antics. When once the theater is complete, there will be a great rehearsal. The rehearsal is what they want me for. The invisible, impalpable wires are everywhere, passing through everything, attaching themselves to objects in which one would never think of looking for them. (330)[96]

While the image suggests the kind of melodrama that made theater such a frequent metaphor for the great actions of the French Revolution, Hoffendahl's plot plays itself out on a diminished stage, and Hyacinth is to appear rather as a puppet understudy than as a genuine actor.[97] Hoffendahl handles the wires of Hyacinth's movements—the threads of the web of action reenvisioned—like a puppeteer, reigning supreme over his little theater of revolution: "he made me see, he made me feel, he made me do, everything he wanted" (330). Yet what Hoffendahl wants will in effect turn one of those "innumerable" wires into a "noose" to slip over Hyacinth's head (331). One is reminded of the puppeteer metaphor used by Thackeray in *Vanity Fair* (1848). Or, given that Hyacinth insists that the plot depends upon "immense coincidence" (334), of the intricacies of Dickensian plotting. Such forms of control, though, are the opposite of the freedom that James had envisioned for his characters.

As the stage metaphor also suggests, Hyacinth needs to have faith because of a problem of perspective: he can't see everything that is happening. But then again, no one can: not the audience, not the performers, not even the director or puppetmaster. And this problem is due to the nature of collective action. Irving Howe complains that "[James] had no larger view of politics as collective action."[98] But part of what James wanted to show was precisely that collective action cannot be "viewed" in the same way one views the deeds of an individual. In his review of *The Princess*, R. H. Hutton pointed to the paradox inherent in James's hidden plot—the way it simultaneously represents an increased focus on action and the repudiation of it—by looking at the role of "incident" in the novel: "It has hardly any incident, unless the tendency of the whole network of circumstance and character to the tragedy with which the third volume abruptly closes [that is, Hyacinth's suicide] may be regarded as in itself constituting a single massive incident."[99] Hutton's use of the word *network* here is striking. His description of the plot recalls Hyacinth's: "he didn't pretend to know what good his little job might do, or what *portee* it might have; he hadn't the data for appreciating it. . . . The thing was to be a feature in a very large plan, of which he couldn't measure the scope—something that was to be done simultaneously in a dozen different countries. The effect was to be very much in this immense coincidence" (334).

Advocacy of such cell-like action, where agents perform in isolation, unaware of the overall structure of the plan, was a well-known and distinguishing feature of radical political organizations. In *Demons,* Dostoevsky described in detail the workings of a "program of action" composed of individual "knots" in "an infinite network of knots," owing "blind obedience to the center."[100] But such networking can also be thought of as typical of the way action works in the laissez-faire world. We saw in chapter 2 how E. S. Dallas attributed the rise of the novel to the predominance in the modern world of acts whose force is cumulative rather than individual—like the working of the marketplace—a shift that brought "the little men and the private men and all the little incidents of privacy" "into repute."[101] The language of social science, which we have already encountered in James's description of Paul Muniment, also slips into Hyacinth's description of the plot, with its dependence on "data." And "Little Hyacinth"—whose smallness renders him suitable to the "little job" (334) at hand—represents the modern little man. Like conspirators in an anarchist plot, all of us can have but the faintest conception of how our little piece of the web of action fits into the whole.

The kind of "half knowledge" that such plotting allows must have fascinated James, given his artistic concern with point of view. So often, the moral interest in his novels comes from characters'—and readers'—attempts to grasp the nature of the thoughts and actions of others: how much does Milly Theale see of Merton and Kate's plan? What does Maisie know? The way that an understanding of *The Golden Bowl* (1904) can be pieced together only by assimilating partial knowledge from a variety of positions resembles the way that actors in anarchist plots can have only partial knowledge of how their deeds fit into the overall plan of action. Plot occurs on a different level from that occupied by the individual consciousness, existing both outside its control and beyond its knowledge. So Hyacinth does not get to see beyond his little piece of the action. But neither do we as readers. To see the whole plot would be to destroy its power. No one really knows everything that is happening, not even (Paul's ambitions suggest) Hoffendahl. One must act on faith.

Yet Hyacinth's tragedy arises explicitly from a crisis of belief, and this crisis derives from the problem of invisibility. His attraction to the products of culture—the attraction that causes him to lose faith in a movement that would willingly sacrifice such products—stems from his susceptibility to the sensory, his supreme capacity for "watching" (34), his participation in his author's delicate sensitivity to beauty. As James writes, expressing the purest form of the conflict between action and vision presented by the novel, "the growth of his reluctance to act for the 'party of action'" had been "the simple extension of his observation" (582). How can someone so committed to the sensory attach himself to a movement that not only has no appreciation for the sensory, but that he is unable to see?

One way to express the strangely apolitical affect of *The Princess* is to say that the Hoffendahl plot, while formally interesting to James, serves as a kind of screening mechanism, covering the emotional heart of the novel. This, it turns out, is personal rather than political—although these two categories will prove hard for James to differentiate between. The crisis of belief his hero suffers demonstrates the conflation. Hyacinth cannot help asking Paul for an explanation of the effect of his part of the plot, "exactly what good" he thinks "it will do" (444). The question indicates how belief becomes tenuous in an atmosphere of obscurity. And Paul recognizes the problem: "If you've ceased to believe we can do anything, it will be rather awkward, you know" (445). Hyacinth responds by declaring his religion: "I don't know that I believe exactly what you believe, but I believe in you, and doesn't that come to the same thing?" (446). It doesn't, as Hyacinth himself discovers. James tells us that in Paris, when Hyacinth undergoes that great change of opinion that marks the "inward revolution" described by the Preface to the novel, he asks himself a question: "'How could he—how *could* he—?' It may be explained that 'he' was a reference to Paul Muniment; for Hyacinth had dreamed of the religion of friendship" (393–94). The end of this dream marks the end of Hyacinth's faith in his part of the plot.

His dilemma comes from his awareness that in Paul Muniment, he has been betrayed by the only real embodiment of the revolution. He may have met Hoffendahl once, but the physical presence of the movement—and the moral weight of James's story—rests squarely on Muniment's monumental shoulders. Paul personifies the revolution not only for Hyacinth, but also for Christina. Even her great question—"I want to know *à quoi m'en tenir.* Are we on the eve of great changes, or are we not?"—suggests that the political plot needs to be approached from a personal angle. She expresses herself in the language of pent-up sexual energy, of a growing underground "force" that she fears will never "burst forth," but will "sputter out and spend itself," leaving "heroism" "sterile" and "movement" "abortive" (200). So while the novel strangely lacks menace in regard to the possible onset of revolution, it succeeds in presenting both the prevailing mode of invisible power and Hyacinth and the Princess's joint longing for a leader who can give expression to that obscure force: that is, their longing for Paul Muniment.

James would have agreed with E. M. Forster's oft-quoted declaration: "if I had to choose between betraying my country and betraying my friend, I hope I should have the guts to betray my country."[102] The emphasis on personal betrayal sets *The Princess Casamassima* apart from many contemporary works that deal with radical political movements.[103] For all the novel's posited opposition between culture and anarchy, it is not really, or at least primarily, about ideology; the moral sense of the novel feels oddly disconnected from its radical politics. To employ the distinction Dostoevsky sets forth in *Demons,* James seems to have eaten—rather than have been eaten by—an idea.[104] Usually, the central ethical dilemma presented by novels of radical politics lies in the threat of random violence. In swearing to take part in an anarchist plot, one demonstrates not only a willingness to sacrifice oneself but also a willingness to sacrifice the innocent. *Demons* concludes with a barrage of deaths—murders, accidents, and suicides—all the result of a botched conspiracy. Among the dead are several significant characters in the novel and many innocents, including a newborn baby. Similarly, in Joseph Conrad's *The Secret Agent,* a young man, Stevie, is blown to bits while unknowingly helping his anarchist brother-in-law Verloc set a bomb in the Greenwich Observatory. Conrad emphasizes Stevie's guiltlessness to the point of making him an "innocent"—"half an idiot."[105] So while the public cost of Conrad's anarchist plot does turn out to be a private one (as the Assistant Commissioner puts it, "From a certain point of view we are here in the presence of a domestic drama"[106]), Conrad leaves the reader with a strong sense of concern for the phenomenon of collateral damage. In contrast, in James's novel the only innocent really harmed by the plot is Hyacinth himself. James's imagination of good and evil is so intensely personal that although Hyacinth has been asked to kill a man, this death seems hardly to figure in the moral balance. Unlike Dostoevsky and Conrad, James never introduces us to the nameless intended victim, who, to an even greater extent than the conspirators, remains in the shadows.

That Hyacinth's recognition that his friendship has been betrayed—not only by Paul, but also by the Princess and by Millicent—stands as the climax of the novel suggests a deep connection between its private and political plotlines. James hints at this link in his Preface in arguing that Hyacinth needed to be given "a social—not less than a socialist connexion."[107] As W. J. Harvey remarks of James's comment: "The word *social,* then, in one direction, leads off to *socialite* and the Princess, in another to *socialist* and Paul Muniment. Trapped in this pun is the hero, Hyacinth Robinson."[108] Yet the pun also contains in it a pointed commentary on the position of politics in modern society. Consider Hannah Arendt's analysis: "with the rise of society, that is, the rise of the 'household' (*oikia*) or of economic activities to the public realm, housekeeping and all matters pertaining formerly to the private sphere of the family have become a 'collective' concern."[109] As George Eliot's writing demonstrated, the tendency to conflate the social and political realms played a large role in the Victorian political imagination, especially with regard to the elevation of the domestic sphere.

In this novel, however, the domestic realm is as embattled as the political realm. Those few biological families we encounter seem doomed to disaster: Lady Aurora feels herself an alien in her own home,[110] and Millicent comes from a house of poverty and chaos to which she never wishes to return. Notably, the strongest family unit we encounter—that of Paul and Rosy— is also the most sinister. Hyacinth, as an orphan, an individual separate from all collective concerns, becomes involved in a series of groups that stand in lieu of a family. He sometimes seems to be "shopping for a family," as Americans now sometimes speak of shopping for a church. Miss Pinnie and Mr. Vetch, the Poupins, Paul and Rosy, the Princess and Madame Grandoni, Millicent, even Lady Aurora: each offers Hyacinth an opportunity to create a substitute family of his own. As the list suggests, these societies do not necessarily exist in opposition to the secret society of the conspirators; Arendt describes how "in the modern world, the social and the political realms are much less distinct." In *The Princess,* family structures appear as flowing and indeterminate—and as insecure—as political ones.

Like family, marriage does not fare well in the novel. The Princess is in England playing at revolution in order to escape from an unhappy marriage. The Poupins, the only really contented couple in the book, are not legally married. Hyacinth's father's unwillingness to marry his mother occasioned the tragedy of his birth. And the potential for marriage seems oddly absent from the work, especially given its strong atmosphere of sexual attraction. In *The Princess,* James has created a complex web of overlapping desire. Everyone desires the Princess, except, maybe, Paul—and he wants her money. Several characters—Christina, Lady Aurora, and Hyacinth—desire Paul. Captain Sholto and Hyacinth also seem to want Millicent. And Millicent feels attracted to both of them, in different ways. She offers Hyacinth the most promising prospect of a love interest—at least she is single—but the prevailing atmosphere of attraction is too confusing to stimulate any particular action. Nor does the reader sense genuine potential for legally sanctioned sexual connections.

In fact, James refuses to indulge in the idea of safe domesticity that so fascinated Eliot, a refusal he indicates in part by conflating his private and his political plot. Both these forms of action are subject to the same danger we saw in *The Portrait of a Lady:* the transformation of a "doing" into a "doing with." In the closing pages of book 1, Mr. Vetch demonstrates the link between the two modes. Worrying about Hyacinth's connection to Millicent, Mr. Vetch turns to the familiar formulation: "'What will she do with you?' he inquired at last" (172). Yet the degree to which the revolution also treats people as means to an end is emphasized by the fact that the Princess, who quite happily considers Hyacinth as a valuable addition to her collection of democrats (346), remains valuable to Paul only as long as her husband's money keeps flowing: "when I find you have nothing more to give to the cause I will let you go" (576), he tells her. Her response: "You are only using me— only using us all" (578). And for all Mr. Vetch's fears that Hyacinth will be trapped in a marriage plot, he recognizes an even greater danger with regard to revolutionary plots. He almost immediately repeats his question, this time turning his attentions toward Paul: "And what will *he* do with you?" (173; James's emphasis).

The conflation between the two plots, political and private, emerges in the metaphor of the "vow" by which Hyacinth enters into his "engagement"; James uses both words to describe Hyacinth's pledge to Hoffendahl. After Hyacinth declares that "he would never marry at all—to that his mind was absolutely made up" (105), the vow to act for the revolution takes the place of a marriage vow in the narrative. The most famous example of the speech act is the "I do" of the marriage vow. Yet a political vow like that pledged by Hyacinth can also be thought of as "the ultimate political speech-act," as Taylor Stoehr has characterized it.[111] So Hyacinth's promise can be looked on as a kind of bridge between word and deed, one James must have found very attractive as a novelist concerned with the moral dilemmas posed by the commitment of one's life to words rather than deeds. The political vow at the center of *The Princess* occasions the same moral dilemma as the marriage vow at the center of *The Portrait:* both Hyacinth and Isabel find themselves pledged to commitments in which, because of personal betrayals, they no longer believe. The connection demonstrates once again the intimacy of the link between revolutionary and courtship plots; the focus on the act of avowal also shows how for James, issues of both ethics and action often become issues of language.

James repeatedly emphasizes the sacramental quality of Hyacinth's vow. Consider Hyacinth's formulations of it: "I pledged myself, by everything that is sacred," "I took a vow—a tremendous, terrible vow—in the presence of four witnesses" (327). Later, the Princess tries to play down the significance of the "famous engagement" or "vow" by comparing it to "some silly humbug in a novel" (485). And if it does often sound as if we were in a novel by Trollope, say, in which Hyacinth finds he has proposed to the wrong girl. His Sun and Moon friends attempt to release him from his pledge— notably, by advocating passivity: "We want you to do nothing, because we know you have changed. . . . [T]hat alters everything." But Hyacinth, as a man of honor, sees things differently: "Does it alter my engagement? There are some things in which one can't change. I didn't promise to believe. I promised to obey" (551)—as if asserting the bride's vow of obedience from the traditional marriage ceremony. Moreover, the positioning of the vow in the narrative contributes to the reader's sense of the political plot as an ersatz marriage plot. After Hyacinth's confused cab ride through the streets of London to meet Hoffendahl, book 2 ends abruptly. When the narrative resumes, we see Hyacinth awakening in the Princess's home at Medley, as though on the first morning of their honeymoon—and in fact, the stay at Medley has something of the sweetness of a honeymoon, a lull before the action of real life must recommence. As James tells us, "Hyacinth . . . felt at times almost as if he were married to his hostess" (482).

But the private aspects of Hyacinth's engagement can also be considered in light of another social phenomenon: that of dandyism. Like Isabel Archer's, Hyacinth's yearning for action belies a deep-seated passivity, an association with "the idea of suffering" (159). But Howe's rather typical complaint about this passivity suggests the new context for understanding it: "Hyacinth Robinson . . . is one of the most passive of James's heroes. . . . It is his languorous passivity, far more than anything he actually says or does, that constitutes his snobbism."[112] Manfred Mackenzie has argued that Hyacinth's desire for exclusivity (a manifestation of his "snobbism") leads to his desire to belong to a secret society.[113] Such "exclusivism" has been identified by Ellen Moers as an essential component of the dandy's code.[114] And James actually describes the Sun and Moon as a kind of "gentleman's club"; as Muniment puts it, it is like one of those "flaming big shops, full of armchairs and flunkies, in Pall Mall" (209). Indeed Hyacinth's very name brands him a dandy.

Moers also points out that "throughout the nineteenth century the rising majority called for equality, responsibility, energy; the dandy stood for superiority, irresponsibility, inactivity." Refusing other forms of action, "the dandy's achievement is simply to be himself." And as Moers recognizes, this insistence on selfhood contains in the denial of conventional standards its own element of revolution.[115] It also represents a preeminently visible statement of identity; the dandy's creed can be seen in the clothes he wears. In fact, Hyacinth becomes more of a dandy after he has taken his revolutionary vow to action. Moers's analysis of the paradox inherent in dandyism—the way in which it implies a form of revolution based on inaction rather than action and closely related to the preservation of a coherent and independent self—suggests why dandies figure so prominently in the works I have considered. The dandy's reign overlaps precisely with the timeframe of this study: it begins in the Romantic period and concludes with the great aesthetes of the fin de siècle—as Moers has it, it lasts from "Brummel to Beerbohm." Hyacinth is a descendant both of Byron's Don Juan and of Clough's Claude, who share many of his dandyish qualities. But Hyacinth's passivity also characterizes many other heroes of revolutionary novels—including, for that matter, Paul Muniment. Nezhdanov's Hamletism (that is, active consciousness and passive body) has already been noted, as has Verloc's luggish laziness. Dostoevsky's Stavrogin, the antihero of *Demons,* also displays both the fastidiousness and the ennui of the dandy. The passive revolutionist represents a personification of the literary trend toward internalizing revolution in order to assert character.

But for all that Hyacinth asserts his identity through his dandyish quality, his membership in the collective of the (albeit exclusive) secret society of revolutionists also divests him of his individual agency. Mackenzie remarks on Hyacinth's desire to enter the plot in order to make up for his orphaned, outsider position in society: "Committing himself to Hoffendahl . . . he might at last be 'more.' He *is.* It is a pathetic and terrible autonomy that James expresses by a remarkable withdrawal; for a moment it is as if there were no story. How can a nobody, who in the effort to give himself a story only depersonalized himself, quite have a story?"[116] Mackenkzie recognizes that the form of selfhood ("terrible autonomy") that Hyacinth's membership in the secret society leads him to is a nightmarish rendition of Moer's selfhood divorced from action or story. "He *is*" rather than "he *does*"—he is patient rather than agent, having lost his agency to the group to which he belongs.

Gilbert Osmond's dandyism (itself a reflection on the dandyism of Eliot's Grandcourt) demonstrates that James was well aware of the moral limitations of the type, and we should remember that Hyacinth questions and combats his own inclinations to be a dandy. James's interest in the dandy continues in his next political novel, *The Tragic Muse,* in which the hero, Nick Sherringham, is convinced by a dandy friend, Gabriel Nash, to give up his political career in order to become an artist. Nash's creed can perhaps best be summed up by himself: "People's actions, I know, are, for the most part, the things they do, but mine are all the things I don't do. . . . My only behavior is my feelings."[117] Calling upon that great Jamesian capacity, consciousness, Nash defines what he means by "the agreeable": "Oh, the happy moments of our consciousness—the multiplication of those moments. We must save as many as possible from the dark gulf."[118] Yet while James may agree with Nash's version of "the agreeable," he would wish it to be expanded to include a moral dimension. Hence James's significant irony in his treatment of Nash, who when asked whether he intends to write, to transform those moments of consciousness into something of more lasting (and communicable) value, responds dismissively in the negative.

Of Hyacinth, in contrast, we hear that "in secret, he wrote" (112).[119] Like James, he values this form of "doing." Turgenev's Nezhdanov is a poet, and James seems to have kept this in mind when he created Hyacinth. James fashioned Hyacinth to serve as his "vessel of consciousness" precisely because of his fine nature, the quality of his crystal, because he is "the person capable of feeling in the given case more than another of what is to be felt for it."[120] Hyacinth is like a Wordsworthian poet, one who sees not differently from other men, but more deeply, "endued with more lively sensibility"—with a greater capacity to feel.[121] Referring to Hyacinth's wish to move from bookbinding to book writing, James informs us that "it had occurred to Hyacinth more than once that it would be a fine thing to produce a brilliant death-song" (404). Whether or not Hyacinth achieves his goal, his final pose in suicide is that of a poet—of Chatterton, the archetypal Romantic icon of wasted youth and genius, as captured in the famous Pre-Raphaelite painting by Henry Wallis (1856): "Hyacinth lay there as if he were asleep. . . . His arm hung limp beside him, downwards, off the narrow couch; his face was white and his eyes were closed" (590).

The act of suicide represents Hyacinth's magnum opus: it is the one thing he does, the one work he completes. It is also the end of his action, as it is the end of his story. We are in fact privy, leading up to the suicide, to a series of requests that Hyacinth refrain from action. First the Princess, responding to Mr. Vetch's sense that she wants Hyacinth "to commit some atrocity, some infamy," insists, "I don't want him to do anything in all the wide world" (468–69).[122] Then Hyacinth's friends at the Sun and Moon tell him "we want you to do nothing, because we know you have changed" (551). Finally, in the boldest statement of this sentiment, Mr. Vetch demands a new vow of Hyacinth: "promise me that you will never, under any circumstances, do anything" (564). Hyacinth qualifies his promise by responding, "I shall never do any of their work" (565). But does his suicide qualify as an act? Derek Brewer sees the suicide as comparable to James's "retreat from the life of action" into the world of art—a way out of the "terrible dilemma[s]" one inevitably faces in the practical realm.[123] Like Francis in *The White Doe of Rylstone,* Hyacinth faces a situation in which his loyalties conflict. On the one hand, he wishes to remain true to his vow to Hoffendahl; on the other hand, his revised beliefs, both political and personal, do not allow him to fulfill his commission honorably. Suicide stands as "the solution of his difficulty" (568). Ironically, the act of suicide, the cessation of all possible future action and vision, replaces that "vision of a great heroism" with which Hyacinth had been so fatally enamored at the Sun and Moon. He fulfills his engagement to murder by turning the weapon inward, upon himself.

The temptation to suicide figures prominently not only in the revolutionary novels of the late-nineteenth century but also in many of the earlier works that deal with the crisis in action. It can be found in characters as diverse as Hamlet, Werther, Arnold's Empedocles, and Eliot's Mirah. *Demons* contains three suicides, of very different natures: a casual incident describing a youthful act of desperation, which is treated as a kind of aesthetic entertainment by the gentry of Dostoevsky's imagined town; Kirillov's ideological suicide—suicide as a Schopenhauerian gospel of "self-will"[124]; and finally, Stavrogin's hopeless garret hanging, the discovery of which (like that of Hyacinth's suicide) concludes the novel. Turgenev's Nezhdanov also finds suicide to be the only escape from his own version of Hyacinth's dilemma: "But what could I do? I could find no other way out of it. I could not simplify myself; the only thing left was to blot myself out altogether."[125] Action, he seems to imply, requires a "simplification" of self that is impossible for the complex—and often, as with Nezhdanov and Hyacinth, hybrid—modern individual.[126] Caught by the web of Hoffendahl's plot, Hyacinth escapes it the only way he knows how, by blotting himself out. Having learnt that action and vision are incommensurable, he decides to forgo both.

Departing from his initial position as advocate for the party of action, Hyacinth has come to recognize that "we must have patience" (517). Henrietta Stackpole's concluding advice to Caspar Goodwood also concerned the need for patience, a patience that Isabel seemed to embrace. Isabel inherited from Mr. Touchett those very means to liberty that James withholds from Hyacinth: "freedom and ease, knowledge and power, money, opportunity, and satiety" (34). But she sacrificed herself to her marriage vow as surely as Hyacinth sacrifices himself to his political pledge. Yet Hyacinth's suicide also parallels Isabel Archer's decision to return to her marriage in a more positive sense: it can be thought of as a gesture of authenticity, a reclamation of his own agency from the hands of the puppeteer Hoffendahl. As Kirillov argues, suicide represents the supreme act of self will, a triumph of the individual in the face not only of the collective conspiracy of the movement, but also of family history. Hyacinth kills himself precisely to avoid repeating the story of his mother's life—"the horror of the public reappearance, on his part, of the embrued hands of his mother." As James tells us,

> This loathing of the idea of a *repetition* had not been sharp, strangely enough, till his summons came; in all his previous meditations the growth of his reluctance to act for the 'party of action' had not been the fear of a personal stain, but the simple extension of his observation. Yet now the idea of the personal stain made him horribly sick; it seemed by itself to make service impossible. (582–83; original emphasis)

In the end, Hyacinth kills himself to reassert himself; the "personal" trumps the political. By proving an ability to act independently of both familial precedent and the structure of Hoffendahl's plotting, Hyacinth creates a space for truly independent action. To steal a phrase from James's description of Isabel, he affronts his destiny.[127] Of course in the process, and to an even greater degree than Isabel Archer did, he destroys himself, and with that, the potential for future action. It is at best a pyrrhic victory. James's experiments in the realm of action in *The Princess Casamassima* lead him only farther and farther underground: to the subterraneous politics of his plot, and ultimately, to Hyacinth's burial.

CODA: "THE BEAST IN THE JUNGLE"

James's attitude toward the dialectic between character and action finds its most allegorical instantiation in "The Beast in the Jungle" (1902). As

Ruth Bernard Yeazell has put it, "it is almost a parody of the classic Jamesian plot, and Marcher, that sensitive, passive, and deeply reserved gentleman, is the quintessential Jamesian hero."[128] Like *The Princess Casamassima,* "The Beast" is structured around a secret: while our first sign of the plot in the novel came when Muniment asked Hyacinth if he could "keep a secret," James's later story develops because John Marcher had "so breathed his secret" to May Bartram.[129] But if *The Princess Casamassima* represented a failed revolutionary plot, this tale represents the apotheosis of the failed marriage plot. Marcher's discovery after May's death that "*she* was what he had missed" proves to be the only thing to "happen" in the story (489). So the beast in the jungle can be thought of as a metaphor for nefarious plot—or really, as it turns out, nefarious plotlessness—finally emerging from the darkness.

"The Beast in the Jungle" is also the work that most frequently tempts James's critics into the realm of biographical speculation. Leon Edel uses it as a model upon which to build his voluminous biography: "Was it true for Henry James, as some have insisted, that like his protagonist in 'The Beast in the Jungle' he was 'the man of his time, *the* man, to whom nothing on earth was to have happened'?"[130] He then quotes Percy Lubbock in defense of a biography based on such a premise: "Looked at from without [James's] life was uneventful enough. . . . Within, it was a cycle of vivid and incessant adventure, known only to himself except insofar as he put it into words."[131] Note how both Lubbock and Edel invoke James's own aesthetic creed of internalized adventure in order to render his life interesting. The corollary of such a reading of James's life is that his repressed active principle must find a way out, and that it does so by being sublimated into his art. So, for example, Edel calls Henry James "a man of action in art": "he was an active and masculine individual who finding direct action impossible . . . realized this activity and individuality through a prodigiously creative and highly productive art."[132]

Many modern critics of James also see repression—especially sexual repression—as essential to his artistic power. Recently, reflecting contemporary cultural concerns, they have concentrated on the issue of his possible homosexuality.[133] Indeed the question of James's sexuality has continued to fascinate, I think legitimately, because of the way suppressed action—sexual and otherwise—figures so prominently in his work. Hyacinth's friendship with Paul provides one example of a homoerotic relationship in James's work that has drawn attention,[134] and *The Princess Casamassima*'s obsession with questions of action in the political realm is closely linked, both structurally and linguistically, to its vision of action in the sexual realm, as I have argued.

But with the avoidance of marriage at its center, "The Beast in the Jungle" has become a focus for the discussion. Eve Kosofsky Sedgwick's groundbreaking essay of 1986, "The Beast in the Closet: Henry James and the Writing of Homosexual Panic," suggests that the tale represents not Marcher's failure to recognize the marriage plot as the event he had been awaiting, but rather his inability—I think the implication is also James's, although Sedgwick does not state this explicitly—to see in himself an unsanctioned and unspeakable homosexual desire that precludes the successful completion of the marriage plot. The failure results from what Sedgwick calls "homosexual panic": "In the last scene of 'The Beast in the Jungle,' John Marcher becomes, in this reading, not the finally self-knowing man who is capable of heterosexual love, but the irredeemably self-ignorant man who embodies heterosexual compulsion."[135] In other words, he has buried his desires so deep that they remain hidden not only on the level of action (he does nothing) but even on that of consciousness (he sees nothing). For all that I think James possesses more self-knowledge than Sedgwick appears to grant him, I believe her reading responds to a real truth about "The Beast in the Jungle," one that would be missed by aligning the tale too closely with works like *The Portrait of a Lady*, in which what is lost in terms of action can be recompensed, at least in part, by gains of consciousness. The question of buried desire remains central to the story: hence its conclusion in the graveyard. In "The Beast in the Jungle," James recognizes with unprecedented clarity that the burial of plot can easily come to coincide with the death of character.

Curiously, James implicitly connects Marcher's views with his own artistic methods. In fact, while Marcher is crucially different from his author (as we shall see), James seems to write the tale in order to confront his personal "beast"—as though to say with Prospero, "This thing of darkness I acknowledge mine." James loads "The Beast" with the terms of his critical writings, words like *real, truth, natural, suspense, catastrophe, sequel, page, story, forms, climax, anticlimax, consciousness,* and *imagination.* Such self-reference also appears in the Jamesian centrality of metaphor to the tale. As Yeazell has commented, Marcher is "a man obsessed with a metaphor."[136] But while James manipulates violent metaphors to stress that "our ordinary lives can be as precarious and breathtaking as any melodrama,"[137] Marcher turns to metaphor precisely in order to escape ordinary life, "to evade immediate reality and its demands."[138] One can in fact think of the central metaphor in "The Beast in the Jungle" as a stage on which James plays out a contest between the kinds of action associated with realism or naturalism and those associated with more extravagant forms like romance and melodrama. When he speaks almost incessantly of the "real" (461, 462, 463) and the "natural" (457), Marcher directs his imagination toward an externalized understanding of the beast. But he is looking the wrong way, gazing out at the jungle when he should be focusing closer to home, both at what is right before his eyes (May) and at what lies within himself. As he finally acknowledges, "he had seen *outside* of his life, not learned it within" (488).

Consider, for example, Marcher's first response on again meeting May Bartram: "Marcher said to himself that he ought to have rendered her some service—saved her from a capsized boat in the Bay, or at least recovered her dressing-bag, filched from her cab, in the streets of Naples, by a lazzarone with a stiletto" (452). In an admittedly limited and ironized manner (the purse snatcher represents a wonderful reduction of the villain of adventure narratives), Marcher imagines the alternative plot of action with which James has so frequently flirted. James believes, though, that these are matters to be understood metaphorically rather than literally—that is, in an internalized manner. In his distinction between realism and romance in the Preface to *The American,* James refuses to recognize as genuine romance adventures like those mentioned by Marcher: "there have been, I gather, many definitions of romance, as a matter indispensably of boats, or of caravans, or of tigers, . . . or of pistols and knives, but they appear for the most part reducible to the idea of the facing of danger."[139] Marcher's false romanticizing of the beast in the jungle leads to his avoidance of a far more ordinary romance with May, what she calls "the expectation—or, at any rate, the sense of danger familiar to so many people—of falling in love" (456).

James's story can be read as an attempt to come to grips with the true meanings of *expectation* and *danger.* Indeed one way to get to the heart of "The Beast" is to ask: why does James let May point right to the moral of the story in part 1? Even if one agrees with Sedgwick's argument that the love Marcher has failed to recognize is homosexual, May's perceptiveness— the accuracy of her early questions and comments—seems to disrupt the ordinary methods of narrative suspense. And yet Marcher's own life is characterized by a "perpetual suspense" (459) (like that experienced by Hyacinth once he is subject to Hoffendahl's plot [335]), by "the simplification of everything but the state of suspense" (465), which one usually thinks of as a condition of plotting. It represents a form of pure expectation, of "something evermore about to be," as Wordsworth put it.

One could argue that suspense functions on two levels in the tale: on the first, Marcher awaits the beast; on the second, we (and May) await Marcher's recognition of the beast. In this reading, we have a typically Jamesian elevation of the internal plot of consciousness over the external plot of action.

But such a reading misses an essential aspect of this tale: its critique of the ordinary mechanisms of suspense and their dependence upon suspended action. James proves once again that in a story, there can be as much adventure in inaction as in action. Yet he also emphasizes that this same equivalence does not necessarily hold for a life. Marcher's state of inaction carries with it none of those benefits of "pure being" that I have been tracing, of which Emily's blessed state in *The White Doe of Rylstone* provided the clearest example. And for all John Marcher's attempt to win "back by an effort of thought the lost stuff of consciousness" (484), James makes it quite clear that he does not really think this kind of Romantic consolation is feasible, that whatever Marcher's final recognition, it cannot make up for "the sounded void of his life" (488). Instead, as Marcher admits, his "was failure" not only to *do* anything, but also "to be anything" (471). Oddly, complete plotlessness leaves as little room for consciousness as total plottedness. This must surely be the point also of Marcher's forgetfulness at the beginning of the tale, the "unaccountably faded" memory of his earlier encounter with May (454). Memory—that favorite device of solace for the poets of Romanticism—can find no ground in an eventless life, a life based exclusively on the principle of expectation; it requires richer soil.[140]

As though to drive home the contrast with Wordsworth, James concludes his tale in the most Wordsworthian of settings (and the setting in which *The White Doe* concludes): a graveyard. And as in Wordsworth, the graveyard is a place from which the stories of the dead speak forth. Yet remarkably, May's grave tells not her own tale but Marcher's. Marcher comes to realize that the "plot of ground" (486) in which May's body rests represents the plot of his own life: it is what "happened" to him.[141] He sees (in the familiar literary terms of the tale) in "the graven tablet" of May's tombstone the "page" (486, 488) of his existence: "*there* were the facts of the past, there the truth of his life, there the backward reaches in which he could lose himself" (486)—as he tries to do at the end of the tale by flinging himself, "on his face, on the tomb" (490). A total nonentity, Marcher must look upon the monument to his friend to read from it "not only for a support but for an identity" (486). And the name to which Marcher's identity has been reduced is not even his own: "he had before him in sharper incision than ever the open page of his story. The name on the tablet smote him" (488). The reader must assume that the slab reads "May Bartram," but James makes it seem uncannily as though Marcher were inhabiting a ghost story of the kind in which the hero recognizes his own death only after encountering his name on a tombstone. In the 1895 "germ" of "The Beast," the woman outlives the man; James records in his *Notebooks* that the "intensity" of the tale is to stem from the fact that "*She is his Dead Self: he is alive in her and dead in himself.*"[142] The tale as a whole can in fact be thought of as one of James's supernatural stories—a tale of the living dead. Marcher experiences such a "shock" from his encounter with "the face of a fellow-mortal" (487) in the graveyard precisely because he sees that he can claim no fellowship with this man's pain. His mortality is at best a bad joke; in himself, he has seen a ghost.

So the plot of John Marcher's life of studied inaction lies in the plot of May Bartram's grave. And James affords Marcher none of that partial compensation that he allotted to Isabel Archer and to Hyacinth Robinson. The tale concludes with an admission of the same "abject anticlimax" of which critics had so often accused James's novels (470). In this late story, which critics have been tempted to read as a parable of its author's life, James seems to have revised subtly his position on inaction. He recognizes that taken to an extreme, the demise of action entails the demise of character. And Marcher is forced to ask his own version of a question that we have encountered many times before: instead of the "What can I do?" of one of Eliot's heroines or James's earlier question of Isabel—"What will she do?"—here, in this tale of expectation, he can only wonder about possible past actions: "What could he have done . . . ?" (483).

Afterword:
Adventure Fiction

Action is consolatory. It is the enemy of thought and the friend of flatter-
ing illusions. Only in the conduct of our action can we find the sense of
mastery over the Fates.

—Joseph Conrad, *Nostromo*

I WISH IN conclusion to consider—albeit very briefly—a competing
genealogy. It, too, can be seen to have roots in a branch of Romanticism:
this time, in the romances of Scott. I refer to the adventure novel, the popularity of which came to something of a head around the turn of the century, under the auspices of writers like Robert Louis Stevenson, Rudyard
Kipling, H. Rider Haggard, and G. A. Henty. As this list suggests, the particular genealogy I am considering here has a very boyish slant to it. One
can think of a line leading from the naval tales of Marryat, through to the
schoolboy novels that developed midcentury, in the wake of *Tom Brown's
Schooldays* (1857) and the movement that came to be known as muscular
Christianity, and into the fully developed adventure novel. Indeed, Elaine
Showalter has argued that the subgenre is born in response to fear of the
feminization of literature: "The revival of 'romance' [a term synonymous
in the context with adventure story] in the 1880s was a men's literary revolution intended to reclaim the kingdom of the English novel for male
writers, male readers, and men's stories."[1] But it might be worth mention-
ing that a parallel line of plot-oriented fiction could be drawn from the sensation novels of the sixties through to the "New Woman" narratives of the
fin de siècle, many of them written by and for women—a line leading to
books like Grant Allen's suggestively entitled *The Woman Who Did*
(1895).[2] Moreover, I also think it is important to recognize the distinction

171

between men and boys: as Showalter herself notes, to a remarkable degree, these books were written for the latter.[3]

The blossoming of the genre at the end of the century was no doubt due to several converging forces. Robert Fraser has pointed to a material cause in the collapse, in 1894, of the agreement between publishers and the circulating libraries under which triple deckers that first appeared in serialized form flourished. When publishers withdrew their subsidies to the libraries, "shorter, one-volume novels with incisive plots became newly attractive."[4] But above all, the rise of adventure fiction can be seen as contiguous with the growth of imperialism; as Martin Green has argued, "to celebrate adventure is to celebrate empire, and vice versa."[5] It is surely no coincidence that muscular Christianity developed alongside the end of the Pax Britannica that had followed the Napoleonic Wars, just as the nation was reentering an imperialist and militaristic mood with the advent of the Crimean War (1854–56), soon to be followed by the Sepoy Uprising or Indian Rebellion (1857).[6] The term "muscular Christianity" was coined in reference to Charles Kingsley's *Two Years Ago* (1857), a novel set in England during the Crimean War, and Kingsley's earlier *Westward Ho!* (1855), a tale of imperialist Elizabethan heroics against the Spanish at home and in the New World, was written in part as wartime propaganda. But the connection between romances and imperialism is an old one: the two great patriarchs of the adventure novel in British literature are Daniel Defoe and Sir Walter Scott, who both wrote stories that reflected on English dominion over other nations, economic and cultural. Still, the dual parentage (like the paradox inherent in the idea of muscular Christianity) suggests that this form, too, was not free from the crisis in action. After all, Scott was the father of the wavering hero, and the Defoe of *Robinson Crusoe* (1719) championed those very economic forces that nineteenth-century writers would see as restraints to epic heroism.

And while imperialism plays a large role in the development of the genre, we can also see adventure fiction in terms of the crisis in action: as John R. Reed puts it, "The popularity of adventure stories late in the century indicates that readers wanted a rendering of the world that allowed for independent and determining action on the part of individual heroes and heroines."[7] In what follows, I want to look at Stevenson's *Treasure Island* (1883)—perhaps the purest example of the adventure novel to be written in English—in light of the issues I have been outlining in these pages.

Henry James's friendship with Robert Louis Stevenson actually developed out of a debate concerning the role of action and character in literature, occasioned by what Stevenson saw as James's too-quick comments in "The Art of Fiction" about *Treasure Island*. The title of James's essay refers in part to his attempt to avoid the "clumsy separations" suggested by such categories (listed here as a chiasmus) as "the novel and the romance, the novel of incident and that of character," an argument he bolsters by denying that there is any less "story" in Edmond de Goncourt's *Chérie* (1884), which tells the tale of "the development of the moral consciousness of a child," than in Stevenson's very different (and according to James, much more successful) tale of a very different child's adventures in *Treasure Island*.[8] But in "A Humble Remonstrance," Stevenson insists on a distinction: his kind of "story" demands a much more basic—and externalized—conception of character:

> Character to the boy is a sealed book; for him, a pirate is a beard, a pair of wide trousers and a liberal complement of pistols. . . . [F]or in this elementary novel of adventure, the characters need to be presented with but one class of qualities—the warlike and formidable. . . . [T]he characters are portrayed only so far as they realize the sense of danger and provoke the sympathy of fear.[9]

The idea is important to Stevenson, who had already outlined a version of it in the modestly entitled "A Gossip on Romance" (1882), which can be seen as a defense of the genre. There he acknowledged that "English people of the present day are apt, I know not why, to look somewhat down on incident, and reserve their admiration for the clink of teaspoons and the accents of the curate. It is thought clever to write a novel with no story at all, or at least with a very dull one." But the mistake of this attitude can be registered, he argues, by the fact that *Clarissa* goes more or less unread in the present, while *Robinson Crusoe* has retained all its charms to contemporary readers. "It is not character but incident that woos us out of our reserves," he concludes, perhaps surprisingly; readers enter into the fiction of a novel only when they place themselves into an exciting story: "Then we forget the characters; then we push the hero aside." It is this effect that the romance can achieve.[10]

Such an understanding of the novel or, rather romance, reader should be contrasted with theories of identification based on character, which, I have argued, ultimately stem from ideas of the Romantic sympathetic imagination. But while Stevenson's theory instead highlights activity, it should be noted that both reader and hero are active only in certain, limited ways. What he (and it is predominately a *he*) is not asked to do is *think,* and in particular, to think about moral issues:

> There is a vast deal in life and letters both which is not immoral, but simply a-moral; which either does not regard the human will at all, or deals with it in obvious and healthy relations; where the interest turns, not upon what a man should choose to do, but on how he manages to do it; not on the passionate slips and hesitations of the conscience, but on the problems of the body and of the active intelligence, in clean, open-air adventure, the shock of arms or the diplomacy of life.[11]

This "vast deal" is the stuff out of which Stevenson crafts the world of *Treasure Island.* His story describes the adventures of a boy, young Jim Hawkins, on the quest for treasure—a boy surrounded by men, both gentlemen and pirates, and far away from the protective confines of home (it was written to amuse his twelve-year-old stepson, who insisted that there be no women or girls in it; petticoats might hamper the action[12]). The novel begins by telling how Jim comes to be in possession of a pirate's map and how he gains the support of the local squire and doctor, who put together a ship and crew to sail after the treasure. But most of it takes place around and on the titular "Island," as the crew—which has been divided into two groups after a mutiny onboard has shown the masquerading pirates for who they are and forced the rest of the crew to choose their allegiances—attempt first to find and then to hold on to the loot. Yet while the tale is full of action and "active intelligence," it achieves action only through its willingness to dispense not only with the home front but also with the moral reasoning that had become associated with the domestic space. And even given this omission, the novel is able to create an amoral (rather than an immoral) universe only by simultaneously jettisoning adulthood and its problems.

The amorality of the tale comes out most forcefully in the fact that, as Robert Fraser has pointed out, it is often difficult to distinguish between the gentlemen and the pirates in the story.[13] Long John Silver's name for *pirate*—"gentleman of fortune"—may initially confuse Jim, but the novel does not altogether undermine the designation.[14] After all, neither group is truly entitled to the silver, and once the action has shifted out of England, the distinctions break down even further. When Silver speaks to the pirates under his command, he reminds them (in "King George's English") of his rights as an elected official (165). Silver's own shifting back and forth between the groups—his double and even triple agency, so to speak—is actually linked to the novel's wider treatment of its characters. Indeed, both groups are seen as representative of "Englishness"; in the very first chapter of the novel, the terrifying "Old Sea-dog" (Billy Bones), whose arrival at Jim's father's inn sets the tale in motion, is spoken of by the locals as "the sort of man that made England terrible at sea" (6). Of the infamous pirate Flint, the squire remarks how "Spaniards were so prodigiously afraid of him that . . . I was sometimes proud he was an Englishman" (33).[15] If you compare this world to that in which Francis was forced to operate in *The White Doe of Rylstone,* say, it becomes clear how much easier agency is; if even enemies are really on the same side, deep conflicts of allegiance—such as make it impossible to know the right thing to do—are impossible.

Since the quest is "morally void," as Fraser puts it, "the point of the journey is not to win, or even to prove a point: it is to play."[16] So it comes as no surprise that a boy should be the hero of this story. His skills are those best suited to the game. In the midst of a tussle with one of the pirates, Jim reminds us of this fact:

> Seeing that I meant to dodge, he also paused; and a moment or two passed in feints on his parts and corresponding movements upon mine. It was such a game as I had often played at home about the rocks of Black Hill Cove, but never before, you may be sure, with such a wildly beating heart as now. Still, as I say, it was a boy's game, and I thought I could hold my own at it against an elderly seaman with a wounded thigh. (150)

Henry James, in reflecting on the absence of "moral motive" in Stevenson's novels, counters that Stevenson's rhapsodic appreciation of "the romance of boyhood," of "the age of heterogeneous pockets," indeed of a boyish pluck that is perhaps the purest form of the "heroism" that James sees as Stevenson's ultimate subject, stands in the novels in lieu of the usual moralizing.[17] In the context of the crisis of action I have been outlining in these pages, we can begin to see James's point; these qualities appear rarely in nineteenth-century British fiction, and their very presence can operate normatively. Reading *Treasure Island,* the fresh sea air seems palpable. Stevenson describes action as natural and unforced—and often unwilled. To quote a characteristic passage of Jim's narration of his adventures:

> Mechanically, I obeyed, turned eastwards, and with my cutlass raised, ran around the corner of the house. Next moment I was face to face with Anderson. He roared aloud, and his hanger went up above his head, flashing

in the sunlight. I had not time to be afraid, but as the blow still hung
impending, leaped in a trice upon one side, and missing my foot in the soft
sand, rolled headlong down the slope. (121)

This is the kind of brisk, unmediated, and effective action that has been
missing in the pages of the works I have looked at thus far, and *Treasure
Island* is chock-a-block full of it.

But the force of the action—the whole impetus of the story—depends
entirely upon Jim, who (like Daniel Deronda, in a more troubled version
of a romance plot) is described as a "born favorite" (198). Jim says as much
in his longest speech in the book, which captures beautifully the fantasy of
boyish agency even as it recapitulates the plot of the novel (thus demonstrating the close connection between these two things):

"Well," said I, "I am not such a fool but I know pretty well what I have
to look for. Let the worst come to the worst, it's little I care. I've seen too
many die since I fell in with you. But there's a thing or two I have to tell
you," I said, and by this time I was quite excited; "and the first is this: here
you are, in a bad way—ship lost, treasure lost, men lost, your whole business gone to wreck; and if you want to know who did it—it was I! I was
in the apple barrel the night we sighted land, and I heard you, John, and
you, Dick Johnson, and Hands, who is now at the bottom of the sea, and
told every word you said before the hour was out. And as for the schooner,
it was I who cut her cable, and it was I that killed the men you had aboard
of her, and it was I who brought her where you'll never see her more, not
one of you. The laugh's on my side; I've had the top of this business from
the first; I no more fear you than I fear a fly. Kill me, if you please, or spare
me. But one thing I'll say, and no more; if you spare me, bygones are
bygones, and when you fellows are in court for piracy, I'll save you all I
can. It is for you to choose. Kill another and do yourselves no good, or
spare me and keep a witness to save you from the gallows." (164)

"It was I," Jim keeps on repeating, and the story is most emphatically his.
He narrates it (with the exception of a brief episode in the middle of the
novel where the doctor takes over to describe events to which Jim could
have no access, because he is off saving the day elsewhere), and—as this
speech shows—he also enacts it. Although it should be added that for all
his centrality to the tale, we don't get much of a sense of him as an individual character. This is because he acts rather as an avatar for our own boyish selves, as Stevenson's theory of readerly identification had suggested.

And perhaps the greatest charm of the novel lies in its willingness to let Jim—and us—maintain this kind of control. He is never forced to learn a lesson—not even the lesson of growing up. Jim starts the tale a boy and finishes it a boy; he has not really matured, although he has become more practiced at playing the game. He has also been made richer, but we don't hear how he spends his loot, just that "All of us had an ample share of the treasure and used it wisely or foolishly, according to our natures" (202). To say more would have been to enter the sordid world of everyday action and consequence, of adult responsibility.

So the remarkable freshness of *Treasure Island* depends upon its boy-protagonist and its fundamental unwillingness to acknowledge the adult world of choice and morality. It's a precarious formula. Stevenson himself never replicated the breeziness of this first foray into the novel. David Balfour, the slightly older protagonist of *Kidnapped* (1886), already has something of the wavering hero about him (Stevenson's Scottish setting and his personal awareness of national history no doubt add to the influence of Scott over the book). Compare this typical moment of action, in which David comes face-to-face with one of his kidnappers, to that quoted above:

> [T]he glass of the skylight was dashed in a thousand pieces, and a man leaped through and landed on the floor. Before he got to his feet, I had clapped a pistol to his back, and might have shot him, too; only at the touch of him (and him alive) my whole flesh misgave me, and I could no more pull the trigger than I could have flown.[18]

The shipboard setting and accoutrements of action remain, but the tone has changed. While David does eventually shoot his attacker, he is able to do so only after deliberation and hesitation that stems from moral consciousness and self-consciousness ("and him alive").

And while *Treasure Island* spawned a slew of adventure novels,[19] it can also be seen to have influenced works of a very different nature, including, I would argue, those of Joseph Conrad, whose own stories in this line are very much matter for grown-ups.[20] At the turn of the century, even the adventure novel was capable of taking a turn inward. So in *Lord Jim* (1900) (whose hero shares Stevenson's hero's name), Jil Larson has argued that "the romantic sea story/adventure novel of the sort Jim himself read as a boy becomes, in Conrad's hands, a narrative that skeptically questions many traditional moral notions—heroism, the effectiveness of a code of conduct, the value of sympathy—by violating the narrative conventions that typically undergird these ethics."[21] Similarly, in *Nostromo* (1904), which picks up on Stevenson's treasure island motif and transplants it into an altogether different artistic landscape, "a novel about political history . . . is reduced, over the course of several hundred pages, to a condition of mind, an inner state," as Edward Said has put it.[22] Once again, the action is internalized, and once again, the story becomes one of failed revolutions and failed marriages. In *Nostromo,* Conrad's eponymous hero (really, one of three central figures, none of whom deserves the title), who begins as much a chosen son as was Jim Hawkins (and as much a figure of action: Harold Bloom calls him a "pure Homeric throwback"[23]), ends up dead, after having been corrupted by the treasure. Conrad's experiences with revolution and imperialism have left him acutely aware of the fact that "There was something inherent in the necessities of successful action which carried with it the moral degradation of the idea"; while "Action is consolatory," as *Nostromo* recognizes, it is not necessarily a consolation to be wished. Still, Conrad also understands that "In our activity alone do we find the sustaining illusion of an independent existence as against the whole scheme of things of which we form a helpless part." When the dandyish Martin Decoud loses "all his belief in the reality of his action past and to come," he commits suicide.[24] Conrad's fiction is suffused with such ambivalence about the moral status of action.

And while Stevenson's *Treasure Island* manages to preserve its atmosphere of free and unfettered action, its very composition contains a final irony: Stevenson's own substantial travels were not entered on in search of buried treasure but rather in quest of elusive health. His books may reflect a persistent interest in action, but in his life, his invalidism becomes the source (because it fosters his imagination) of what Henry James identifies as his *character:*

> "Character, character is what he has!" These words may be applied to Mr. Robert Louis Stevenson; in the language of that art which depends most on direct observation, character, character is what he has. He is essentially a model, in the sense of a sitter.[25]

Even though Stevenson's own writing may embrace the idea of a literature of action, under James's gaze, he is transformed into the hero of a novel: one whose inability to run allows him to sit still enough for the portraitist—or the novelist: it comes to much the same thing here—to capture his essence.

NOTES

INTRODUCTION

1. William Wordsworth, Preface to *Lyrical Ballads* (1800), in *The Prose Works of William Wordsworth*, 3 vols., ed. W. J. B. Owen and Jane Worthington Smyser (Oxford: The Clarendon Press, 1974), I: 128; Matthew Arnold, Preface to first edition of *Poems* (1853), in *On the Classical Tradition*, ed. R. H. Super, vol. 1 of *The Complete Prose Works of Matthew Arnold* (Ann Arbor: University of Michigan Press, 1960), 2; and Henry James, Preface to *The Portrait of a Lady*, in Henry James, *The Art of the Novel*, intro. Richard P. Blackmur (New York: Charles Scribner's Sons, 1962), 42, 48, 56.

2. Aristotle, *Poetics*, in *The Basic Works of Aristotle*, ed. and intro. Richard McKeon, trans. Ingram Bywater (New York: Random House, 1941), 1461 (chapter 6, 1450a)

3. Benjamin Disraeli, *Lothair* (Westport, Conn.: Greenwood Press, 1970), 422.

4. Aristotle, *Nicomachean Ethics*, in *The Basic Works of Aristotle*, 952 (book II, chapter 1, 1103a).

5. Aristotle, *Poetics*, in *The Basic Works of Aristotle*, 1462 (chapter 6, 1450b).

6. W. B. Yeats, "The Circus Animals' Desertion," in *The Poems*, Vol. 1 of *The Collected Works of W. B. Yeats*, ed. Richard J. Finneran (New York: Scribner's, 1997), 356.

7. Immanuel Kant, *Foundations of the Metaphysics of Morals*, trans. Lewis White Beck (Indianapolis: Bobbs-Merrill, 1959), 23.

8. Thomas Hardy, *Tess of the D'Urbervilles*, ed. Tim Dolan, intro. Margaret R. Higonnet (London: Penguin Classics, 1998), 340.

9. As Stephen Halliwell argues, "If the categories of action and character have come to seem unavoidable or indispensable to many readers and critics of drama, it is a historical fact that their fundamental place in the theory of drama was first established and explored in the *Poetics*. Yet such an observation carries the risk of importing a preconception into the reading of the treatise. . . . In fact, . . . the heritage and apparent influence of the *Poetics* has often been a matter more

of superficial and terminological alignment than of serious continuity of thought. . . . Modern readers of the *Poetics* are likely to continue to experience dissatisfaction and unease over Aristotle's pronouncements on action and character, and particularly his firm subordination of the latter to the former, on account of the wide discrepancy between the view of drama which this subordination represents and the dominant post-Romantic belief in the centrality of psychological characterization both to drama and to other forms of literature (above all, the novel)." Stephen Halliwell, *Aristotle's "Poetics"* (London: Duckworth, 1986), 138.

10. *The Loeb Classical Library: Quintilian,* 4 vols., ed. and trans. H. E. Butler (Cambridge: Harvard University Press, 1969), II: 421 (book VI, chapter 2, sections 8–9). I am indebted to Emily Wilson for help with this and other classical sources.

11. Harold Bloom, *Wallace Stevens: The Poems of Our Climate* (Ithaca: Cornell University Press, 1977), 139.

12. Aristotle, *Poetics,* in *The Basic Works of Aristotle,* 1462 (chapter 6, 1450b); 1466 (chapter 11, 1152b). For more on the distinction between *ethos* and *pathos,* see D. A. Russell's commentary on Longinus 9.15 (*On the Sublime,* ed., intro, and commentary D. A. Russell [Oxford: The Clarendon Press, 1964], 99). At times, Aristotle himself sets up the opposition. Referring to Homer, he argues that "his two poems are each examples of construction, the *Iliad* simple and a story of suffering, the *Odyssey* complex and a story of character" (*Poetics,* 1481 [chapter 22, 1459b]). This contrast, which is simultaneously a contrast between a work of plot and one of character, shows the degree to which Aristotelian *pathos* cannot be distinguished from what we think of as action today—the *Iliad* represents the archetypal action narrative. But the designation of the *Odyssey* as a tale of character (rather than of plot) is perhaps more intuitive for us; its modern appeal tends to be romantic rather than classical.

13. Robert L. Caserio, *Plot, Story, and the Novel: From Dickens and Poe to the Modern Era* (Princeton: Princeton University Press, 1979), xiii.

14. See in reference to this J. L. Austin's *How To Do Things with Words* (Oxford: The Clarendon Press, 1975) on performative language. The authors I consider wonder just how possible it is to "do things with words."

15. For versions of the phrase, see George Eliot, *Felix Holt, The Radical,* ed. and intro. Fred C. Thomson (Oxford: Oxford University Press, 1988), 388; and Henry James, Preface to *The Princess Casamassima,* in Henry James, *The Art of the Novel,* 72.

16. Matthew Arnold, "Dover Beach," line 37, in *The Poetical Works of Matthew Arnold,* ed. C. B. Tinker and H. F. Lowry (London: Oxford University Press, 1950).

17. Kenneth Burke, *A Grammar of Motives* (Berkeley: University of California Press, 1969), 14.

18. Henry James, Preface to *The Portrait of a Lady,* in *The Art of the Novel,* 42.

19. Much more can be said about Dickens than I will have space for in this study, which will deal with him only in passing. In part, I have chosen to defer to Caserio, who looks in some detail at how Dickens's plots demonstrate his allegiance to the concept of meaningful action (see *Plot, Story, and the Novel,* esp. "The

Featuring of Act as 'The Rescue': Story in Dickens and George Eliot," 91–132). But here I note that while I take Dickens as a proponent of action—largely on the basis of his neatly resolved plots—he, too, participates in the crisis. His novels—especially the later ones—are full of signs of it. Activity is not always a good, as Steerforth (whose name brands him) demonstrates. Pip's passivity is no doubt an evil, but it results from his immersion in an atmosphere of "expectation" that—while debased through its connection with the financial realm—cannot be entirely divorced from a positive form of romantic expectation, a Wordsworthian "something evermore about to be." And while his laziness must also be contrasted with Joe's prelapsarian labor at the forge and Biddy's ceaseless activity (suggestively, female domestic activity always fares well in Dickens, for reasons that I will address in what follows), neither Joe nor Biddy can serve as role models for Pip. Even these brief reflections show both the endemic nature of the crisis and the complicated ways in which its symptoms manifest themselves.

20. Jil Larson defines the project thus: "to read ethics through narrative by reflecting on ethical concepts or problems as they take shape in the telling of a story." Jil Larson, *Ethics and Narrative in the English Novel, 1880–1914* (Cambridge: Cambridge University Press, 2001), 3. Larson's treatment of agency is particularly relevant to my concerns, although like Caserio's, her study restricts itself to prose and looks forward from the Victorians to the turn of the century rather than backward to the Romantics. But Larson's breakdown of a "*fin-de-siècle* emphasis on subjectivity and inward agency in contrast to Victorian conceptions of freedom as external" strikes me as both underestimating high-Victorian anxieties about agency and overexternalizing their understanding of the concept, as my readings of Clough and Eliot should make clear (36).

21. M. M. Bakhtin, "Epic and Novel," in *The Dialogic Imagination,* ed. Michael Holquist, trans. Caryl Emerson and Michael Holquist (Austin: University of Texas Press, 1981), 37.

22. An exception to this rule is Alexander Welsh's groundbreaking study of Scott, *The Hero of the Waverley Novels* (first published in 1963). Welsh's anatomizing of Scott's passive hero identifies his passivity as the product of historical anxieties about preserving social stability (his passivity comes from "his submission of his individual interests to the accepted morality and order of society"), especially anxieties concerning the role of property. Welsh contrasts Scott's wavering heroes with the "dark" heroes and heroines of the novels, whom he sees as agents of the plot. His discussion resonates forcefully with much of what follows. Scott's prose romances share in some of the ambiguities of Dickens's novels: while their protagonists are passive, their form contributes much to the development of adventure fiction. See Alexander Welsh, *The Hero of the Waverley Novels, with New Essays on Scott* (Princeton: Princeton University Press, 1992), esp. 106, 79ff., 40ff.

23. Caserio, *Plot, Story, and the Novel,* xvii.

24. I must emphasize that although my own focus is on English (and one quasi-American) writers, the phenomenon I address has wider cultural resonance in the period. In particular, Russian and French nineteenth-century literature is full of examples of the conflict between passive and active modes of existence. The eponymous hero of Goncharov's *Oblomov* (1858), who is unable to motivate himself to leave his bed, is the epitome of the passive hero. Much that I have neither

the expertise nor the space to develop could be said on the topic, but I will note that the version of the crisis that manifests itself in England is especially attuned to commercial influences.

25. These include Caserio, Larson, Leo Bersani in *A Future for Astyanax: Character and Desire in Literature* (Boston: Little, Brown and Co., 1976), and John Kucich in *Repression in Victorian Fiction: Charlotte Brontë, George Eliot, and Charles Dickens* (Berkeley: University of California Press, 1987). A notable instance of a critic who looks at both prose and poetry is Jay Clayton in *Romantic Vision and the Novel* (New York: Cambridge University Press, 1987). His examination of the connection between Romantic poetry and the novel via their shared interest in the experience of transcendence has been extremely helpful to me, but his concerns are less historically and biographically oriented than mine.

26. An exception here, and a great influence on me, is Robert Langbaum's classic study, *The Language of Experience* (New York: W. W. Norton and Co., 1963), which in its treatment of the role of the dramatic in poetry frequently touches on issues of action.

Chapter One

1. Wordsworth, Preface to *Lyrical Ballads* (1800), in *The Prose Works of William Wordsworth,* 3 vols., ed. W. J. B. Owen and Jane Worthington Smyser (Oxford: The Clarendon Press, 1974), I: 128. Hereafter *Prose.*

2. Samuel Taylor Coleridge, *The Friend,* 2 vols., ed. Barbara E. Rooke, volume 4 of *The Collected Works of Samuel Taylor Coleridge* (London: Routledge and Kegan Paul, 1969), I: 368.

3. Quoted in Kenneth Johnston, *William Wordsworth: Poet, Lover, Rebel, Spy* (New York: Norton, 1998), 465–66.

4. William Wordsworth, *The Prelude, 1799, 1805, 1850,* ed. Jonathan Wordsworth, M. H. Abrams, and Stephen Gill (New York: Norton, 1979), X.236–37 (1805). All further references will be to this edition (in the 1805 version, unless otherwise noted) and will be internally documented.

5. This mystery has been the object of much scholarly speculation, of which two recent and extensive examples can be found in Nicholas Roe's *Wordsworth and Coleridge: The Radical Years* (Oxford: The Clarendon Press, 1990), and Kenneth Johnston's biography of the young Wordsworth. The fascination with Wordsworth's revolutionary involvements is part of a wider critical concern with what I call the myth of revolutionary disenchantment, perhaps most concisely explored by E. P. Thompson in "Disenchantment or Default? A Lay Sermon" (in *Power and Consciousness,* ed. Conor Cruise O'Brien and William Dean Vanech [London: University of London Press, 1969]). One can see why these topics appeal so strongly to intellectuals, especially left-leaning ones. The question of the comparative effectiveness of action and thought—or even writing—in reforming institutions, and the specter of the reactionary intellectual complacency that can accompany the abandonment of active involvement, hovers over much Wordsworth scholarship, including my own. Is thinking (as opposed to doing) necessarily a conservative activity? What good can thought achieve? These are some of the worries that stand behind this study.

6. See, for example, David Erdman, "Wordsworth as Heartsworth; or, Was Regicide the Prophetic Ground of Those 'Moral Questions'?" in *The Evidence of the Imagination: Studies of Interactions between Life and Art in English Romantic Literature,* ed. Donald Reiman, Michael Jaye, and Betty Bennet (New York: New York University Press, 1978), 12–41.

7. William Wordsworth, letter to Anne Taylor, 9 April 1801, in *The Letters of William and Dorothy Wordsworth: The Early Years,* ed. Ernest de Selincourt, rev. Chester L. Shaver (Oxford: The Clarendon Press, 1967), 327. Hereafter *Early Years.*

8. Wordsworth, Preface to *Lyrical Ballads* (1800), in *Prose,* I: 128.

9. See Johnston, *William Wordsworth,* 387–88.

10. See Johnston, *William Wordsworth,* chapter 15.

11. Many critics and biographers have both recognized the importance of action in *The Borderers* and linked this theme to Wordsworth's involvement with the French Revolution. See, for example: Kenneth Johnston (*William Wordsworth*), David Erdman ("Wordsworth as Heartsworth"), Mary Jacobus ("'That Great Stage Where Senators Perform': Macbeth and the Politics of Romantic Theatre" in *Romanticism, Writing, and Sexual Difference* [Oxford: The Clarendon Press, 1989]), and David Bromwich (*Disowned by Memory: Wordsworth's Poetry of the 1790s* [Chicago: University of Chicago Press, 1998]). Of these, Bromwich's reading has been most important to my own, as what follows should indicate. On action in *The White Doe of Rylstone,* see Willard Spiegelman (*Wordsworth's Heroes* [Berkeley: University of California Press, 1985]), and Evan Radcliffe ("Wordsworth and the Problem of Action: *The White Doe of Rylstone,*" in *Nineteenth-Century Literature* 46.2 [September 1991]: 157–80). Radcliffe's excellent account of the poem points to many of the same features and passages that I do, but his focus tends toward the question of Wordsworth's religious influences and affiliations rather than the biographical reading with which I am concerned.

12. William Wordsworth, *The Borderers,* ed. Robert Osborn (Ithaca: Cornell University Press, 1982), III.v.60–65 (1797–99). All future references to this text will be internally documented.

13. William Hazlitt, "Mr. Wordsworth," in *Selected Writings,* ed. Jon Cook (Oxford: Oxford University Press, 1991), 355.

14. See, for instance, the much-discussed addition of the "Genius of Burke!" passage in *The Prelude,* VII.512 (1850).

15. Geoffrey Hartman, *Wordsworth's Poetry: 1787–1814* (Cambridge: Harvard University Press, 1987), 15.

16. Wordsworth changes the names of his characters between the original 1796–97 manuscript of the play and the published 1842 version: for example, Mortimer becomes Marmaduke and Rivers becomes Oswald. I do not think the play's revisions are systematically significant, and I will refer back and forth to the two versions as necessary, but I will use the earlier names. I will indicate which edition is being cited by conforming with Osborn's method of referring to the early, unproduced play by act, scene, and line reference and to the later, published poem by a running line reference.

17. See Johnston, *William Wordsworth,* 464.

18. The essay is included in the Osborn edition of the play, 62–68, 62.

19. See Mary Moorman, *William Wordsworth: A Biography,* 2 vols. (Oxford: Oxford University Press, 1957–65), I: 304. As Kenneth Johnston has shown, Wordsworth actually published two poems under the name "Mortimer" around the time he was writing *The Borderers* (*William Wordsworth,* 501).

20. I take the concept of the "second self" from "Michael," line 39. In *William Wordsworth: The Oxford Authors,* ed. Stephen Gill (Oxford: Oxford University Press, 1986). All references to Wordsworth's poems, with the exception of the longer works (i.e., *The Prelude, The Borderers, The White Doe,* and *The Excursion*), will be to this edition unless otherwise noted.

21. Charles Rzepka, *The Self as Mind: Vision and Identity in Wordsworth, Coleridge, and Keats* (Cambridge: Harvard University Press, 1986), 25. See also Edward Bostetter, *The Romantic Ventriloquists* (Seattle: University of Seattle Press, 1963), 66–81. The Solitary never leaves England during the Revolutionary period, so avoiding the betrayals into action from which Wordsworth—and some of his more honest fictional selves—suffer: "The tranquil shores / Of Britain circumscribed me; else perhaps / I might have been entangled among deeds, / Which now, as infamous, I should abhor." See William Wordsworth, *The Excursion,* III.812–25, in *William Wordsworth: The Poems,* 2 vols., ed. John O. Hayden (New Haven: Yale University Press, 1981), II: 115. All future references to *The Excursion* will be to this edition and will be internally documented by book and line number.

22. William Wordsworth, Fenwick Note to *The Borderers,* reprinted in *The Borderers,* ed. Osborn, 814–15, 815.

23. Wordsworth, Preface to *Lyrical Ballads* (1800), in *Prose,* I: 128.

24. See Bromwich, "The French Revolution and 'Tintern Abbey,'" in *Disowned by Memory,* 69–91.

25. William Wordsworth, "On the Character of Rivers," in *The Borderers,* ed. Osborn, 65.

26. *Othello,* I.iii.319–20, in *The Riverside Shakespeare* (Boston: Houghton Mifflin Co., 1974). All future references to Shakespeare's plays will be to this edition. William Wordsworth, "On the Character of Rivers," in *The Borderers,* ed. Osborn, 66.

27. See Immanuel Kant, "The Analytic of the Sublime," in *Critique of Judgement,* trans. and intro. J. H. Bernard (New York: Hafner Press, 1951), esp. §26.

28. Bromwich, *Disowned by Memory,* 62, 63.

29. See René Descartes, *Meditations on First Philosophy, With Selections from the Objections and Replies,* trans. John Cottingham, intro. Bernard Williams (Cambridge: Cambridge University Press, 1986), 20–23. Descartes's cogito, his discovery that he can defeat skepticism by building upon his conviction that "I think, therefore I am," marks a radical shift from earlier belief systems, such as Aristotle's, in which actions generate a sense of character. In a way, the Cartesian world picture lies behind the work of all the writers I consider in this study.

30. See Johnston, *William Wordsworth,* 503.

31. Mary Wollstonecraft, "Letter on the Present Character of the French Nation," in *A Wollstonecraft Anthology,* ed. and intro. Janet M. Todd

(Bloomington: University of Indiana Press, 1977), 122. Quoted in Johnston, *William Wordsworth,* 339.

32. For Wordsworth's ongoing interest in the concept of habit, see James Chandler, *Wordsworth's Second Nature: A Study of the Poetry and Politics* (Chicago: University of Chicago Press, 1984). Chandler points out that Wordsworth's emphasis on habit in his poetry increases after 1797—that is, after the revolutionary period (xviii).

33. Wordsworth, Preface to *Lyrical Ballads* (1800), in *Prose,* I: 126.

34. William Wordsworth, "On the Character of Rivers," in *The Borderers,* ed. Osborn, 63.

35. Shakespeare, *Macbeth,* II.ii.70.

36. Nevertheless, Mortimer regrets the forgetfulness more than any other aspect of his crime, because it shows that he did not commit fully to his act of abandonment and so decreases the recompense available to him: "If I had done it with a mind resolved, / There had been something in the deed / To give me strength to bear the recollection" (V.iii.109). The implication is that an action committed halfheartedly can only half-fill with self-consciousness the vacancy it creates. Crimes of omission will also play an essential role in George Eliot's imagination of action, as we shall see.

37. Wordsworth, *A Letter to the Bishop of Llandaff,* in *Prose,* I: 48.

38. Wordsworth, "Home at Grasmere," lines 989–90; the latter comment is quoted in Martin Greenberg, *The Hamlet Vocation of Coleridge and Wordsworth* (Iowa City: University of Iowa Press, 1986), 147.

39. Shakespeare, *Hamlet,* III.i.86–87.

40. Coleridge, "The Character of Hamlet" (1813), in *Lectures 1808–1819 on Literature,* 2 vols., ed. R. A. Foakes, Volume 5 of *The Collected Works of Samuel Taylor Coleridge* (Princeton: Princeton University Press, 1987), II: 539.

41. Erdman, "Wordsworth as Heartsworth," 17.

42. Rzepka sees a comparable echo of Hamlet's father's ghost in Wordsworth's repeated invocations to Dorothy in "Tintern Abbey" to remember him (*Self as Mind,* 88).

43. See Roe, *Wordsworth and Coleridge,* 73–75.

44. See "The Ruined Cottage," MS. B, in William Wordsworth, *The Ruined Cottage and The Pedlar,* ed. James Butler (Ithaca: Cornell University Press, 1979), 58, and "Hart-leap Well," line 97. The phrase echoes *Othello,* I.iii.97: "Of moving accidents by flood or field."

45. For a discussion of *The Borderers* as closet drama, and of closet drama in general, see *Studies in Romanticism* 27.3 (Fall 1988), especially William Jewett, "Action in *The Borderers*" (399–400); and David Marshall, "The Eyewitnesses of *The Borderers*" (391–98); see also Mary Jacobus, *Romanticism, Writing, and Sexual Difference.*

46. William Wordsworth, the 1842 Note to *The Borderers,* in *The Borderers,* ed. Osborn, 813.

47. Wordsworth, Preface to *Lyrical Ballads* (1800), in *Prose,* I: 128.

48. Charles Lamb, "On the Tragedies of Shakspeare Considered with Reference to their Fitness for Stage Representation," in *The Collected Works of Charles Lamb,* 8 vols., ed. E. V. Lucas (London: Methuen, 1912), I: 114–15.

49. Lamb, "On the Tragedies," 123.

50. As Annabel Patterson has pointed out to me, "unjust tribunals" echoes Milton's "unjust tribunals, under change of times" in *Samson Agonistes*. Milton is generally taken to be referring to the trials and executions of regicides such as Sir Henry Vane; Wordsworth may well have had in mind connections with the English Treason Trials of 1794, in which radicals like Thomas Holcroft and John Thelwall were arrested and charged. Like *The Borderers, Samson Agonistes* is a closet drama very much concerned with the roles of action and inaction in the political realm. As we shall see in relation to *The White Doe*, Milton's influence on Wordsworth's treatment of action is considerable. John Milton, *Samson Agonistes*, in *Complete Poems and Major Prose*, ed. Merritt Y. Hughes (New York: Macmillan, 1957), line 695. All future references to Milton will be to this edition.

51. Hannah Arendt, *Thinking*, in *The Life of the Mind* (New York: Harcourt Brace, Jovanovich, 1978), 185.

52. Arendt alludes to the connection between these two mental categories, noting that "It took language a long time to separate the word 'consciousness' from 'conscience,' and in some languages, for instance, in French, such a separation was never made" (*Thinking*, 190). Consider Hamlet's "conscience"—really "consciousness"—that causes the current of his resolve to turn awry in the great soliloquy.

53. Bromwich, *Disowned by Memory*, 137.

54. S. T. Coleridge, letter to George Coleridge, 10 March 1798, in *The Collected Letters of Samuel Taylor Coleridge*, 6 vols., ed. Leslie Griggs (Oxford: Oxford University Press, 1956–71), I: 397; emphasis added.

55. Arendt, *Thinking*, in *The Life of the Mind*, 192; emphasis added.

56. Wordsworth, Preface to *Lyrical Ballads* (1800), in *Prose*, I: 126.

57. Lionel Trilling, *The Liberal Imagination* (London: Secker and Warburg, 1964), xi.

58. Mortimer's response to Rivers's suggested crusade is much expanded in the later version of the play. This brings the end of the drama more in line with Wordsworth's later, more coherent, anti-action stance, which I will discuss in relation to *The White Doe of Rylstone*.

59. From *Moral Essays, Epistle I*. Wordsworth, *The Borderers*, ed. Osborn, 72.

60. William Wordsworth, letter to Francis Wrangham, 19 February 1819, in *The Letters of William and Dorothy Wordsworth: The Middle Years*, 2 vols., ed. Ernest de Selincourt, rev. Mary Moorman and Allan Hill (Oxford: Clarendon Press, 1969), II: 524. Hereafter *Middle Years*.

61. The purpose behind this abandoned framing narrative is rather perplexing, but it seems to function in part as a warning not to treat the Doe as a symbol of hermeneutic uncertainty. We are left in no doubt as to the real center of truth in the poem, rather as in the case of Pompilia's narrative in Robert Browning's *The Ring and the Book* (1868–69).

62. Milton, Sonnet XIX, "When I consider how my light is spent." William Wordsworth, *The White Doe of Rylstone; or The Fate of the Nortons*, ed. and intro Kristine Dugas (Ithaca: Cornell University Press, 1988), line 1070. All further references to this text will be to this edition of the text, based on the 1815 printed version, and will be internally documented by line number (unless reference is

made to other versions, in which case a page number will be given, indicating the footnoted amendment in Dugas's edition).

63. S. T. Coleridge, letter to William Wordsworth, 21 May 1808, in *Collected Letters*, ed. Griggs, III: 107–8. Kristine Dugas points out in her introduction to *The White Doe* how close the terms of Coleridge's objections to Wordsworth's poem are to Wordsworth's criticisms of "The Rime of the Ancient Mariner," of whose principal character he famously complained: "he does not act, but is continuously acted upon" ("Note to the Ancient Mariner" in the 1800 edition of *Lyrical Ballads*) (Introduction, 12). *The White Doe* and "The Rime" bear comparison, perhaps unsurprisingly given how fundamentally problems of action and the will figure in both. Obviously, we should note the ballad form and the central importance of a white beast that acts as genius loci to both poems. But Wordsworth also seems to invoke Coleridge's ballad at two crucial moments in his text: first, when Francis stands apart gazing on the field of battle and the banner below him, as solitary and alone as ever the Mariner is on his "wide, wide sea," he is compared to a "tutelary Power" (Coleridge calls the albatross a "Tutelary Spirit") and to "mariners" gazing for guidance at a distant light (775ff.); second, when Emily sees the White Doe after her return from her Mariner-like wanderings, her relief in tears recalls the relief the Mariner finds when he blesses the sea monsters "unawares." See also David Bromwich's discussion of the relationship between "The Rime" and *The Borderers* (*Disowned by Memory*, 66–68). Wordsworth laid claim to suggesting to Coleridge the nature of the Mariner's original sin, and, as Bromwich argues, both works are interested in examining the consequences of acts of motiveless malignity. Bromwich goes so far as to ponder the possibility that the Ancient Mariner was a portrait of Wordsworth (116 n. 7)—a reading that resonates with the theme of betrayals into action that I explore here.

64. Hartman, *Wordsworth's Poetry*, 325.

65. William Wordsworth, letter to Coleridge, 19 April 1808, in *Middle Years*, I: 221–22.

66. Much of the criticism of *The White Doe* has treated the relationship between the banner and the Doe, symbols of the Catholic and Protestant imagination, respectively (see, for example, Martin Price, "Imagination in *The White Doe of Rylstone*," *Philological Quarterly* 33.2 [April 1954]: 189–99). The Doe's whiteness in this context emphasizes its lack of thingliness, so indicating the lesser dependency of the Protestant imagination on gross materiality (and thus its visionary superiority). While I will not concentrate my discussion on these two objects, it should be noted that the banner is also associated closely with battle and the world of external action, while the Doe is linked to passivity and inaction by its ties to Emily.

67. Wordsworth, letter to Coleridge, 19 April 1808, in *Middle Years*, I: 221–22.

68. [Josiah Condor], review of *The White Doe*, *The Eclectic*, n.s. 5 (January 1816): 38. Quoted in Dugas, Introduction, 61.

69. Dugas reproduces the Fenwick Note in her Introduction, 62–63; I quote from page 62.

70. William Wordsworth, *The Convention of Cintra*, in *Prose*, I: 339.

71. See Christopher Wordsworth, *Memoirs of William Wordsworth*, 2 vols., ed.

Henry Reed (New York: AMS Press, 1966), II: 313. This edition is a reprint of the 1851 original.

72. Shakespeare, *Hamlet,* III.ii.213.

73. See Christopher Wordsworth, *Memoirs,* II: 313. Quoted in Mary Moorman, *William Wordsworth,* II: 113.

74. Willing can be thought of as self-empowered hoping—we *will* something to happen when we not only hope that it happens, but engage in an act of mind that could contribute to its happening. In contrast, when we *hope* that something will happen, our act of mind is not causally related to the occurrence or non-occurrence of the desired outcome, which depends upon the activities of forces outside our control. Wordsworth plays with these two categories in a sophisticated fashion not only in *The White Doe* but also elsewhere in his poetry. Here it is enough to note that both willing and hoping are in themselves internal activities.

75. Spiegelman, *Wordsworth's Heroes,* 168.

76. In regarding the "debate" between the forms of action espoused by the brother and sister as the central concern of Wordsworth's poem, I am agreeing with Evan Radcliffe's treatment of action in *The White Doe* ("Wordsworth and the Problem of Action"). For Radcliffe's suggestive remarks on Spiegelman, see his note 8. I do not include the Doe herself in the list of protagonists, as she lacks the capacity for struggle implicit in the term (from *agon,* "contest"). Nevertheless, her role is central to Wordsworth's narrative, as we shall see.

77. As we shall see, Clough places the hero of *Amours de Voyage* in a similar situation, atop the Pincian Hills, sightseeing alongside his fellow tourists at the war below. While the two passages differ vastly in tone, they both represent the hero's disengagement from the traditional life of action: battle.

78. Jewett, "Action in *The Borderers,*" 409.

79. Marshall, "The Eyewitnesses of *The Borderers,*" 398.

80. I quote from the expanded 1827 version of the text, although the implications are the same in earlier drafts. Note that the dating still places the composition of the passage before the time at which Wordsworth affixes the epigraph from *The Borderers* to *The White Doe.*

81. Robert Langbaum, *The Poetry of Experience* (New York: W. W. Norton and Co., 1963), 63.

82. Immanuel Kant, *Foundation of the Metaphysics of Morals,* trans. Lewis White Beck (Indianapolis: Bobbs Merrill, 1959), 23.

83. Radcliffe makes the same observation: "as a woman she has in the poem no martial role, no clear avenue for action" ("Wordsworth and the Problem of Action," 176). The exemption from battle also extends to the old; hence the presence of the elderly man Emily sends out to scout on the events at the front. Wordsworth's concern in his poetry for female and elderly subjects is linked to his interest in the merits of inaction.

84. Wordsworth's choice of a female center of consciousness for his narrative connects it to the genre of the novel, where female characters will play an increasingly important role. In her seminal study, *Desire and Domestic Fiction: A Political History of the Novel* (Oxford: Oxford University Press, 1987), Nancy Armstrong considers in detail the implications, political and cultural, of the rise of domestic fiction (that is, fiction that centers on and exalts the figure of the domestic

woman). Like Armstrong, I am interested in the new attention granted to "qualities of mind" in such fiction. But while Armstrong contrasts these qualities with
the earlier focus on social status as constitutive of selfhood, I wish to contrast the
nineteenth-century concern for a life of the mind with the earlier focus on a life
of action (4–5).

    85. Milton, *Paradise Lost,* VIII.173.

    86. Wordsworth, *The White Doe,* ed. Dugas, Introduction, 63.

    87. Hartman, *Wordsworth's Poetry,* 324.

    88. See Radcliffe, "Wordsworth and the Problem of Action," 172–73.

    89. Radcliffe considers Wordsworth's attitude toward the relationship
between art and action by looking at the role of the narrator of the tale, whom he
sees as "passive" in a way that differentiates him from many of Wordsworth's other
narrators ("Wordsworth and the Problem of Action," 178–80).

    90. Milton, *Paradise Lost,* I.19–22)

    91. The phrase is best known from the patriotic conclusion of Tennyson's
Maud (1855). In *Tennyson's Poetry,* ed. Robert W. Hill Jr. (New York: Norton,
1971), 248.

    92. Price, "Imagination in *The White Doe,*" 193.

    93. Wordsworth, letter to Coleridge, 19 April 1808, in *Middle Years,* I: 222.

    94. Radcliffe, "Wordsworth and the Problem of Action," 169.

    95. Wordsworth, "Essay, Supplementary to the Preface," in *Prose,* III: 81–82.

    96. Wordsworth, letter to Anne Taylor, 9 April 1801, in *Early Years,* 327.

    97. Wordsworth, letter to Coleridge, 19 April 1808, in *Middle Years,* I:
222–23.

    98. As always in reading Wordsworth, one should note his use of the word
revolution.

    99. Wordsworth, Preface to *Lyrical Ballads* (1850), in *Prose,* I: 138.

    100. John Keats, letter to the George Keatses, 14 February–3 May 1819, in
The Letters of John Keats: A Selection, ed. Robert Gittings (Oxford: Oxford
University Press, 1970), 249–50.

    101. Lionel Trilling, "The Morality of Inertia," in *The Moral Obligation to be
Intelligent,* ed. and intro. Leon Wieseltier (New York: Farrar, Straus, Giroux,
2000), 337.

CHAPTER TWO

    1. Arthur Hugh Clough, "Lecture on the Poetry of Wordsworth," in *The
Poems and Prose Remains of Arthur Hugh Clough,* 2 vols., ed. and intro. Blanche
Clough (London: Macmillan and Co., 1869), I: 315. Hereafter, these volumes will
be referred to as *PPR* and will be internally documented. For the quotation, see
chapter 1 n. 44.

    2. For an early source of the distinction between subjective and objective
poetry that influenced Arnold, see Friedrich Schiller's *On Naive and Sentimental
Poetry* (1795) (naive poetry is objective; sentimental poetry is subjective).

    3. A. H. Clough, letter to F. T. Child, 16 April 1858, in *The Correspondence
of Arthur Hugh Clough,* 2 vols., ed. F. L. Mulhauser (Oxford: The Clarendon Press,

1957), II: 546. Hereafter *Correspondence.* There is no complete edition of Clough's letters. Where possible, I will quote from *Correspondence,* but it is often necessary to turn to other sources for letters not included by Mulhauser.

4. See, for example, Henry Sidgwick, review of Clough's life and work, *Westminster Review* 92 (October 1869): 382; rpt. in *Arthur Hugh Clough: The Critical Heritage,* ed. Michael Thorpe (London: Routledge, 1972), 287. See also J. M. Robertson, "Clough" (1887), which includes an extended reflection on Clough's relationship to contemporary novelists. In John Mackinnin Robertson, *New Essays towards a Critical Method* (London: The Bodley Head, 1897); rpt. in *The Critical Heritage,* ed. Thorpe, 343–65.

5. The standard biography of Clough is Katherine Chorley's *Arthur Hugh Clough: The Uncommitted Mind* (Oxford: Oxford University Press, 1962). Critical monographs that incorporate significant amounts of biographical material include: R. K. Biswas, *Arthur Hugh Clough: Towards a Reconsideration* (Oxford: Oxford University Press, 1972); Wendell V. Harris, *Arthur Hugh Clough* (New York: Twayne Publishers, 1970); Michael Timko, *Innocent Victorian* (Athens: Ohio University Press, 1966); Paul Veyriras, *Arthur Hugh Clough* (Paris: Didier, 1964); and Isobel Armstrong, *Arthur Hugh Clough* (London: Longman, 1962). One notable exception to this biographical trend is Walter E. Houghton's *The Poetry of Clough: An Essay in Revaluation* (New Haven: Yale University Press, 1963). Houghton begins his study with the bold declaration: "I am not concerned in this book with Clough's poetry as a biographical document, or as a record of his thought, or as an index to the age" (xi).

6. Timko, *Innocent Victorian,* 3.

7. Matthew Arnold, "Thyrsis," lines 221–26, in *The Poetical Works of Matthew Arnold,* ed. C. B. Tinker and H. F. Lowry (London: Oxford University Press, 1950). All future references to Arnold's poetry will be to this edition and will be internally documented by line number.

8. For a discussion of the events surrounding the renaming of this poem, originally published as *The Bothie of Toper-na-Fuosich*—literally, the hut of the bearded well, and a euphemism for the female genitalia—see Biswas, *Arthur Hugh Clough,* 264–66. Clough's poems routinely underwent processes of editing for their frequently explicit sexual content, especially under the direction of his wife, Blanche.

9. G. H. Lewes, review of *Poems* (1862), *Cornhill Magazine* 6 (September 1862): 398; rpt. in *The Critical Heritage,* ed. Thorpe, 155.

10. Clough would come to describe Dr. Arnold as one of those men who are "too . . . practical to be literally theoretical; too eager to be observant, too royal to be philosophical; too fit to head armies and rule kingdoms to succeed in weighing words and analyzing emotion; born to do, they know not what they do" ("Review of Mr. Newman's *The Soul,*" in *PPR* I: 294). With its invocation of the language of Jesus on the Cross (Luke 23.34), the statement shows the characteristic ambivalence Clough felt toward his teacher in later life, and also how much of that ambivalence centered on the relationship between action and speculation. The great schoolmaster represented for Clough uncomplicated action of a kind he found it hard to imagine. While Clough always recognized that useful activity is central to the living of a good life (his debt to Aristotle's *Ethics,* as will become

apparent, was enormous), he implied that Dr. Arnold's kind of activity has something childlike, even unwilled about it—not only innocent but also ignorant. There is no struggle in such activity, and for this reason, it seems almost involuntary, and less valuable for that. As Clough wrote in a review entitled "Recent Social Theories," "There are many, surely, who looking back into their past lives, feel most thankful for those acts which came least from their own mere natural volition" (*PPR* I: 414). In the postlapsarian world, action is most valuable when it runs counter to desire, perhaps because it is then that one feels one's moral freedom.

11. Thomas Carlyle, *Chartism,* in *Critical and Miscellaneous Essays in Six Volumes: Volume Five,* Volume 10 of *The Library Edition of the Collected Works of Thomas Carlyle,* 30 vols. (London: Chapman and Hall, 1869), 381. The section is entitled "Not laissez-faire."

12. A. H. Clough, letter to Anne Clough, 4–23 May 1847, in *Correspondence,* I: 149.

13. "He who does not pray, does not labor." Unsigned review of *Ambarvalia* and *The Strayed Reveller and Other Poems,* in *The Guardian* 4 (28 March 1849): 209; rpt. in *The Critical Heritage,* ed. Thorpe, 83.

14. Thomas Carlyle, "Characteristics" (1831), in *Critical and Miscellaneous Essays in Six Volumes: Volume Three,* vol. 8 of *The Library Edition* (London: Chapman and Hall, 1869), 361–62.

15. William Hazlitt, *An Essay on the Principles of Human Action* (Gainsville, Fla.: Scholars' Facsimiles and Reprints, 1969), 66–67.

16. See Charles Taylor, *Sources of the Self: The Making of the Modern Identity* (Cambridge: Harvard University Press, 1989), especially chapters 1–3, and Alasdaire MacIntyre, *After Virtue* (Notre Dame: University of Notre Dame Press, 1984), and *Whose Justice? Which Rationality?* (Notre Dame: University of Notre Dame Press, 1988).

17. Arthur Hugh Clough, letter to E. Hawkins, 23 January 1848, in *Correspondence,* I: 196.

18. Quoted in Evelyn Barish Greenberger, *Arthur Hugh Clough: The Growth of a Poet's Mind* (Cambridge: Cambridge University Press, 1970), 161; from "Fragment on America." Clough's first major poem, *The Bothie,* composed immediately after his renunciation of his fellowship, concludes with its heroes' marriage and emigration to New Zealand, to begin a new life there. The emigration is based on that of Clough's friend Tom Arnold, and Clough himself seriously considered following the same route. *The Bothie* stands alone in Clough's canon of longer works as a poem in which action is allowed to be realized—Tom Arnold commented on its "action," calling it "among the boldest and purest" he had known (Tom Arnold, letter to Clough, 24 September 1849, in *Correspondence,* I: 272). And even Matthew, after criticizing the poem for its use of slang, praises its "true Homeric ring" of phrase and "out-of-doors freshness, life, naturalness, [and] buoyant rapidity" ("On Translating Homer," in *On the Classical Tradition,* vol. 1 in *The Complete Prose Works of Matthew Arnold,* ed. R. H. Super [Ann Arbor: University of Michigan Press, 1960], 216). Yet while the marriage plot finds a happy resolution, the real "actions" of its heroes cannot take place within the framework of the narrative—or even of Great Britain. What Elspie and Philip will achieve on their virgin soil must be left to the imagination. I will again consider this need for

virgin territory as a consequence of the crisis of action when I look at the conclusion of *Daniel Deronda*. The impulse can be traced also from Coleridge and Southey's plans to create a Pantisocraticy on the banks of the Susquehanna; in fact, Tom Arnold refers to Pantisocracy in writing of his emigration (*Passages in a Wandering Life* [London: E. Arnold, 1900], 64–65).

Henry James's novels on the clashing of cultures display the Victorian sense of the difference between Europe and America as potential grounds of action. Isabel Archer, the paradigmatically active American, becomes hopelessly entangled in the web of past deeds when she goes to Europe.

19. A. H. Clough, letter to Tom Arnold, 16 May 1851, in *Correspondence,* I: 290.

20. Clough, letter to Blanche Smith, February 1852. Bodleian MS Eng. Lett. e. 77, fol. 123—Feb. 1852. Original italics. Quoted in Evelyn Barish Greenberger, *Arthur Hugh Clough: The Growth of a Poet's Mind* (Cambridge: Cambridge University Press, 1970), 130.

21. Descartes's cogito is in some sense the epistemological root of Clough's problem, as it is the source of all modern definitions of consciousness. See chapter 1 n. 29.

22. Clough's one substantial late poem, *Mari Magno* (a series of tales of marriage recounted by shipboard travelers and resembling Chaucer's *Canterbury Tales* in structure), on which he working at the time of his death, is generally regarded by modern critics as lacking the interest and originality of his earlier work. Blanche, though, approved of its conventionalities and positive expression of "the daily problems of social life" (*PPR* I: 41).

23. George Eliot, *Middlemarch,* ed. David Carroll, intro. Felicia Bonaparte (Oxford: Oxford University Press, 1998), 785.

24. A. H. Clough, letter to Blanche Smith, 4 February 1853, in *Correspondence,* II: 376.

25. See esp. *PPR* I: 44–45. Biswas is particularly good at discussing Blanche's influence on her husband's activity, both poetic and otherwise. See Biswas, *Arthur Hugh Clough,* 417–69.

26. Lytton Strachey, *Eminent Victorians* (London: Penguin, 1948), 164. As Nightingale herself argued in *Cassandra,* "The family? It is too narrow a field for the development of an immortal spirit, be that spirit male or female." Florence Nightingale, *Cassandra and other selections from Suggestions for Thought,* ed. Mary Poovey (London: Pickering and Chatto, 1991), 216.

27. Arthur Hugh Clough, *Dipsychus and the Spirit,* in *Clough's Selected Poems,* ed. J. P. Phelan (London: Longman, 1995), 3.2.131–34. Further references to Clough's poems will be to this edition and will be internally documented (by section and line number, as appropriate), unless otherwise noted.

28. Strachey, *Eminent Victorians,* 165.

29. Carlyle, "Characteristics," in *Critical and Miscellaneous Essays,* 356. The quotation alludes to the primary argument of Aristotle's *Ethics.*

30. Thomas Carlyle, "The Everlasting No," in *Sartor Resartus,* vol. 1 of *The Library Edition of the Complete Works,* 30 vols. (London: Chapman and Hall, 1870), 159. Original emphasis.

31. Carlyle, "The Everlasting Yea," in *Sartor Resartus,* 188. Original emphasis.

32. Joseph Bristow, "'Love, let us be true to one another': Matthew Arnold, Arthur Hugh Clough, and 'our Aqueous Ages,'" *Literature and History* 4.1 (Spring 1995): 36.

33. Johann Wolfgang von Goethe and Friedrich Schiller, "On Epic and Dramatic Poetry" (1797), in *Goethe's Literary Essays,* ed. and trans. J. E. Spingarn, intro. Viscount Haldane (New York: Harcourt, Brace and Company, 1921), 101.

34. [Clough], "Recent English Poetry," *North American Review* 77 (1853): 3; in *PPR* I: 360, 361.

35. Just to emphasize how remarkable—and how significant—the anticlimax of this plot is, one can compare it to two preceding works: Longfellow's *Evangeline* (1847) (Clough's purported source for his hexameters) and Goethe's *Hermann und Dorothea* (1797). *Evangeline* relates the disrupted courtship of a young French couple in Acadia (Nova Scotia), who have been forced south from their homeland by eighteenth-century English political tyranny only to lose each other in the confusion. It actually includes a long description of Evangeline's hunt for her lost lover but ends in a deathbed reunion of the couple in old age amidst great religious fanfare. Like *Amours, Hermann und Dorothea* sets an explicitly bourgeois courtship plot to epic hexameters against the background of French political tyranny; Dorothea has fled her homeland to escape the forces of the French Revolution. But Goethe also ensures that his poem concludes with a wedding.

36. R. W. Emerson, letter to Clough, 17 May 1858, in *Correspondence,* II: 548.

37. Matthew Arnold, letter to A. H. Clough, 21 March 1853, in *The Letters of Matthew Arnold to Arthur Hugh Clough,* ed. and intro. Howard Foster Lowry (London: Oxford University Press, 1932), 132.

38. Matthew Arnold, Preface to the first edition of *Poems* (1853), in *On the Classical Tradition,* ed. R. H. Super, 4.

39. Matthew Arnold, letter to A. H. Clough, 12 Feb. 1853, in *Arnold-Clough Letters,* ed. Lowry, 130.

40. See Lionel Trilling, *Matthew Arnold* (New York: Columbia University Press, 1949), 23–35.

41. Matthew Arnold, letter to A. H. Clough, 30 November 1853, in *Arnold-Clough Letters,* ed. Lowry, 146.

42. Aristotle, *Poetics,* in *The Basic Works of Aristotle,* 1461 (chapter 6, 1450b).

43. William Wordsworth, Preface to *Lyrical Ballads* (1800), in *Prose,* I: 128.

44. Matthew Arnold, Preface to the first edition of *Poems* (1853), in *On the Classical Tradition,* ed. Super, 1.

45. Matthew Arnold, Preface to the first edition of *Poems* (1853), in *On the Classical Tradition,* ed. Super, 4.

46. Wordsworth, Preface to *Lyrical Ballads* (1850), in *Prose,* I: 123, 125.

47. For a detailed treatment of the phenomenon of Spasmody, see Mark A. Weinstein, *William Edmonstoune Aytoun and the Spasmodic Controversy* (New Haven: Yale University Press, 1968); for the connection with Arnold's Preface, see page 110. The word "spasmodic" was first applied to a group of poets by Charles Kingsley, whose "muscular Christianity" represents a school of thought (and a literature produced by that school) that starkly contrasted with the sentimental drift

of the Spasmodics. See "Thoughts on Shelley and Byron," *Fraser's Magazine* 48 (November 1853): 568–76.

48. The strangely uneven tone of the lyrical passages that begin and end each canto adds to the confusion of voice: while sometimes they seem to represent Claude's own effusions, at other points they read like a third-person-narrator's reflections on Claude's progress.

49. See Eugene R. August, "*Amours de Voyage* and Matthew Arnold in Love: An Inquiry," *Victorian Newsletter* 60 (Fall 1981): 15–20.

50. Clough, "Blank Misgivings of a Creature moving about in Worlds not realized" (V.1–8), in *The Poems of Arthur Hugh Clough*, 2nd ed., ed. F. L. Mulhauser (Oxford: The Clarendon Press, 1974), 30. The poem's title is a quotation from Wordsworth's Intimations Ode. The language of the clue also permeates *Amours de Voyage*, in which, as we shall see, the epic quest is translated into Claude's chase across Italy and Switzerland in search of Mary. In an early letter of *Amours*, Claude acknowledges that life is a "labyrinth" but insists that "Yet in my bosom unbroken remaineth the clue; I shall use it" (I.xii.241). We do not quite believe him, though, and the "clue" here metamorphosizes quickly into a cord from which Claude dangles dangerously over a crag-lined void. He claims he will again "plant firm foot" on "the great massy strengths of abstraction," but these abstractions, unsurprisingly, prove inadequate foothold (I.xii.251). Later, the clue is transformed once again by the voice of the narrator of the elegiacs that conclude Canto IV, the canto describing Claude's chase after Mary across Italy and Switzerland: "Italy, unto thy cities receding, the clue to recover, / Hither, recovered the clue, shall not the traveller haste?" (concluding elegiacs, IV.82–83). Mary should have provided direction for Claude, but he lost the clue; as I have suggested, Clough's own marriage to Blanche Smith can be seen as his attempt to keep hold of it.

51. Matthew Arnold, *Culture and Anarchy*, vol. 5 of *The Complete Prose Works*, ed. Super (Ann Arbor, University of Michigan Press, 1965), 175, 225.

52. Clough, *The Bothie of Tober-na-Vuolich*, in *Arthur Hugh Clough: Everyman's Poetry*, ed. John Beer (London: J. M. Dent, 1998), IX.49–53. Further references to *The Bothie* will be to this edition and will be internally documented.

53. Isobel Armstrong, *Victorian Poetry: Poetry, Poetics and Politics* (London: Routledge, 1993), 174.

54. [Walter Bagehot], review of Tennyson's *Idylls of the King, National Review* 9 (October 1859): 378.

55. John Henry Newman, *Fifteen Sermons Preached before the University of Oxford, between A.D. 1826 and 1843*, 3rd ed. (London: Longmans Green, 1919), 201.

56. Armstrong, *Victorian Poetry*, 175.

57. See William Wordsworth, *The Prelude*, X.64

58. A. H. Clough, letter to J. P. Gell, 13 July 1844, in *Correspondence*, I: 130.

59. A. H. Clough, letters to A. P. Stanley, 14, 19 May 1848, in *Correspondence*, I: 206, 207.

60. A. H. Clough, letter to Tom Arnold, 15 February 1849, in *Correspondence*, I: 243

61. A. H. Clough, letter to J. C. Shairp, 18 June 1849, in *PPR* I: 151.

62. Politicians made much of this empowerment of the common man, as conservative legislators still do today—the rhetoric has not changed at all. See, for

example, Gladstone's Budget Speech of 10 February 1860: "in legislation of this kind [i.e., laissez-faire] you are not forging mechanical helps for men, nor endeavoring to do for them what they ought to do for themselves; but you are enlarging their means without narrowing their freedom, you are giving value to their labour, you are appealing to their sense of responsibility, you are not impairing their sense of honourable self-dependence." In *Hansard's Parliamentary Debates, Third Series,* 41 vols., *Volume CLVI: First Volume of Session 1860* (January–March 1860) (London: Cornelius Buck, 1860), 871. See also Samuel Smiles's best-selling book, *Self-Help with Illustrations of Conduct and Perseverance* (1859), which declares that "National progress is the sum of individual industry, energy, and uprightness. . . . [T]he highest patriotism and philanthropy consist, not so much in altering laws and modifying institutions, as in helping and stimulating men to elevate and improve themselves by their own free and independent individual action." Centenary edition, intro. Asa Briggs (London: John Murray, 1958), 36.

63. See the notes to Patrick Scott's edition of *Amours* (Clough, *Amours de Voyage,* ed. and intro. Patrick Scott [St. Lucia: University of Queensland Press, 1974]), 54. Much of Clough's most radical poetry was not included in the published versions of his work, so I will often refer to such canceled lines in my discussion.

64. Thomas Carlyle, "The Menads," in *The French Revolution,* 3 vols., vols. 2–4 of *The Library Edition,* I: 313.

65. Walter Bagehot, "Letters on the French Coup d'Etat of 1851," in *Literary Studies* (London, 1898), III: 6. Quoted in John Goode, "1848 and the Strange Disease of Modern Love," in *Literature and Politics in the Nineteenth Century,* ed. John Lucas (London: Methuen, 1971), 48. Bagehot's letter first appeared in the *Inquirer* in early 1852.

66. John Stuart Mill, "Civilization," in *Essays on Politics and Society,* ed. J. M. Robson, intro. Alexander Brady, vol. XVIII of *The Collected Works of John Stuart Mill* (Toronto: University of Toronto Press, 1977), 129.

67. Carlyle, "Characteristics" (1831), in *Critical and Miscellaneous Essays,* 361. Compare Arnold's declaration that his age is "wandering between two worlds, one dead, / The other powerless to be born" ("Stanzas from the Grande Chartreuse," lines 85–86).

68. E. S. Dallas, *The Gay Science,* 2 vols. (London: Chapman and Hall, 1866) (reprinted by Johnson Reprint Corporation), II: 285, 295. While the title of Dallas's work, with its reference to the art of the Spanish troubadours, tries to set itself apart from the more prevalent contemporary "dismal science" of political economy, economic discourse nevertheless pervades the final section of the work, which begins with an extended comparison of the Venetian commercial empire of the early Renaissance to the current state of England.

69. "And accustomed as we are to regard life as action, . . .—Is it life to think? . . . How shall a man be—be a man, not a puppet; a reality, not a seeming." Dallas, *The Gay Science,* II: 301.

70. Dallas, *The Gay Science,* II: 277–83.

71. *Plutarch's Lives: The Translation called Dryden's,* 5 vols., trans. and revised by A. H. Clough (London: John C. Nimmo, 1893), I: xxviii.

72. Dallas, *The Gay Science,* II: 282. From the beginning of the "Life of

Alexander." The popularity of Plutarch in the nineteenth century is worth remarking upon. To name just a couple more instances of it: George Eliot makes Mary Garth an author of a children's edition of the *Lives* at the end of *Middlemarch,* and Mary Shelley's monster looks to Plutarch for his moral and historical education in *Frankenstein* (1818).

73. Dallas, *The Gay Science,* II: 301. What Dallas describes resembles the "butterfly effect" of modern chaos theory.

74. Dallas, *The Gay Science,* II: 274–75.

75. See Walter Bagehot, *Physics and Politics,* ed. and intro. Roger Kimball (Chicago: Ivan R. Dee, 1999), esp. 75, 175.

76. Walter Bagehot, *The English Constitution,* intro. R. H. S. Crossman (Ithaca: Cornell University Press, 1966), II: 82, 86.

77. Clough, "Sixth Letter to Parapedimus," in *Selected Prose Works of Arthur Hugh Clough,* ed. Buckner B. Trawick (University: University of Alabama Press, 1964), 223–24.

78. Carlyle, "Characteristics," in *Critical and Miscellaneous Essays,* 374; original emphasis.

79. H. Sidgwick, review of Clough, *The Westminster Review* 92: 382–83; in *The Critical Heritage,* ed. Thorpe, 287.

80. See the introduction to Isobel Armstrong, *Victorian Scrutinies: Reviews of Poetry, 1830–1870* (London: Athlone Press, 1972), esp. 38–42. This debate also relates to the phenomenon of closet drama addressed in chapter 1.

81. W. C. Roscoe, review of Arnold's *The Strayed Reveller and Other Poems* (1849*)*, *Empedocles on Etna and Other Poems* (1852), and *Poems* (1853), and Alexander Smith's *Poems* (1853), *Prospective Review* X (February 1854): 111–12; rpt. in Isobel Armstrong, *Victorian Scrutinies,* 195.

82. [C. Edmunds], review of Browning's *Poems* (1849) and *Sordello* (1840), in *The Eclectic Review* 26 (August 1849): 211; quoted in Armstrong, *Victorian Scrutinies,* 42.

83. [Richard Simpson], review of Robert Browning's *The Ring and the Book, North British Review* 51 (October 1869): 112; rpt. in Armstrong, *Victorian Scrutinies,* 274.

84. See Isobel Armstrong, *Victorian Scrutinies,* 53–55. The debate about spasmodic poetry in the 1850s helped set the stage for this shift in attitude.

85. [William Johnson Fox], review of Tennyson's *Poems, Chiefly Lyrical, Westminster Review* 14 (January 1831): 213–14; rpt. in Armstrong, *Victorian Scrutinies,* 74–75.

86. Fox, review of Tennyson, 213; in Armstrong, *Victorian Scrutinies,* 74.

87. Ibid., 221; in Armstrong, *Victorian Scrutinies,* 81.

88. Charles Peter Chretien, review of *The Princess, Christian Remembrancer* 17 (April 1849): 393, 388; in Armstrong, *Victorian Scutinies,* 208.

89. Unsigned review of Arnold's *Poems* (1853) and *Poems, Second Series, The Eclectic Review* n.s. 9 (March 1855): 279. Quoted in Weinstein, *William Edmonstoune Aytoun and the Spasmodic Controversy,* 156.

90. George Eliot, *Felix Holt, the Radical,* ed. and intro. Fred C. Thomson (Oxford: Oxford University Press, 1988), 388. Henry James, Preface to *The Princess Casamassima,* in *The Art of the Novel,* intro. Richard P. Blackmur (New York: Charles Scribner's Sons, 1962), 72.

91. J. F. Waller, signed Anthony Poplar, "Midsummer Muses," review of Matthew Arnold, Gerald Massey, and others, *Dublin University Magazine* (June 1854): 737; quoted in Armstrong, *Victorian Scrutinies,* 44.

92. Clough, letter to Blanche, 31 Dec. 1851, Bodleian MS Eng. Lett. e. 77. Quoted in Chorley, *Arthur Hugh Clough,* 235.

93. Arnold, "Dover Beach," lines 29–30.

94. See Scott's notes to his edition of *Amours de Voyage,* 33.

95. The notes have been very usefully collated by Paul Scott into Appendix 3 (81–82) of his edition of *Amours de Voyage;* I quote from this appendix.

96. I quote from the "1849 (Roma) notebook" version in Clough, *The Poems,* ed. Mulhauser, 673, which includes alternate material not in the revised version of the poem printed in Phelan. Further quotations are from *The Poems,* ed. Mulhauser, 195–98.

97. See cancelled passage at lines 183–86, in the textual notes to *Amours de Voyage,* ed. Scott, 42.

98. See notes to *Amours,* ed. Scott, 81.

99. Nightingale, *Cassandra,* 217; original emphasis. In another example of the contemporary discussion concerning the distinction between individual and collective action, she continued by observing, "and is it a wonder that all individual life is extinguished?"

100. See the textual notes to *Amours de Voyage,* ed. Scott, 42. Parenthetical lines omitted.

101. Carlyle, "The Hero as Man of Letters," in *Heroes and Hero-Worship* (1840), volume 12 of *The Library Edition* (London: Chapman and Hall, 1869), 206.

102. See the notes to Scott's edition of *Amours de Voyage,* 60.

103. James Buzard, *The Beaten Track: European Tourism, Literature, and the Ways to Culture, 1800–1918* (Oxford: The Clarendon Press, 1993), 90.

104. Goethe's *Roman Elegies,* his sequence of poems relating a happy love affair with Rome—and also with a lovely Roman prostitute—are behind this aspect of *Amours* (see John Goode, "*Amours de Voyage:* The Aqueous Poem," in *The Major Victorian Poets: Reconsiderations,* ed. Isobel Armstrong [London: Routledge and Kegan Paul, 1969], 285–86). Goethe finds himself completely at home in the city; he puns on the German word for wonder or inspiration to suggest a total possession by and of his surroundings—"Froh empfind ich mich nun auf klassischen Boden begeistert"—as he taps the meter of his poetry onto the body of his beloved (my own translation: "Joyful, I now find myself inspirited on classical ground"). In contrast, Claude experiences radical alienation in Rome, fueling his desire for someone to "Utter . . . the word that shall reconcile Ancient and Modern!" (I.x.200). See Johann Wolfgang Goethe, *Römische Elegien* (v.1), in *Gedichte 1,* vol. 1 of *Goethe's Werke,* 12 vols., ed. Jochen Golz (Leipzig: Aufbau-Verlag Berlin und Weimar, 1981).

105. See A. H. Clough, letter to his mother, 28 May 1849, in *Correspondence,* I: 257.

106. See also Isobel Armstrong's account of this incident: "Despite the comedy the 'event' is sickening in its confusion, ambiguity, and brutality, not the least because it undermines the idea of coherent action altogether" (*Victorian Poetry,* 200).

107. Eliot, *Middlemarch,* 180.

108. Shakespeare, *Julius Caesar,* IV.iii.218–19.

109. Lord Byron, *Don Juan,* ed. T. G. Steffan, E. Steffan, and W. W. Pratt (London: Penguin Classics, 1986), VI.2.1–2.

110. Clough, letter to A. P. Stanley, 19 May 1848, in *Correspondence,* I: 207.

111. John Addington Symonds, "Arthur Hugh Clough," *Fortnightly Review* 10 (1 December 1868): 604; rpt. in *The Critical Heritage,* ed. Thorpe, 234–35.

112. See Caserio, *Plot, Story, and the Novel,* 92–132. Put simply, for Dickens, belief in "Providence" supports a faith in one's "own efforts," as Jarndyce's advice to Richard Carstone (used as an epigraph to this chapter) suggests. Still, as always with Dickens, the author's proclaimed faith in deeds is countered by an awareness of the problem of action in the period, as Carstone's all too apparent inability to do much of anything shows. See Charles Dickens, *Bleak House,* ed. Nicola Bradbury (London: Penguin, 1996), 213.

113. John Forster, *The Life of Charles Dickens,* 2 vols. (London: J. M. Dent and Sons, 1927), II: 182.

114. Shakespeare, *Hamlet,* III.i.77–79, 87.

115. For more on Hamlet's role in nineteenth-century literature, see Alexander Welsh, *Hamlet in His Modern Guises* (Princeton: Princeton University Press, 2001), esp. chapters 3 (on Goethe and Scott) and 4 (on Dickens).

116. Ralph Waldo Emerson, "Shakspeare; or, the Poet," in *Representative Men,* ed. and intro. Wallace E. Williams and Douglas Emory Wilson, vol. 4 of *The Collected Works of Ralph Waldo Emerson* (Cambridge: Harvard University Press, 1987), 117. Clough much admired this volume of his friend's writing.

117. A. S. McDowell, "On Osborne's *Arthur Hugh Clough,*" *The Times Literary Supplement* (4 March 1920): 153; rpt. in *The Critical Heritage,* ed. Thorpe, 400.

118. Arnold's Preface refers to the "discouragement, of Hamlet and of Faust." Matthew Arnold, Preface to the first edition of *Poems* (1853), in *On the Classical Tradition,* 1. Clough also makes good use of the Faust legend, with its emphasis on the connection between sin and action ("Es irrt der Mensch solang er strebt" ["Man sins as long as he strives"])—it provides the framework for *Dipsychus and the Spirit.* See "Prolog im Himmel," in Goethe, *Faust: Erster Teil,* in *Die natürliche Tochter, Pandora, Faust,* vol. 4 of *Goethes Werke,* ed. Golz, 166. My own translation.

119. John Addington Symonds, "Arthur Hugh Clough," 604; rpt. in *The Critical Heritage,* ed. Thorpe, 235. Symonds's review of Clough's poem *Dipsychus* turns to Aristotle (from book 10 of the *Nicomachean Ethics*) as an authority on the Faustian connection between striving and sin: "Reflection, it was long ago said by the philosophers, belongs to God and to godlike men. But action is proper to mankind and to the mass of human beings. By cleaving to action we renounce our heavenly birthright of contemplation. Yet if we confine ourselves to reflection and aspiration, we separate ourselves from the mass of men. No one has yet solved the problem of acting without contracting some stain of earth" (*The Critical Heritage,* ed. Thorpe, 236–37).

120. [W. Y. Sellars], review of Clough's *Poems* (1862), *North British Review* 37 (November 1862): 341; rpt. in *The Critical Heritage,* ed. Thorpe, 192. This remark emphasizes the relationship of the poem to a realistic novel.

121. See Shakespeare, *Hamlet,* III.i.154.

122. See Shakespeare, *Hamlet,* II.ii.559–60.

123. Stopford A. Brook, "Arthur Hugh Clough," in *Four Poets: A Study of Clough, Arnold, Rossetti and Morris* (1908); rpt. in *The Critical Heritage,* ed. Thorpe, 373.

124. See headnote to *Maud,* in *Tennyson's Poetry,* 214. Tennyson's poem shares in both the tendency of *Amours* toward generic hybridity and its psychological insight. Both works can be thought of as case studies of the Hamletism of the times, and both were tainted by accusations of spasmody. Unlike Claude, though, the hero of *Maud* chooses to escape from his speculative nature by abrogating individuality in his embrace of the collective activity of the Crimean War:

> We have proved we have hearts in a cause, we are noble still,
> And myself have awakened, as it seems to a better mind;
> It is better to fight for the good than to rail at the ill;
> I have felt with my native land, I am one with my kind,
> I embrace the purpose of God, and the doom assigned. (III.5)

The horrifying conclusion to Tennyson's poem is as much a response to the crisis of action as was Clough's decision to help Florence Nightingale following her efforts to nurse soldiers in the Crimea. In fact, responses to the Crimean War often reflect the contemporary uneasiness about action.

125. See William Hazlitt, *Character of Shakespeare's Plays,* intro. Arthur Quiller-Couch (Oxford: Oxford University Press, 1952), xxvii.

126. Roscoe, review of Arnold and Smith, 112; rpt. in *The Critical Heritage,* ed. Thorpe, 195.

127. H. Sidgwick, review of Clough, 382; rpt. in *The Critical Heritage,* ed. Thorpe, 287.

128. Johann Wolfgang von Goethe, *Wilhelm Meister's Apprenticeship,* ed. and trans. Eric A. Blackall, with Victor Lange (Princeton: Princeton University Press, 1995), 5.7.185–86. Schopenhauer makes a related but broader point when he states that "The art [of the novel] lies in the setting of the inner life into the most violent motion with the smallest possible expenditure of outer life" (Arthur Schopenhauer, *Essays and Aphorisms,* sel. and trans. R. J. Hollingdale [London: Penguin, 1970], 165).

129. H. Sidgwick, review of Clough, 382; rpt. in *The Critical Heritage,* ed. Thorpe, 287.

130. Bagehot, *The English Constitution,* 108.

131. Walter Bagehot, "Mr. Clough's Poems," in *National Review* 15 (October 1862): 323; rpt. in *The Critical Heritage,* ed. Thorpe, 171.

132. Barbara Hardy, "Clough's Self-Consciousness," in *The Major Victorian Poets: Reconsiderations,* ed. Isobel Armstrong (London: Routledge and Kegan Paul, 1969), 261.

133. Robertson, *New Essays,* 306, 307; in *The Critical Heritage,* ed. Thorpe, 347.

134. Robertson, *New Essays,* 315, 317, 319; in *The Critical Heritage,* ed. Thorpe, 353–54, 355, 356.

Chapter Three

1. Wilkie Collins, Preface to the 1861 edition of *The Woman in White,* in *The Woman in White,* ed. and intro. Harvey Peter Sucksmith (London: Oxford University Press, 1975), xxxviii.

2. Wilkie Collins, Preface to *The Moonstone,* in *The Moonstone,* ed. and intro. Sandra Kemp (London: Penguin, 1998), 3. In part, the growing vogue for detective fiction, beginning in the latter half of the nineteenth century, can be attributed to the sense of "having lost the clue" that I discussed in reference to Clough in the previous chapter and that surfaces frequently in Eliot's heroines. Detective stories are all about finding clues that lead to answers. They narrate the discovery of an obscured plot. When the murderer or thief is revealed by the detective at the end of the tale, a world that appeared to be full of confusions and irrationalities is proven to be coherent and knowable. As Collins suggests, though, the recovery of plot in *The Moonstone* turns out to be orthogonal to the real knowledge that the novel espouses: a knowledge of Rachel's character. As Lady Verinder tells Sergeant Cuff, "My knowledge of her [Rachel's] character dates from the beginning of her life. . . . I am sure, beforehand, that (with all your experience) the circumstances have fatally misled you in this case" (171). If *The Moonstone* really is the first detective novel, it contains within it a startling ambivalence about the priorities the genre would seem to embrace.

3. [William Henry Smith], "Mr. Thomas Trollope's Italian Novels," *Blackwood's Edinburgh Magazine* 43 (Jan. 1863): 92; quoted in Richard Stang, *The Theory of the Novel in England, 1850–1870* (New York: Columbia University Press, 1959), 130.

4. "W. M. Thackeray and Arthur Pendennis, Esquires," unsigned review, *Fraser's Magazine* 43 (Jan. 1851): 88; quoted in Stang, *The Theory of the Novel,* 129.

5. [R. H. Hutton], review of *North and South, National Review* 6 (Oct. 1855): 336–37.

6. See also Robert Caserio's observation that in "some of the most prestigious novelistic fiction of the past and the present centuries, the imitation of actuality becomes opposed to the imitation of acts." Caserio, *Plot, Story, and the Novel,* xiii.

7. Ibid., 105. Caserio's excellent analysis has been extremely helpful to me. Oddly enough, though, especially given his concentration on *Felix Holt* and *Daniel Deronda,* he does not directly address the political implications of Eliot's treatment of action. Another related discussion comes in John Kucich's *Repression in Victorian Fiction: Charlotte Brontë, George Eliot, and Charles Dickens* (Berkeley: University of California Press, 1987). Kucich looks at what he calls "a general Victorian tendency to make matters of intense feeling—primarily, but not exclusively, sexual feeling—matters of secrecy and self-reflexiveness, and to withhold them from speech and action" (3). Kucich's "repression," which positively heightens "a sense of the self's importance," can be usefully compared to my concept of "inaction." Notably for my argument in what follows, Kucich sees the role of repression in *Daniel Deronda* to be a particularly vexed one (177).

8. See George F. Ford, *Dickens and His Readers: Aspects of Novel Criticism since 1836* (Princeton: Princeton University Press, 1955), 182.

9. George Eliot, *Felix Holt, the Radical,* ed. and intro. Fred C. Thomson

(Oxford: Oxford University Press, 1988), 388. Hereafter, references to this text will be internally documented by FH followed by the page number. For discussions of *Felix Holt* and political activism, see: Arnold Kettle, "Felix Holt the Radical," in *Critical Essays on George Eliot,* ed. Barbara Hardy (London: Routledge and Kegan Paul, 1970), 99–115; William Myers, "George Eliot: Politics and Personality," in *Literature and Politics in the Nineteenth Century,* ed. and intro. John Lucas (London: Methuen, 1971), 105–30; Linda Bamber, "Self-Defeating Politics in George Eliot's *Felix Holt,*" *Victorian Studies* 18 (June 1975): 419–35; Ruth Bernard Yeazell, "Why Political Novels Have Heroines: *Sybil, Mary Barton,* and *Felix Holt,*" *Novel* 18 (Winter 1985): 126–44; Rosemarie Bodenheimer, *The Politics of Story in Victorian Social Fiction* (Ithaca: Cornell University Press, 1988). Contemporary critics also noticed the misleading title. E. S. Dallas remarked that it "is not, as its title would lead one to suppose, a political novel, though it necessarily touches on politics. . . . [B]ut the purpose of the author is not, as is usual in a political novel, to advocate or to render palatable any constitutional doctrines— it is rather to exhibit the characters of men as they conduct themselves in a political struggle." [E. S. Dallas], review of *Felix Holt, The Times* (26 June 1866), 6; rpt. in *George Eliot: The Critical Heritage,* ed. David Carroll (London: Routledge and Kegan Paul, 1971), 265. And Henry James somewhat scathingly noted of Felix, "We find him a Radical and leave him what?—only 'utterly married'; which is all very well in its place, but which by itself makes no conclusion." [Henry James], review of *Felix Holt, Nation* 3 (16 August 1866): 127–28; rpt. in *The Critical Heritage,* ed. Carroll, 273.

　10.　Aristotle, *Nicomachean Ethics,* 953 (book II, chapter 1, 1103b).

　11.　*George Eliot's Life, As Related in Her Letters and Journals,* 3 vols., ed. J. W. Cross (Boston: Dana Estes and Company, n.d.; republished Grosse Pointe, Michigan: The Scholarly Press, 1968), III: 170. Hereafter Cross.

　12.　George Eliot, *Daniel Deronda,* ed. and intro. Graham Handley (Oxford: Oxford University Press, 1988), 407. Hereafter internally documented by DD followed by the page number.

　13.　Henry James, "Daniel Deronda: A Conversation," *Atlantic Monthly* 38 (December 1876): 684; rpt. in *Henry James: Literary Criticism,* 2 vols., ed. Leon Edel and Mark Wilson, *Volume 1: Essays, American and English Writers* (New York: Library of America, 1984), 975. Hereafter *Literary Criticism.*

　14.　See Caserio, *Plot, Story, and the Novel,* 91–132.

　15.　V. S. Pritchett, "George Eliot," in *Discussions of George Eliot,* ed. and intro. Richard Stang (Boston: D. C. Heath and Co., 1960), 60.

　16.　Aristotle, *Nicomachean Ethics,* 1106 (book X, chapter 8, 1178b).

　17.　George Eliot, *Middlemarch,* ed. David Carroll, intro. Felicia Bonaparte (Oxford: Oxford University Press, 1998), 34. Hereafter internally documented as M, followed by the page number.

　18.　Arendt, *The Human Condition,* 184.

　19.　George Eliot, "Address to Working Men, by Felix Holt," in *George Eliot, Selected Critical Writings,* ed. Rosemary Ashton (Oxford: Oxford University Press, 1992), 341.

　20.　Arendt, *The Human Condition,* 185.

　21.　George Eliot, *Adam Bede,* ed. and intro. Valentine Cunningham

(Oxford: Oxford University Press, 1996), 313. Hereafter internally documented as AB followed by the page number.

22. George Eliot, *Romola,* ed. and intro. Andrew Brown (Oxford: Oxford University Press, 1994), 97, hereafter internally documented as R, followed by the page number. *Romola* was first published in 1862–63.

23. Eliot, letter to Charles Bray, 5 July 1859, in *The George Eliot Letters,* 9 vols., ed. Gordon S. Haight (New Haven: Yale University Press, 1954–78), III: 111. Hereafter *Letters.*

24. George Eliot, "The Progress of the Intellect," in *Selected Critical Writings,* ed. Ashton, 21.

25. John Stuart Mill, *Autobiography,* ed. and intro. John M. Robson (London: Penguin, 1989), 135. George Eliot read the *Autobiography* in November 1873. For a close analysis of Eliot's relation to determinism, including her relationship to Mill, see George Levine's excellent essay, "Determinism and Responsibility in the Works of George Eliot," *PMLA* 77 (June 1962): 268–79.

26. Eliot, letter to Mrs. Ponsonby, 19 August 1875, in Cross, III: 216; in *Letters,* VI: 166.

27. Eliot, letter to Mrs. Ponsonby, 10 December 1874, in *Letters,* VI: 98. See also the letter to Mrs. Stuart, in which she argued with W. H. Mallock's statement that "there is nothing in the constitution of things to produce, to favour, or to demand a course of action called right." Again, Eliot resorted to what can be called her "argument from hygenic habits": she advised her friend to "put the words 'cleanliness' and 'uncleanliness' for 'virtue' and 'vice,' and consider how fully you have come not only to regard cleanliness as a duty, but to shudder at uncleanliness" (Eliot, letter to Mrs. Stuart, 5 February 1877, in *Letters,* VI: 339).

28. Eliot, letter to Mrs. Houghton, 9 February 1850, in Cross, I: 185; in *Letters,* I: 328.

29. Thomas Carlyle, *Past and Present,* volume 13 of *The Library Edition* (London: Chapman and Hall, 1870), 158.

30. John Stuart Mill, *A System of Logic: Ratiocinative and Inductive,* 2 vols. (London: Longman's, Green, and Company, 1879), II: 429.

31. See Gordon Haight, *George Eliot: A Biography* (London: Penguin, 1986), 464.

32. G. W. F. Hegel, *Introduction to the Philosophy of History, with an Appendix from The Philosophy of Right,* trans. and intro. Leo Rauch (Indianapolis: Hackett Publishing Company, 1988), 78.

33. William Godwin, *An Enquiry Concerning Political Justice,* ed. and intro. Isaac Kramnick (New York: Penguin, 1985), 125.

34. Levine, "Determinism," 271. The concept of gradualism also stands behind Darwin's evolutionary theory: "As natural selection acts solely by accumulating slight, successive, favorable variations, it can produce no great or sudden modification; it can act only by very short and slow steps." Charles Darwin, *On the Origin of Species,* "Recapitulation," in *The Origin of Species and The Descent of Man* (New York: Modern Library, 1936), 361. For Eliot's debt to Darwin, see Gillian Beer, *Darwin's Plots: Evolutionary Narrative in Darwin, George Eliot and Nineteenth-Century Fiction* (London: Ark, 1985).

35. George Eliot, "The *Antigone* and Its Moral," in *Selected Critical Works,* ed. Ashton, 246.

36. Eliot, letter to John Blackwood, 27 April 1866, in *Letters,* IV: 247–48.

37. Rosemarie Bodenheimer, *The Real Life of Mary Ann Evans: George Eliot, Her Letters and Fiction* (Ithaca: Cornell University Press, 1994), 111, 87.

38. Eliot, letter to Mrs. Pears, 31 March 1842, in Cross, I: 83; in *Letters,* I: 133.

39. Quoted in Oscar Browning, *Life of George Eliot* (London: Walter Scott, Limited, 1892), 119.

40. George Eliot, *The Mill on the Floss,* ed. Gordon S. Haight, intro. Dinah Birch (Oxford: Oxford University Press, 1996), 151. Hereafter internally documented by MF followed by the page number. The book was first published in 1860.

41. [W. H. Mallock], review *of Impressions of Theophrastus Such, Edinburgh Review* 105 (October 1879): 563; rpt. in *The Critical Heritage,* ed. Carroll, 454. The phrase could apply equally well to Clough.

42. Cross, I: 247.

43. Eliot, letter to Mrs. Bray, 4 September 1855, in Cross, I: 246; in *Letters,* II: 213.

44. Henry James, "The Life of George Eliot," *Atlantic Monthly* 55 (May 1885): 671; rpt. in Henry James, *Literary Criticism,* 999–1000.

45. Henry James, "The Life of George Eliot," 671. In part, James is responding here to the relative lack of action in Eliot's writings, but he is also hinting at a related issue: her tendency to interrupt her tales with moralizing commentary, like those "wise, witty and tender sayings" collected by Alexander Main in 1872. Eliot's complicated relationship to maxims, parables, and proverbs—her distrust of their generalizing tendencies but appreciation for their ability to foster the work of sympathy by drawing connections between different instances of similar phenomena—can be compared to her complicated relationship to action. As Walter Benjamin has written, "A proverb . . . is a ruin which stands on the site of an old story and in which a moral twines about a happening like ivy around a wall." In other words, a proverb is a story from which the action has been obscured by time. Walter Benjamin, *Illuminations,* ed. and intro Hannah Arendt, trans. Harry Zohn (New York: Schocken Books, 1969), 108. For Eliot and epigrams, maxims, etc., see also Leah Price, "George Eliot and the Production of Consumers," *Novel: A Forum on Fiction* 30.2 (Winter 1997): 145–69.

46. Eliot, letter to John Chapman, 15 October 1854, in *Letters,* IV: 124–25.

47. Eliot, letter to Sara Hennell, 5 June 1857, in *Letters,* II: 341–42.

48. Eliot, letter to Durade, 18 October 1859, in *Letters,* III: 186.

49. For Eliot on vocation, see Alan Mintz, *George Eliot and the Novel of Vocation* (Cambridge: Harvard University Press, 1981).

50. Walter E. Houghton, *The Victorian Frame of Mind, 1830–1870* (New Haven: Yale University Press for Wellesley College, 1957), 242.

51. Carlyle, *Past and Present,* 192 (III.iv, "Happy"), 308 (IV.i, "Aristocracies").

52. Arendt, *The Human Condition,* 7, 143–44.

53. Eliot, letter to Mrs. Ponsonby, 10 December 1874, in *Letters,* VI: 99.

54. George Eliot, "Address to the Working Men, by Felix Holt," in *Selected Critical Writings,* ed. Ashton, 347.

55. Arendt, *The Human Condition*, 233, 190.

56. George Eliot, "Address to the Working Men, by Felix Holt," in *Selected Critical Writings*, ed. Ashton, 349.

57. Eliot, letter to Mrs. Congreve, 28 November 1863, in *Letters*, IV: 115

58. Eliot, letter to Charles Bray, 5 July 1859, in *Letters*, III: 111.

59. Wordsworth's influence on Eliot has been thoroughly documented and researched: Cross's *Life* already remarks on the importance of the poet to Eliot's development (I: 45). One recent contribution to the discussion comes in Stephen Gill's *Wordsworth and the Victorians* (Oxford: The Clarendon Press, 1998).

60. William Wordsworth, Preface to *Lyrical Ballads* (1800), in *Prose*, I: 126.

61. Percy Byshe Shelley, *A Defense of Poetry*, in *Shelley's Poetry and Prose*, ed. Donald S. Reiman and Sharon B. Powers (New York: W. W. Norton and Co., 1977), 487, 508.

62. Eliot, letter to Charles Bray, 15 November 1857, in *Letters*, II: 403.

63. Keats, letter to Richard Woodhouse, 27 October 1818, in *Letters of John Keats*, sel. and ed. Robert Gittings (Oxford: Oxford University Press, 1992), 157.

64. W. H. Mallock, review of *Impressions of Theophrastus Such*, 560; in *The Critical Heritage*, ed. Carroll, 451. Note again the reference to *Hamlet* in the context of a lack of outer action and its relationship to the debate about genre.

65. [E. S. Dallas], review of *Felix Holt*, *The Times* (26 June 1866), 6; rpt. in *The Critical Heritage*, ed. Carroll, 263–64.

66. Quoted in Browning, *Life*, 164.

67. Eliot, letter to Mrs. Bray, 4 December 1863, in Cross, II: 292; in *Letters*, IV: 120.

68. Bodenheimer, *The Politics of Story*, 212.

69. Dallas, *The Gay Science*, II: 186, 251. See also Nancy Armstrong, *Desire and Domestic Fiction: A Political History of the Novel* and chapter 1 n. 84.

70. Dallas, *The Gay Science*, II: 295.

71. Ibid., 296–97. Consider also George Meredith's version of this idea, as stated by the heroine of *Diana of the Crossways* (1885): "We women are the verbs passive of the alliance, we have to learn, and if we take to activity, with the best intentions, we conjugate a frightful disturbance. We are to run on lines, like the steam-trains, or we come to no station, dash to fragments. I have the misfortune to know I was born an active. I take my chance." Diana Warwick bears more than a passing resemblance to both Gwendolen Harleth and Isabel Archer. George Meredith, *Diana of the Crossways* (New York: The Modern Library, 1931), 68–69.

72. See Eliot, letter to Major Blackwood, 27 May 1860, in *Letters*, III: 299.

73. Sarah Stickney Ellis, *The Women of England, Their Social Duties, and Domestic Habits*, 2 vols. (Philadelphia: A. L. Carey and A. Hart, n.d.), I: 45, 49. Original emphasis.

74. Eliot, letter to John Morley, 14 May 1867, in *Letters*, IV: 364.

75. Dinah Craik, "Something To Do," in *A Woman's Thoughts about Women* (Philadelphia: T. B. Peterson and Bros., n.d.), 20.

76. George Eliot, *Impressions of Theophrastus Such*, ed. Nancy Henry (Iowa City: University of Iowa Press, 1994), 130–31.

77. Eliot, *Impressions*, 131.

78. This passage represents but one of several places in the novel where Eliot

uses evolutionary language of Rosamond. She often appears as a kind of paragon of Darwinian fitness, as her survival at the end of the novel suggests. For example, Lydgate twice refers to her as belonging to a "different species" with "opposing interests" to his (M 587, 657). Eliot uses Rosamond to suggest a subtle critique of the moral blankness of the Darwinian world.

79. Cross, III: 344.

80. [R. H. Hutton], "George Eliot's Moral Anatomy," review of book VI of *Middlemarch, Spectator* 45 (5 October 1872): 1273; rpt. in *The Critical Heritage,* ed. Carroll, 303.

81. For Henry James, the "question" of Gwendolen is whether "the Dorothea element or the Rosamond element is to prevail" in her. [Henry James], review of *Daniel Deronda, The Nation* 23 (24 February 1876): 131; rpt. in James, *Literary Criticism,* 974.

82. I put *political* in scare quotes because I am arguing that there is something deeply antiactivist and therefore antipolitical in Eliot's stance. But in all these novels, Eliot tests the possibility for political action.

83. See Wordsworth, Preface to *Lyrical Ballads* (1800), in *Prose,* I: 128, and "The Ruined Cottage," MS. B, in *The Ruined Cottage and The Pedlar,* ed. James Butler, 58. *Silas Marner* (1861), with its unusually allegorical style and format (most obviously represented by the replacement of Silas's gold with Effie's golden locks) should be distinguished from Eliot's longer works in its attitudes toward plot and character. In this novella, as in a fable, Eliot's plot neatly portions out success and failure according to the merits. While Godfrey Cass finds, like most of Eliot's characters, that the past comes back to haunt him, Silas himself is allowed to begin anew in Raveloe after his false conviction for theft had driven him from the city. Although *Silas Marner* allows plot to succeed in a way that makes it anomalous, it does demonstrate the extraordinary Wordsworthian influence—indicated in part by Eliot's use of a quotation from Wordsworth's "Michael" as its epigraph—that is particularly apparent in her earlier works. In fact, the story seems to revise (and restore) "The Ruined Cottage."

84. Note Eliot's use of the metaphor that so appealed to Clough and Arnold.

85. Dorothea's "unhistoric acts" are obviously related to Wordsworth's "little, nameless, unremembered acts / Of kindness and of love" that form "that best portion of a good man's life" in "Tintern Abbey" (lines 34–36).

86. As does the proliferation of questions in the text, the first of which forms the opening sentence to the novel. As Gillian Beer has argued, "the interrogative is the form of speech which most invokes the future," the realm of possibility so necessary to a conception of action (*Darwin's Plots,* 187).

87. Arendt, *The Human Condition,* 9.

88. R. E. Francillon first employs this distinction in 1876. He calls the novel "George Eliot's first Romance," and recognizes Mirah as "heroine of the Romance as Gwendolen is of the reality," although the distinction breaks down somewhat in his analysis of Gwendolen, whom he also compares to the romance heroine Undine. R. E. Francillon, "George Eliot's First Romance," review of *Daniel Deronda, Gentleman's Magazine* 17 (October 1876): 424, 414; rpt. in *The Critical Heritage,* ed. Carroll, 382, 395, 386.

89. James, "*Daniel Deronda:* A Conversation," 684; in *Literary Criticism,* 974.

90. Eliot recounts the germination of her poem, on seeing an annunciation by Titian, in her "Notes to *The Spanish Gypsy*," which have been reprinted in full in Browning's *Life*. I quote from Browning, 101. They are also reprinted in Cross, III: 31–37.

91. George Eliot, *The Spanish Gypsy*, in *The Complete Poems of George Eliot* (New York: Frederick A. Stokes Co., n.d.), 109. Hereafter SG, internally documented.

92. Eliot, "Notes on *The Spanish Gypsy*," in Browning, *Life*, 104.

93. Ibid.

94. Ibid., 105. She is probably referring most specifically to "The Human Spirits Saw I On a Day," of which the most crucial line is "I know not, I will do my duty, said the last" (line 25).

95. Eliot, "Notes to *The Spanish Gypsy*," in Browning, *Life*, 106.

96. See Eliot's journal entry of 6 September 1864 (in Cross, II: 305). But it is "eminently suited for an opera," according to Lewes, who wrote that he hoped it would eventually be made to "take that shape." George Henry Lewes, letter to John Blackwood, 23 June 1868, in *Letters*, IV: 453.

97. James, "*Daniel Deronda*: A Conversation," 690; in *Literary Criticism*, 985; Blackwood, letter to Eliot, 10 November 1875, in *Letters*, VI: 182.

98. Auguste Comte, *Introduction to Positive Philosophy*, ed., trans., and intro. Frederick Ferré (Indianapolis: Bobbs-Merrill, 1970), 19. In a letter to Mrs. Congreve of 16 December 1868, Eliot referred to *The Spanish Gypsy* as a "mass of Positivism." In *Letters*, IV: 496; in Cross, III: 54.

99. Eliot, letter to John Blackwood, 4 October 1872, in *Letters*, V: 314.

100. These include the Romantic Pantisocratics, Clough, and his hero Philip Hewson of *The Bothie*. The colonies frequently provide characters in Victorian literature with an escape from their pasts. Before writing *Daniel Deronda*, Eliot had herself used the idea of a fresh start on virgin territory: at the end of *Adam Bede*, Arthur runs away to France while Hetty avoids death by being sent to one of the penal colonies. Nevertheless, Eliot shows her awareness of the difficulties of building a "second life" in *Middlemarch* when Bustrode discovers (through Raffles's return from America) that "a man's past is not simply a dead history . . . : it is a still quivering part of himself" (M 605).

101. Early on, there was actually some talk (probably initiated by Lewes) of writing *Daniel Deronda* as a dramatic piece. See Haight, *Biography*, 471–72.

102. James, "*Daniel Deronda*: A Conversation," 686; in *Literary Criticism*, 978.

103. Suicide represents both the cessation of all action and the culmination of it. I will return to the theme of suicide in chapter 4.

104. Barbara Leigh Smith Bodichon, *Reasons for the Enfranchisement of Women* (1866); rpt. in *Victorian Prose: An Anthology*, ed. Rosemary J. Mundhenk and LuAnn McCracken Fletcher (New York: Columbia University Press, 1999), 379. An activist in women's causes, philanthopist, landscape painter, and cofounder of Girton College, Cambridge, Bodichon herself is notable for having come up with a good solution to the problem she described.

105. Her name represents another take on the active woman as "archer."

106. Eliot's own attitude toward nursing is revealing. In January 1843 she

wrote to a friend: "I think it almost enviable as far as one's self is concerned not of course when the sufferer is remembered, to have the care of a sickroom, with its twilight and tiptoe stillness and helpful activity" (Eliot, letter to Sara Hennell, 7 January 1843, in *Letters,* I: 156). Nursing is perhaps the apotheosis of the kind of activity Eliot favors—it is both sympathetic and habitual—but her awareness of the degree to which it depends on the suffering of others seems to trouble her. For more on Eliot's attitude toward nursing, see also Catherine Judd, "Nursing and Female Heroics: George Eliot and Florence Nightingale (1835–1837)," in *Bedside Seductions: Nursing and the Victorian Imagination, 1830–1880* (New York: St. Martin's Press, 1998), 123–52. Judd tells how disappointed Nightingale was by Dorothea's "home epic" in *Middlemarch;* Eliot should have shown a more successful outcome for youthful idealism, one more clearly grounded in socially useful "work" (124). Judd sets Nightingale's sense of the nurse as a symbol of activity against Eliot's sense of her as the embodiment of "the patience and self-sacrifice necessary for ideal social change" (151). In a footnote, she even speculates that Florence and her sister Parthenope may have been the models for Dorothea and Celia Brooke (182).

107. Beer, *Darwin's Plots,* 234.

108. This phrase also contains an allusion to Carlyle's "Donothingism," or laissez-faire, which I discussed in reference to Clough. Eliot's casual use of the term hints at how Gwendolen's crisis of action reflects contemporary cultural forces.

109. Eliot actually suggests a comparison between Gwendolen's and Hamlet's crimes: "There is a way of looking at our daily life as an escape, and taking the quiet return of morn and evening . . . as a salvation that reconciles us to hardship. Those who have a self-knowledge prompting such self-accusation as Hamlet's can understand this habitual feeling of rescue" (DD 682). Hamlet's self-accusation ("O what a rogue and peasant slave am I!" [II.ii.550 ff.]) is, of course, prompted by his inaction, linking it to Gwendolen's more complicated crime of inaction, the "murder" of Grandcourt. Moreover, for both, inaction creates self-knowledge. Here, as elsewhere in Eliot, habit serves as a balm to ease the frustrations inherent in action.

110. Shifra Hochberg, "*Daniel Deronda* and Wordsworth's *The White Doe of Rylstone,*" *English Language Notes* 31 (March 1994): 46.

111. James, "*Daniel Deronda:* A Conversation," 687–88; in *Literary Criticism,* 981.

112. The idea of a "banner" once again surfaces here in the context of the crisis of action, as it did in the writings of Wordsworth and Carlyle.

113. Alexander Welsh helpfully uses the term "ideology" to describe the nature of Daniel's mission. But there is one place in his account on which I would put a slightly different emphasis: his assertion that the ideas of the mission are "explicit." Although it is true, as Welsh notes, that the ideas are written down by Mordecai, I think that Eliot strives to preserve some of their vagueness precisely because she is much more interested in the general concept of ideology than in the specific ideology of Zionism. See Alexander Welsh, *George Eliot and Blackmail* (Cambridge: Harvard University Press, 1985), 314.

114. Graham Martin, "Daniel Deronda: George Eliot and Political Change," in *Critical Essays on George Eliot,* ed. Hardy, 149.

115. Benjamin Disraeli, *Tancred, or, The New Crusade* (London: Peter Davies, 1927), 496, 136.

116. Disraeli, *Tancred*, 473, 499–500. The novel closes abruptly when Tancred's parents' arrival in Jerusalem is announced just after Eva has fainted on hearing his declaration.

117. Robert Preyer—like Alexander Welsh, a critic who sees *Daniel Deronda* as Eliot's effort at redefining and so revitalizing political activism—argues that the novel is her attempt to show, in what could be called proto-Marcusean fashion, how ideas presented in the form of visions can help "us to break free from the tyranny of habitual responses" and effect significant change. See "Beyond the Liberal Imagination: Vision and Unreality in *Daniel Deronda*," *Victorian Studies* 4 (September 1960): 48.

118. Shelley, *Prometheus Unbound*, II.iii.36–42, in *Shelley's Poetry and Prose,* ed. Reiman and Powers, 169.

119. Immanuel Kant, *Critique of Judgement* (New York: Hafner Press, 1951), 150ff.

120. James, "*Daniel Deronda*: A Conversation," 686; in *Literary Criticism,* 981.

121. The novel was also accused of wanting in plot, although Richardson defended the slow progress of the story by arguing it was necessary to allow for development of character: "The letters and conversations, where the story makes the slowest progress, are presumed to be *characteristic.*" Samuel Richardson, *Clarissa,* ed. and intro. Angus Ross (London: Penguin, 1985), 1499, 425.

122. Jay Clayton, *Romantic Vision and the Novel* (New York: Cambridge University Press, 1987), 32.

123. R. E. Francillon, review of *Daniel Deronda,* 420; in *Critical Heritage,* 391.

124. Caserio, *Plot, Story, and the Novel,* 129.

125. Eliot, letter to Sara Hennell, 26 December 1862, in *Letters,* IV: 71.

126. [R. R. Bowker], review of *Daniel Deronda, International Review* iv (January 1877), 70; rpt. in *The Critical Heritage,* ed. Carroll, 435.

127. Dorrit Cohn, *Transparent Minds: Narrative Modes for Presenting Consciousness in Fiction* (Princeton: Princeton University Press, 1978), 5.

128. M. M. Bakhtin, *The Dialogic Imagination,* ed. Michaeld Holquist, trans. Caryl Emerson and Michael Holquist (Austin: University of Texas Press, 1981), 37.

129. James, "*Daniel Deronda*: A Conversation," 692; in *Literary Criticism,* 990.

130. See Hannah Arendt, *Thinking,* in *The Life of the Mind* (San Diego: Harcourt Brace Jovanovich, 1978), 190–93.

131. See also David Bromwich's comments on this passage: "The possibility that Wordsworth's dread may have sprung from an obscure self-knowledge, or from something about his past that he now wished forgotten or undone, is suggested by the hope earlier in the poem that, in judging him now, we will hold in mind 'that best portion of a good man's life; / His little nameless unremembered acts / Of kindness and of love'" (*Disowned By Memory,* 72).

132. Eliot, letter to John Blackwood, 18 February 1857, in *Letters,* II: 299.

133. James, *"Daniel Deronda:* A Conversation," 692; in *Literary Criticism,* 998–99.

134. James mentions Gwendolen (in a list of Eliot's heroines) in his Preface to *The Portrait of a Lady* (in Henry James, *The Art of the Novel,* intro. Richard P. Blackmur [New York: Charles Scribner's Sons, 1962], 49). Many critics have also noted the obvious connection. See, for example, Richard Freadman, *Eliot, James and the Fictional Self: A Study in Character and Narration* (London: Macmillan, 1986), 62ff.

135. James, Preface to *The Portrait of a Lady,* in *The Art of the Novel,* 53.

CHAPTER FOUR

1. Henry James, "The Art of Fiction," in Henry James, *The Future of the Novel,* ed. Leon Edel (New York: Vintage, 1956), 15–16.

2. Henry James, letter to Mrs. Humphry Ward, 3 July 1888, in *The Letters of Henry James,* 4 vols., ed. Leon Edel (Cambridge: Harvard University Press, 1974–84), III: 235 (hereafter *HJL*). *Robert Elsmere,* the story of a young minister's crisis of doubt and subsequent work in London as a social reformer, reflects in part its author's desire to revise the public perception of men like Clough, to whom the novel makes several oblique and explicit references and who was a good friend of Ward's father and uncle. Mrs. Ward's novel argues that inner doubts need not hamper outward deeds. James's comments play down the social-activist tendencies of the book.

3. George Eliot, *Daniel Deronda,* 102–3.

4. See Leon Edel, *Henry James,* 5 vols. (Philadelphia: J. B. Lippincott, 1953–72), I: 175 (hereafter *Life*). Henry James, Preface to *Portrait of a Lady,* in Henry James, *The Art of the Novel,* intro. Richard P. Blackmur (New York: Charles Scribner's Sons, 1962), 47–48 (hereafter Blackmur).

5. Henry James, Preface to *Portrait of a Lady,* in Blackmur, 48

6. [W. C. Brownell], "James's *Portrait of a Lady,"* *Nation* 34 (2 February 1882): 102. Reprinted in *Henry James: The Contemporary Reviews,* ed. Kevin J. Hayes (Cambridge: Cambridge University Press, 1996), 146.

7. See also Dorothea Krook's account of F. R. Leavis's reading of James, which she sees as criticizing him for "an excess of 'doing' over what is actually 'done.'" Dorothea Krook, *The Ordeal of Consciousness in Henry James* (Cambridge: Cambridge University Press, 1962), 11; F. R. Leavis, *The Great Tradition* (New York: Doubleday, 1954), esp. 196.

8. Henry James, Preface to *Roderick Hudson,* in Blackmur, 8. See also James's letter to Henry Adams of 21 March 1914: "You see I still, in presence of life (or of what you deny to be such), have reactions—as many as possible—and the book I sent you [*Notes of a Son and Brother*] is a proof of them. It's I suppose, because I am that queer monster the artist, an obstinate finality, an inexhaustible sensibility. Hence the reactions—appearances, memories, many things go on playing upon it with consequences that I note and 'enjoy' (grim word!) noting. It all takes doing—and I *do.* I believe I shall do yet again—it is still an act of life" *(HJL* IV: 706). The "act of life," the "doing" that is writing, comes from a reaction to the world rather than an action in the world.

9. Henry James, Preface to *The Portrait of a Lady*, in Blackmur, 52, 53, 56. Emphasis in original.

10. George Eliot, *Daniel Deronda*, 382; *Middlemarch*, 27, 272.

11. Henry James, Preface to *The Portrait of a Lady*, in Blackmur, 55.

12. Yvor Winters, *In Defense of Reason* (London: Routledge, 1960), 308. Note how Winters suggests that (as in Eliot and Wordsworth) the internal process of "choice" stands at the center of James's sense of freedom of action. See also Richard Freadman's account, "Choice: 'Daniel Deronda' and 'The Portrait,'" in *Eliot, James and the Fictional Self: A Study in Character and Narration* (London: Macmillan, 1986), 87–122.

13. W. D. Howells, "Henry James, Jr.," *Century Illustrated Monthly Magazine* 3 (November 1882): 28. Reprinted in *Henry James: The Critical Heritage*, ed. Roger Gard (London: Routledge and Kegan Paul, 1968), 133–34.

14. Unsigned review of American fiction, in *Quarterly Review* 114 (January 1883); rpt. in *The Critical Heritage*, ed. Gard, 137.

15. William James, "The Dilemma of Determinism," in *The Will to Believe and Human Immortality* (New York: Dover Publications, Inc., 1956), 146.

16. In his biography of Henry James, Leon Edel frequently uses William, whom he tends to regard as a "man of action," as a foil to Henry, a "man of art." As what follows should indicate (and as Edel often suggests), such a strict contrast of the brothers irons out many of the complexities inherent in Henry's position (and no doubt also in William's). But for an example of William James's beliefs about the life of action, consider the following: "There is no more contemptible type of human character than that of the nerveless sentimentalist and dreamer, who spends his life in a sea of sensibility and emotion, but who never does a manly concrete deed" (William James, *The Principles of Psychology*, 2 vols. [New York: Dover Publications, Inc., 1950], I: 125). William appears to have recognized the threat to action posed by current cultural forces, and his philosophy of pragmatism—with its emphasis on *praxis*—was developed largely in response. The fundamental conclusion he drew regarding modern physiology concerned the primacy of action, the recognition that "consideration or contemplation or thinking is only a place of transit, the bottom of a loop, both of whose ends have their point of application in the outer world" (William James, "Reflex Action and Theism," in *The Will to Believe and Human Immortality*, 114).

17. Henry James, Preface to *The Portrait of a Lady*, in Blackmur, 56.

18. Ibid., 51.

19. Ibid., 56.

20. Ibid., 57. Isabel's midnight vigil can be compared both in its climactic centrality and in its emphasis on the internal acts of consciousness to Dorothea's after she discovers Ladislaw and Rosamond in a compromising position (chapter 80).

21 Ibid., 48.

22. Ibid., 42.

23. Peter Brooks, *Reading for the Plot: Design and Intention in Narrative* (New York: Vintage, 1985), 12.

24. Because of the links I have been drawing to the Preface, I have decided to use the revised New York edition of *The Portrait*. Internal page references are to

the Norton reprint of this edition, which includes an appendix of alterations made to the text (ed. Robert D. Bamberg [New York: W. W. Norton and Co., 1975]). As Anthony J. Mazzella's analysis of James's revisions indicates, James makes several slight but significant changes to his novel that increase its tendency to emphasize internalized action. Mazzella points to two moves that are particularly relevant to my argument: first, the later Isabel seems more explicitly invested in her "freedom" on the level of consciousness; second, the later Isabel has a greater tendency to see life "through the pages of a book." See Mazzella, "The New Isabel," in Henry James, *The Portrait of a Lady*, ed. Bamberg, 611–13. I believe, though, that James was honest to the spirit of his work when he altered it for the New York edition. The changes seem to me not to introduce new elements to *The Portrait* but rather to highlight preexisting elements. For further analysis of James's revisions, see Philip Horne, *Henry James and Revision: The New York Edition* (Oxford: The Clarendon Press, 1990).

25. See Richard Freadman, *Eliot, James and the Fictional Self,* 62ff., and *Life,* II: 432. George Levine makes the connection not only to Gwendolen but also to Dorothea in "Isabel, Gwendolen, and Dorothea," *ELH* 30 (September 1963): 244–57. Contemporary critics also linked Isabel to Eliot's heroines. See the unsigned review in the *Californian* 5 (January 1882): 87; rpt. in *The Contemporary Reviews,* ed. Hayes, 139 (comparison to Gwendolen); and William Dean Howells, "Henry James, Jr.," 26; rpt. in *The Critical Heritage,* ed. Gard, 130 (comparison to Dorothea).

26. James's attitude toward the courtship plot is mixed. As critics have noted, he breaks from the conventional wedding-bells ending in most of his major novels. I have been arguing all along that the successful courtship plot tends to coincide with a positive realization of the concepts of plot and action, while the unsuccessful marriage or the failed courtship plot often indicates an underlying fear of action. For women, though, the active avoidance of the marriage plot of the kind Gwendolen Harleth and Isabel Archer seem initially to undertake usually suggests, in its expression of a desire to escape the bonds of conventional action, a particularly aggressive pursuit of free agency. Just how adroit James is at manipulating the marriage plot to suit his interests can be seen in *The Bostonians* (1885–86). James plays upon the fact that as novel readers, we have been trained both to expect and to desire the story to end in marriage. By making Basil and Verena's wedding such an unattractive option, he forces us to reconsider our usual habits of reading the courtship plot. Of course, the political plot of *The Bostonians,* in which Verena serves rather as a passive than as an active participant, does not really provide a more attractive option.

27. Isabel's response, "No I haven't the least idea, and I find it very pleasant not to know. A swift carriage, of a dark night, rattling with four horses over roads that one can't see—that's my idea of happiness," resembles Henry James's often-quoted remarks on history: "I regard the march of history very much as a man placed astride of a locomotive, without knowledge or help, would regard the progress of that vehicle. To sit on, somehow, and even to enjoy the scenery as we pass, is the sum of my aspirations" (Henry James, letter to Charles Eliot Norton, 31 March 1873, in *HJL* I: 362–63). The crucial difference, of course, is that James's eyes are wide open to what goes on outside. But for both author and heroine, the stance is one of a passive experience of great activity.

28. Henry James, letter to A. C. Benson, 1896, in Henry James, *Letters to A. C. Benson and August Monod,* ed. E. F. Benson (London: Elkin Matthews and Marrot, 1930), 35. Lionel Trilling picks up on and makes use of the phrase in his essay, "The Princess Casamassima," in *The Liberal Imagination* (London: Secker and Warburg, 1964), 60.

29. Isabel's feelings about Rome seem to have resembled closely those of her author, although the young James rang a slightly more worldly note in describing his responses to the city by actually quoting Clough: "I do find Rome '*rubbishy*'— magnificently, sublimely so." Henry James, letter to Grace Norton, 11 November 1869, in *Henry James: A Life in Letters,* ed. Philip Horne (New York: Viking, 1999), 29. Hereafter *Life in Letters.*

30. The most shocking of these narrative gaps concerns the birth and death of Isabel's baby, which we hear of only through a casual remark of Madame Merle's to Ned Rosier (305).

31. Many critics have noticed the connection between Grandcourt and Gilbert Osmond, beginning with the critic in the *Saturday Review* 52 (December 1881): 703; rpt. in *The Critical Heritage,* ed. Gard, 99.

32. Henry James, letter to Mrs. Humphry Ward, March or April 1888, in *Life in Letters,* 203.

33. Henry James, Preface to *The Portrait of a Lady,* in Blackmur, 43.

34. George Eliot, *Middlemarch,* 183. For discussion of the relationship between James's and Eliot's metaphors, see Barbara Hardy, *The Novels of George Eliot: A Study in Form* (London: Athlone Press, 1959), 222, and Ruth Bernard Yeazell, *Language and Knowledge in the Late Novels of Henry James* (Chicago: University of Chicago Press, 1994), 49–51.

35. See Milton, *Paradise Lost,* XII.646–47.

36. [R. H. Hutton], review of *The Portrait of a Lady, Spectator* 54 (26 November 1881): 1506; rpt. in *The Critical Heritage,* ed. Gard, 96.

37. Unsigned review of *The Portrait of a Lady, Athenaeum* 2822 (26 November 1881): 699; rpt. in *The Contemporary Reviews,* ed. Hayes, 121.

38. [John Hay], "James's *The Portrait of a Lady,*" *New York Tribune* (25 December 1881), 8; rpt. in *The Contemporary Reviews,* ed. Hayes, 134.

39. Leavis, *The Great Tradition,* 116.

40. Henry James, letter to Edith Wharton, 13 October 1908, in *HJL* IV: 495. Note the striking resemblance to so many of George Eliot's letters to her suffering friends, brought out in particular by the notion of "hygiene."

41. Henry James, letter to T. S. Perry, 24 January 1881, in *HJL* II: 332–34.

42. Henry James, letter to T. S. Perry. Quoted in Edel, *Life,* III: 84. I have been unable to locate a more specific source or date for this letter.

43. Jacques Barzun seems to be the source of most modern critics' application of the term "melodrama" to James's work. See "Henry James, Melodramatist," in *The Question of Henry James,* ed. F. W. Dupee (New York: Holt, 1947). See also Dorothea Krook, *The Ordeal of Consciousness,* 195. The most extensive discussion of James's use of melodrama comes in Peter Brooks, *The Melodramatic Imagination: Balzac, Henry James, Melodrama, and the Mode of Excess* (New Haven: Yale University Press, 1976).

44. George Eliot, *Daniel Deronda,* 615.

45. Leo Bersani, *A Future for Astyanax: Character and Desire in Literature* (Boston: Little, Brown and Co., 1976), 142. As Joyce Taylor Horrell puts it, "It has long been recognized that his plots are mainly reworkings of such never-fail formulas as seduction with sentiment, and his characters have their origins in the villains, heroes, and poor little rich girls common to novelists of all ages." Joyce Taylor Horrell, "A 'Shade of Special Sense': Henry James and the Art of Naming," *American Literature* 42 (1970): 212.

46. Krook, *The Ordeal of Consciousness,* 20–23.

47. Brooks, *The Melodramatic Imagination,* 157.

48. Ibid., 157.

49. Caserio adopts this story's title for his chapter analyzing James's stance toward action.

50. Henry James, "The Story in It," in *Daisy Miller, Pandora, The Patagonia, and Other Tales,* vol. 18 of *The New York Edition of the Novels of Henry James* (New York: Augustus M. Kelley, 1971), 424–25.

51. James, "The Story in It," 434–35.

52. See also Ruth Bernard Yeazell, "Podsnappery, Sexuality, and the English Novel," *Critical Inquiry* 9 (December 1982): 339–357. Yeazell uses the tale to demonstrate the tension in James's work between the Continental "adultery-plot" and the English "courtship-plot."

53. Henry James, Preface to *The Princess Casamassima,* in Blackmur, 65.

54. Brooks, *The Melodramatic Imagination,* 206. His reading has particular force in the context of the crisis of obscurity I discussed in regard to Clough.

55. This general tendency in James has been called many things: *difficulty, obscurity,* and *ambiguity,* to name but a few of the labels. See, for example, Edmund Wilson, "The Ambiguity of Henry James," in *The Triple Thinkers: Ten Essays on Literature* (New York: Harcourt, Brace and Company, 1938), 122–64; and Allon White, *The Uses of Obscurity: The Fiction of Early Modernism* (London: Routledge and Kegan Paul, 1981).

56. The parallel has been much commented upon. See, for example, Hugh Stevens, *Henry James and Sexuality* (Cambridge: Cambridge University Press, 1998), 34.

57. Robert Caserio, in a compelling discussion of the role of action in James's work, suggests that one can trace a distinct change from the earlier works, such as *The Portrait,* which advocate passivity because of its relationship to consciousness, to the later works in which action figures positively: "He shifts his allegiance from subjects and persons who are valuably innocent by virtue of their freedom from plot, understood as intrigue and action, to those who are valuably experienced by commitment to the intriguing and plotting enactments of story." Caserio chooses to build his argument on what he sees as Milly's education in intrigue and Densher's final act of quasi-refusal to the marriage with Kate. I think that a stronger basis for claiming a shift could be found in the more sympathetic portrayals of schemers, from Kate to both Charlotte Stant and Maggie Verver, in late James—as well as a slightly more sinister view of passive characters, including Merton (and even, I believe, *contra* Caserio, the blessèd Milly Theale). But in general, the move in James from his earlier to his later work is not so much a move from the passive to the active stance but rather a greater and greater sense

of the complexities and dangers of both. Caserio, *Plot, Story, and the Novel,* 199, 220–22.

58. Arnold Kettle, "Henry James: *The Portrait of a Lady,*" in Henry James, *The Portrait of a Lady,* ed. Bamberg, 674. Actually, George Meredith was working with methods of opacity even before James. He also shared James's concern with the role of action in modern life. Consider the protagonist of *Beauchamp's Career* (1874–75). Nevil Beauchamp begins his career as a hero of the Crimean War but dies in a boating accident after a failed attempt at politics. Meredith describes his life as a failed attempt at epic: "His indifferent England refused it [that is, a hero's role in an epic] to him. That is all I can say. The greater power of the two, she seems, with a quiet derision that does not belie her amiable passivity, to have reduced in Beauchamp's Career the boldest readiness for public action, some stout good efforts besides, to the flat result of an optically discernable influence of our hero's character in the domestic circle." George Meredith, *Beauchamp's Career* (Oxford: Oxford University Press, 1950), 34–35.

59. Leon Edel notes of the reception of the dramatic version of *The American,* "A. B. Walkley, admiring the amount of busy action Henry had infused into his drama, exclaimed: "What, Mr. James? All this 'between dinner and the suburban trains'?" (*Life,* III: 298). James's relative failure as a writer of dramas owed much to his difficulty with representing action, as Edel relates, but his desire to do work for the stage, while partially motivated by pecuniary concerns, also attests to his genuine interest in the realm of action.

60. As Ruth Bernard Yeazell has pointed out to me, this plot closely resembles the conclusion to James's own earlier novel, *Roderick Hudson* (1876). Henry James, *The Princess Casamassima,* ed. and intro. Derek Brewer, notes Patricia Crick (London: Penguin, 1986), 195. This edition uses the text of the 1886 first edition. Future references to this text will be internally documented.

61. R. L. Stevenson, letter to Henry James, 8 December 1884. Quoted in *Life in Letters,* 167.

62. Henry James, letter to William James, 9 October 1885, in *HJL* II: 101–2.

63. Henry James, Preface to *The Princess Casamassima,* in Blackmur, 64.

64. Ibid., 62. But Hamlet's slashing out in Act V of the play finds only a rather meager equivalent in Hyacinth's suicide at the end of James's novel. In Turgenev's *Virgin Soil* (1877), a novel long recognized as an inspiration for *The Princess Casamassima,* the revolutionary hero's relationship to Hamlet is even more pronounced. The connection of *The Princess* to Turgenev's novel via the link of Hamletism was made by a critic in *The Saturday Review* 62 (27 November 1886): 229; rpt. in *The Contemporary Reviews,* ed. Hayes, 183. Oscar Cargill also explores the relationship in "*The Princess Casamassinia:* A Critical Reappraisal" *PMLA* 71 (1956): 97–117, especially 114–16.

65. Unsigned review of *The Princess* (and three other novels), *Saturday Review* 62 (27 November 1886): 728; rpt. in *The Contemporary Reviews,* ed. Hayes, 182.

66. "H. B.," "London Letter," *Critic,* n.s. 6 (December 1886): 252–53; rpt. in *The Critical Heritage,* ed. Gard, 179.

67. Unsigned review of *The Princess, Graphic* 35 (18 December 1886): 646; rpt. in *The Contemporary Reviews,* ed. Hayes, 184.

68. Unsigned review of *The Princess, Times* (London) 26 (November 1886): 13; rpt. in *The Contemporary Reviews,* ed. Hayes, 181.

69. "Socialism in Three Volumes," unsigned review, *Punch* 911 (20 November 1886): 245; rpt. in *The Contemporary Reviews,* ed. Hayes, 178.

70. W. J. Harvey, *Character in the Novel* (London: Chatto and Windus, 1965), 89.

71. This concern is especially strong in the work of critics of the postwar period, for whom radical ideology was very much a live issue. Is the plan James devised for his revolutionaries a realistic one, what Lionel Trilling calls "a brilliantly precise representation of social actuality," or does it reflect his ignorance of the real methods of the time and his lack of genuine interest in the political scene, as Irving Howe argues? For discussions of these issues, see, among others, John Lucas, "Conservatism and Revolution in the 1880s," in *Literature and Politics in the Nineteenth Century,* ed. and intro. John Lucas (London: Methuen, 1971), 173–219; Irving Howe, *Politics and the Novel* (New York: Horizon, 1957), esp. 145–46; Lionel Trilling, "The Princess Casamassima," esp. 74; and Derek Brewer in the Introduction to the edition I am using (28).

72. Henry James, Preface to *The Princess Casamassima,* in Blackmur, 77.

73. Howe, *Politics and the Novel,* 146.

74. His description of hidden action has become sadly resonant in the current political climate. For many of us who were lucky enough to escape unscathed from the more immediate horrors of September 11, 2001, one of the most intellectually disturbing elements of the experience was its impenetrability: what was happening behind the scenes? Was bin Laden a mastermind? Did the government have information it was keeping from us, or were our leaders just pretending to know something, to avoid mass hysteria? In the aftermath of September 11, *The New York Times* published an article on *The Princess Casamassima, Demons,* and *The Secret Agent.* See Emily Eakins, "Novels Gaze into Terror's Dark Soul," *New York Times,* September 22, 2001. The article cites James's lack of "a clear political agenda" as one of the elements that make his novel seem "unnervingly up to date."

75. Henry James, Preface to *The Princess Casamassima,* in Blackmur, 65.

76. In his Foucauldian reading of the novel, Mark Seltzer has pointed to the prevalence of images and instances of spying in *The Princess Casamassima.* He argues that James's book, while it may advertise "a radical conflict between politics and the novel"—where the novel represents the world of culture embraced by Hyacinth as he loses faith in the revolutionary enterprise—works "against this simple polarization" by suggesting "a criminal continuity between the techniques of the novel and the social technologies of power that inhere in these techniques." For it is in the "vigorous continuity established in James's novels between seeing, knowing, and exercising power that the politics of the Jamesian text appears." While I think that Seltzer focuses on the correct paradigm, I would like to shift the emphasis slightly: real political power is represented in this book not so much by surveillance (which we rarely get to experience in the novel, although we can intimate it) as by its counterpart, invisibility, and in particular, by invisibility identified with plot *in contrast to* the Jamesian visionary consciousness. Both plot and consciousness are "techniques of the novel," in Seltzer's sense, but James finds that his preferred technique of vision is threatened by the underground plotting of

modern politics—just as Hyacinth, who like his author is "a youth on whom noth-
ing was lost" (164), who has "more impressions than he knew what to do with"
(158), discovers that his entanglement within such a plot threatens his vision.
Mark Seltzer, "Surveillance in *The Princess Casamassima*," in *Henry James: A
Collection of Critical Essays,* ed. Ruth Bernard Yeazell (Englewood Cliffs, N.J.:
Prentice Hall, 1994), 117, 164, 158.

77. Henry James, Preface to *The Princess Casamassima,* in Blackmur, 70

78. Ibid., 72; emphasis added. See George Eliot, *Felix Holt, the Radical* for
Eliot's use of the same phrase (388).

79. It represents one of several connections between the novels. I have already
suggested a similarity in the kind of critical debate the two novels opened up. One
should also note the role of "race" (62) in Hyacinth's destiny. The degree to which
his fate is determined by the "extraordinarily mingled current in his blood" (165)
recalls Deronda's blood-legacy of Judaism. But Deronda, being a purebred Jew
(although one raised in a Christian environment) escapes the kind of schizophre-
nia poor Hyacinth faces.

80. George Eliot, *Daniel Deronda,* 445.

81. [R. H. Hutton], review of *The Princess, Spectator* 60 (1 January 1887):
15; rpt. in *The Contemporary Reviews,* ed. Hayes, 186, 188.

82. See Kate Croy's name for Mrs. Lowder in *The Wings of The Dove.*

83. See Benjamin Disraeli, *Lothair* (Westport, Conn: Greenwood Press,
1970), 273–74.

84. Ibid., 310.

85. Ibid., 422.

86. Ibid., 101–2.

87. Henry James, *The Notebooks of Henry James,* ed. F. O. Matthiessen and
Kenneth B. Murdock (New York: Oxford University Press, 1947), 68.

88. See Mark Seltzer, who is interested in "Hoffendahl's god-like power of the
omniscient narrator, a power of unlimited overseeing" ("Surveillance," 115).

89. Julia Wedgewood, from a review of social novels, *Contemporary Review* 1
(December 1886): 900; rpt. in *The Critical Heritage,* ed. Gard, 174.

90. Ivan Turgenev, *Virgin Soil,* trans. Constance Garnett, intro. Charlotte
Hobson (New York: New York Review Books, 2000), 332.

91. Fyodor Dostoevsky, *Demons,* trans. Richard Pevear and Larissa
Volokhonsky (New York: Knopf, 2000), 253. The title of this novel is also translated as *The Possessed* or *The Devils.* Stenka Razin was a Robin Hood-like hero of
the Russian peasant revolt of 1670.

92   Ibid., 422.

93. William James, "The Will to Believe," 2–3.

94. Ibid., 27.

95. In spite of the fact that many revolutionists of the period belonged to the
class of skilled tradesmen (as we see at both the Hand and Banner and the Sun
and Moon), James emphasizes that Hyacinth's two "trades"—the bookbinding and
the revolution making—represent incommensurable alternatives for him.

96. In *The Secret Agent* (1907), Joseph Conrad's later novel about underground radical politics, the Assistant Commissioner of Police—who is in charge
of an investigation into the anarchist bombing that stands in place of the plot in

James's novel—yearns for the control that Hoffendahl is said to possess: "Here I am stuck in a litter of paper . . . supposed to hold all the threads in my hands, and yet I can but hold what is put in my hand, and nothing else. And they fasten the other end of the threads where they please." The Assistant Commissioner unmasks the fiction of such control precisely by demonstrating his reliance on his own "agents," including the pedestrian Chief Inspector Heat (indicated by his "they" in the quotation). Joseph Conrad, *The Secret Agent,* ed. Roger Tennant (Oxford: Oxford University Press, 1998), 115.

97.   As in so many of the works of the period, attitudes to the theater in this novel reveal attitudes about action both generally and in relation to character. Hyacinth is at best an unnatural actor. Consider his response to Millicent's comment that he would do well in fancy dress: "he was on the point of replying that he didn't care for fancy costumes, he wished to go through life in his own character. But he checked himself, with the reflection that this was exactly what apparently he was destined not to do. His own character? He was to cover that up as carefully as possible; he was to go through life in a mask, in a borrowed mantle, he was to be, every day and every hour, an actor" (109). To Hyacinth, action is essentially unnatural because it does not reveal genuine character. The Princess, though, is a consummate actor, unsurprisingly, given that in *Roderick Hudson* we learnt that "she's an actress, but she believes in her part while she's playing it." Henry James, *Roderick Hudson,* volume 1 in *The New York Edition* (New York: Augustus M. Kelley, 1971), 196.

98.   Howe, *Politics and the Novel,* 150.

99.   [R. H. Hutton], review of *The Princess Casamassima,* 14; rpt. in *The Contemporary Reviews,* ed. Hayes, 186.

100.   Dostoevsky, *Demons,* 546–47.

101.   Dallas, *The Gay Science,* II: 186, 251.

102.   E. M. Forster, "What I Believe," in *Two Cheers for Democracy* (London: Edward Arnold and Company, 1951), 78.

103.   For the role of betrayal in the novel, see also Peter Faulkner, "*The Princess Casamassima* and the Politics of Betrayal," *Durham University Journal* 80 (June 1988): 287–93. Faulkner argues that the novel portrays "a culture of betrayal" engulfing both the social and the political realms (293).

104.   See Pyotr Verkhovensky's comment to Kirillov regarding the latter's ideology of suicide: "I also know that it was not you who ate the idea, but the idea that ate you, and so you won't put it off." Dostoevsky, *Demons,* 558.

105.   Conrad, *The Secret Agent,* xxxiv. Conrad's novel bears more than a passing resemblance to James's—one metaphoric echo has already been discussed (see note 96). Both novelists claim that their works were born out of walks through the streets of London (James, Preface to *The Princess Casamassima,* in Blackmur, 59; Conrad, *The Secret Agent,* xxxvii)—and for both novelists, these perambulations produced novels with uncharacteristic settings. But a broader similarity appears in James and Conrad's shared concern for the role of action in the moral life. Verloc's indolence, his "inert fanaticism" (12) appears as a negative reading of Hyacinth's more inwardly lively inaction. And when Conrad says of him that "his part in revolutionary politics having been to observe, he could not all at once . . . take the initiative of action," he seems to be offering a parodic reinterpretation of James's

more likable hero (52). For connections between the two novels, see also Eileen Sypher, "Anarchism and Gender: James's *The Princess Casamassima* and Conrad's *The Secret Agent*," *The Henry James Review* 9.1 (Winter 1988): 1–16, and Eloise Knapp Hay, *The Political Novels of Joseph Conrad* (Chicago: University of Chicago Press, 1963), esp. 237–38.

106.   Conrad, *The Secret Agent*, 222.

107.   Henry James, Preface to *The Princess Casamassima*, in Blackmur, 73.

108.   W. J. Harvey, *Character in the Novel*, 81.

109.   Hannah Arendt, *The Human Condition*, 33.

110.   Lady Aurora represents a different model of political action in the novel, one closer to the small acts of benevolence advocated by George Eliot. Her role as nurse is notable in this regard. As the Princess recognizes in a sentence that sounds like it belongs in an Eliot novel, "She has merged herself in the passion of doing something for others" (451). It might be fairer to say, though, that she tries to lose herself in this passion.

111.   Taylor Stoehr, "Words and Deeds in *The Princess Casamassima*," *ELH* 37 (March 1970): 126. Stoehr has demonstrated that late-nineteenth-century anarchists and nihilists, whose writings James may well have read in preparation for *The Princess*, frequently debated the relationship between words and deeds as forms of propaganda. In particular, they were interested in what Henry B. Brewster called (in 1887) "propaganda by the deed" (125).

112.   Howe, *Politics and the Novel*, 152.

113.   In *Communities of Honor and Love in Henry James* (Cambridge: Harvard University Press, 1976), Manfred Mackenzie claims that the secrecy of Hoffendahl's movement attracts Hyacinth to it: "But what finally draws him to the conspirators is their use of secrecy" (10). In another take on the collapse of political and private spheres in the book, Mackenzie sees it as "a story of society qua secret society" (17) in which "James, as a social observer of his time, can imagine a secret society so well that he inevitably borders on the political" (184 n. 7). While it appears a lot like the obscurity by which I see Hyacinth as being so disturbed, *secrecy* actually suggests a kind of "being-in-the-know" that represents the opposite condition of the unknowability I am describing.

114.   Ellen Moers, *The Dandy: Brummel to Beerbohm* (New York: The Viking Press, 1960), 25. She does not mention Hyacinth.

115.   Moers, *The Dandy*, 13, 18, 13.

116.   Mackenzie, *Communities*, 17.

117.   Henry James, *The Tragic Muse* (London: Rupert Hart-Davies, 1948), 29.

118.   Ibid., 30.

119.   He also works at bookbinding. As he tells Millicent, who seems to consider manual labor beneath Hyacinth, "you must understand I like my work. You must understand that it's a great blessing for a young fellow like me to have it" (252). James's description of Hyacinth's attitude toward his trade may be understated, but it actually makes the work sound rather like Jane Austen's famous labors over her "little piece of ivory": "the only faculty he possessed was the faculty of doing his little piece of work, whatever it was, of liking to do it skillfully and prettily, and of liking still better to get his money for it when he was done" (266). The bookbinding trade seems to connect Hyacinth to Eliot's good workers (like

Adam Bede) and the Carlylean gospel of work that they espoused, but the new emphasis on aesthetic concerns does mark a shift in the type.

120. Henry James, Preface to *The Princess Casamassima*, in Blackmur, 63, 67.

121. Wordsworth, Preface to *Lyrical Ballads* (1850), in *The Prose Works of William Wordsworth*, ed. Owen and Smyser, I: 138.

122. Note how similar Mr. Vetch's worry is to Caspar Goodwood's remark to Isabel: "One would think you were going to commit some atrocity" (143).

123. Derek Brewer, Introduction to *The Princess Casamassima*, 17.

124. "It is my duty to shoot myself because the fullest point of my self-will is—for me to kill myself." Dostoevsky, *Demons*, 617.

125. Turgenev, *Virgin Soil*, 342.

126. It is worth highlighting the number of such hybrid (of mixed cultural or racial background) individuals, both successful and unsuccessful, we have encountered in the course of examining the nineteenth-century crisis of action. In addition to Nezdhanov and Hyacinth, these include Francis and Emily in *The White Doe*, Deronda, and Fedalma.

127. James, Preface to *The Portrait of a Lady*, in Blackmur, 48.

128. Yeazell, *Language and Knowledge*, 40.

129. Henry James, "The Beast in the Jungle," in *Great Short Works of Henry James*, intro. Dean Hower (New York: Harper and Row, 1966), 454. This text is based on the original edition. All future references to it will be internally documented.

130. Edel, *Life*, I: 13; he is quoting page 489 of the edition used.

131. See Edel, *Life*, I: 14.

132. Edel, *Life*, I: 311, I. 65. Perhaps the event in James's life that has drawn the most speculative interest, from an early date, is the "obscure hurt" that he suffered in the spring of 1861. The phrase is his own, from *Notes of a Son and Brother* (1914), and his description of the accident rivals *The Princess Casamassima* for obscurity of plot. One thing, though, is clear: James associates his memory of the injury (which has long been rumored to be some form of castration, but which Edel premises to have been a back injury [see Edel, *Life*, I: 176]) with his memory of the Civil War. The "passage of personal history the most entirely personal" in his life connects ineluctably to "the great public convulsion" by which he was surrounded. Edel argues that "in some way [James] seems to have felt that by vagueness and circumlocution he might becloud the whole question of his non-participation in the Civil War" (I: 175). He describes a form of guilt that recalls Wordsworth's more complex guilt (because it was as much for what he did as what he refrained from doing) over his complicity with the forces of the French Revolution; both writers develop their attitudes toward action in response to political upheavals. Henry James, *Notes of a Son and Brother*, in *Henry James: Autobiography*, ed. and intro. F. W. Dupee (New York: Criterion, 1956), 914–15.

133. See, for example, Donna Przybylowicz, *Desire and Repression: The Dialectic of Self and Other in the Late Works of Henry James* (University, AL: University of Alabama Press: 1986). For a clear instance of this kind of critical discourse, consider Nicholas Buchele's comments on James's artistic motivation: "James, being a non-penetrative sort [i.e., an abstinent homosexual], had mixed responsibilities: he could not pretend to penetrate as other men penetrate (in the

sexual sense), hence the lack of confrontations. Yet the books were the only place where he could do his penetrating (in the cognitive sense): hence the internal revelations" ("Renunciations in James's Late Novels," in *Henry James and Homo-Erotic Desire*, ed. John R. Bradley, intro. Sheldon M. Novick [New York: St. Martin's Press, 1999], 37–38).

134. See Joseph Litvak, *Caught in the Act: Theatricality in the Nineteenth-Century English Novel* (Berkeley: University of California Press, 1992), 235–40; Wendy Graham, "Henry James's Subterranean Blues: A Reading of *The Princess Casamassima,*" in *Modern Fiction Studies* 40.1 (1994): 51–84; and Hugh Stevens, *Henry James and Sexuality* (Cambridge: Cambridge University Press, 1998), esp. chapter 5, "Queer Plotting: *The Princess Casamassima* and *The Bostonians.*"

135. Eve Kosofsky Sedgwick, "The Beast in the Closet," in *Henry James: A Collection of Critical Essays,* ed. Ruth B. Yeazell, 168.

136. Yeazell, *Language and Knowledge,* 37.

137. William Veeder, *Henry James—The Lessons of the Master: Popular Fiction and Personal Style in the Nineteenth Century* (Chicago: University of Chicago Press, 1975), 131.

138. Yeazell, *Language and Knowledge,* 37.

139. James, Preface to *The American,* in Blackmur, 32.

140. James places an unusual emphasis on time in the story. The atmosphere is suffused with Marcher's sense of Romantic belatedness: "What did everything mean . . . unless that, at this time of day, it was simply, it was overwhelmingly too late?" (471). But here, the focus on temporality hints toward future artistic movements more than past ones. As in so many modernist texts, time in "The Beast" seems almost to substitute for plot. Just think of the "Time Passes" section of *To the Lighthouse* (1927), in which so many events of the novel, including Mrs. Ramsay's death, occur offstage. *Marcher* and *May* meet at Weatherend in October, and James carefully conveys all the seasons of their subsequent encounters. As Marcher reasons, "Since it was in Time that he was to have met his fate, so it was in Time that this fate was to have acted" (471). James's allegorical capitalization, unusual for him, turns "Time" into a major figure—almost an agent—in the drama. Time marches on while Marcher waits.

141. In *Reading for the Plot,* Peter Brooks argues for a connection between plots of land and the plotting of stories through his reading of Arthur Conan Doyle's "The Musgrave Ritual" as "an allegory of plot" (26): "The central part of the tale displays a problem in trigonometry in action, as Holmes interprets the indications of the ritual as directions for laying out a path on the ground, following the shadow of the elm when the sun is over the oak, pacing off measurements, and so forth: he literally plots out on the lawn the points to which the ritual, read as directions for plotting points, refers him, thus realizing the geometrical sense of plotting and the archaic sense of plot as a bounded area of ground" (24). I am suggesting that James's story can be read similarly as an allegory of Jamesian plot. If Conan Doyle's plots demonstrate his commitment to reenactment as a form of action, James's plot reveals the connection between inaction and death.

142. Henry James, *The Notebooks,* 184. See also Sedgwick, "The Beast in the Closet," 160 n. 9.

AFTERWORD

1. Elaine Showalter, *Sexual Anarchy: Gender and Culture at the fin de siècle* (New York: Viking, 1990), 78–79.

2. Recall E. S. Dallas's comments about active women in fiction: "When women are . . . put forward to lead the action of a plot, they must be urged into a false position. . . . This is what is called sensation" (*The Gay Science,* II: 296–97). Allen's book, telling the story of a "New" woman who decides to live with her lover and bear his children out of wedlock, ends in tragedy. It was something of a *succès de scandale.* Jil Larson considers the role of agency in the New Woman novel (especially in relation to marriage) in her third chapter: "New Woman writing betrays an insecurity about choice and agency, provoked in this case by the political and social consequences of gender inequity" (44). For her, far from showing unfettered female action, these novels demonstrate the fictiveness of the new freedom. She also notes that "It is no coincidence that the New Woman materialized alongside the decadent and the dandy" (45)—all three pose threats to Victorian gender stereotypes (angel in the house and muscular Christian). I might add here that in its attitude toward plot, one can think of the detective tale as the offspring of sensation fiction and the adventure story.

3. Showalter argues that the focus on boys came in part from male writers' desire to exclude the feminine: "Boyhood, for these writers, was also an allusion to the boyish world of male bonding." But her concern is primarily with the sexual politics of the form, so its gendering is far more interesting to her than its "aging." Showalter, *Sexual Anarchy,* 80.

4. Robert Fraser, *Victorian Quest Romance: Stevenson, Haggard, Kipling and Conan Doyle* (Plymouth: Northcote Publishing House, 1998), 11.

5. Martin Green, *Dreams of Adventure, Deeds of Empire* (London: Routledge and Kegan Paul, 1980), 37. Showalter also remarks that "boys' fiction was the primer for Empire." Showalter, *Sexual Anarchy,* 80.

6. Suggestively, the periodical debates about the status of action in literature that I discussed in chapter 2 directly preceded these momentous events; the call for action was not limited to the literary front but can also be seen as having helped propel the nation into the Crimean War.

7. John R. Reed, *Victorian Will* (Athens: Ohio University Press, 1989), 384.

8. Henry James, "The Art of Fiction," in Henry James, *The Future of the Novel,* ed. Leon Edel (New York: Vintage, 1956), 23.

9. Robert Louis Stevenson, "A Humble Remonstrance," in *R. L. Stevenson on Fiction: An Anthology of Literary and Critical Essays,* ed. Glenda Norquay (Edinburgh: Edinburgh University Press, 1999), 87. Note again the echoes of Aristotle.

10. Stevenson, "A Gossip on Romance," in *R. L. Stevenson on Fiction,* 57, 61.

11. Ibid., 54.

12. See Stevenson, letter to W. E. Henley, August, September 1881, reprinted in *Robert Louis Stevenson: The Critical Heritage,* ed. Paul Maixner (London: Routledge and Kegan Paul, 1981), 125.

13. See Fraser, *Victorian Quest Romance,* 20–21.

14. Robert Louis Stevenson, *Treasure Island,* intro. R. H. W. Dillard (New York: Signet Classic, 1998), 63, 165. Hereafter internally documented by page number.

15. For all the general amorality of the tale, it is possible to read it as commentary on—and even perhaps a critique of—English imperialism. If we stand outside of the perspective of the novel and of the "fun and games" it describes, the identification of gentlemen and pirates can be seen as quite disturbing, to say the least. In this context, the description of the loot reads as an account (a "counting up") of the colonial project; in its diversity, the loot represents the breadth and scope of British imperial history and ambition: "It was a strange collection, like Billy Bone's hoard for the diversity of coinage, but so much larger and so much more varied that I think I never had more pleasure than in sorting them. English, French, Spanish, Portuguese, Georges, and Louises, doubloons and double guineas and moidores and sequins, the pictures of all the kings of Europe for the last hundred years, strange Oriental pieces stamped with what looked like wisps of string or bits of spider's web, round pieces and square pieces, and pieces bored through the middle, as if to wear them round your neck—nearly every variety of money in the world must, must have found a place in that collection; and for number, I am sure they were like Autumn leaves, so that my back ached with stooping and my fingers with sorting them out" (198–99). In this passage, Jim has been transformed into a British colonial administrator, laboring (albeit with pleasure) under the burdens of his dominions. In the context, the epic Virgilian metaphor of the autumn leaves is particularly suggestive.

16. Fraser, *Victorian Quest Romance,* 22. In Kipling's *Kim* (1901), the colonial enterprise is also treated as a "Great Game," although that novel seems far more aware of the seriousness of the play.

17. Henry James, "Robert Louis Stevenson," in *Partial Portraits* (London: Macmillan and Co., 1888), 144, 146, 145, 147; first printed in *Century Magazine,* April 1888.

18. Robert Louis Stevenson, *Kidnapped,* ed. Donald McFarlan (London: Penguin Books, 1994), 68.

19. Including, for example, *King Solomon's Mines* (1885), which was written in response to a bet between Rider Haggard and his brother as to whether or not he could equal Stevenson's great achievement. See Fraser, *Victorian Quest Romance,* 28.

20. Conrad suffered throughout his career from comparisons to Stevenson, which annoyed him greatly (he himself thought of Henry James as his "*cher maître*"—see Ian Watt's discussion in *Joseph Conrad: Nostromo* [Cambridge: Cambridge University Press, 1988], 83). Consider, for example, this response (in an unsigned review in the *National Observer,* 18 April 1896, 680) to *An Outcast of the Islands* (1896): "It is like one of Mr. Stevenson's South Sea stories, grown miraculously long and miraculously tedious. There is no crispness about it and the action is not quick enough, a serious charge to make against a book of adventure." Reprinted in *Conrad: The Critical Heritage,* ed. Norman Sherry (London: Routledge and Kegan Paul, 1973), 70. For more on Conrad's ambivalent relationship to Stevenson, see Hugh Epstein, "*Victory's* Marionettes: Conrad's Revisitation of Stevenson," in *Conrad, James and Other Relations,* ed. Keith Carabine, Owen Knowles, and Paul Armstrong (Boulder: Social Science Monographs, 1998).

21. Larson, *Ethics and Narrative,* 14. Suggestively, Larson's treatment of Conrad focuses not on bodily action but on the ethics of speech acts.

22. Edward Said, *Beginnings: Intention and Method* (New York: Basic Books, 1975), 110. As with James's experience in writing *The Princess Casamassima,* such internalization seems not to have been part of Conrad's original plan of the novel. On 2 January 1903 (in a letter to Ford Madox Ford) he was thinking of *Nostromo* as something "silly and salable," while by 4 June (in a letter to John Galsworthy) he has recognized that "Nostromo grows . . . but the story has not yet even begun." *The Collected Letters of Joseph Conrad: Volume 3 (1903–1907),* ed. Frederick R. Karl and Laurence Davies (Cambridge: Cambridge University Press, 1988), 4, 40.

23. Harold Bloom, "Introduction," in *Joseph Conrad's Nostromo,* ed. Harold Bloom (New York: Chelsea House Publishers, 1987), 4.

24. Joseph Conrad, *Nostromo,* ed. Martin Seymour Smith (London: Penguin Books, 1990), 431, 86, 413.

25. Henry James, "Robert Louis Stevenson," in *Partial Portraits,* 139.

WORKS CITED

EARLY CRITICISM AND REVIEWS

(All attributions come from the *Wellesley Index to Victorian Periodical Literature*, unless another source is cited in the text; unattributed reviews are listed first and alphabetized according to author and work reviewed.)

Unsigned review of American fiction. *Quarterly Review* 145 (January 1883): 212–17.

Unsigned review of Arnold's *Poems* (1853) and *Poems, Second Series. The Eclectic Review* n.s. 9 (March 1855): 276–84.

Unsigned review of *Ambarvalia* and *The Strayed Reveller and Other Poems*, poetry by A. H. Clough and Matthew Arnold. *The Guardian* 4 (28 March 1849): 208–9.

Unsigned review of Joseph Conrad's *An Outcast of the Islands. National Observer* 18 April 1896, 680.

Unsigned review of Henry James's *The Portrait of a Lady. Athenaeum* 2822 (26 November 1881): 699.

Unsigned review of Henry James's *The Portrait of a Lady. Californian* 5 (January 1882): 86–87.

Unsigned review of Henry James's *The Portrait of a Lady. Saturday Review* 52 (December 1881): 703–4.

"London Letter." Review of Henry James's *The Princess Casamassima* by "H. B." *Critic* n.s. 6 (December 1886): 252–53.

"Socialism in Three Volumes." Unsigned review of Henry James's *The Princess Casamassima. Punch* 911 (20 November 1886): 245.

Unsigned review of Henry James's *The Princess Casamassima. Graphic* 35 (18 December 1886): 646.

Unsigned review of Henry James's *The Princess Casamassima. Saturday Review* 62 (27 November 1886): 728–29.

Unsigned review of Henry James's *The Princess Casamassima. Times* (London), 26 November 1886, 13.

"W. M. Thackeray and Arthur Pendennis, Esquires." Unsigned review. *Fraser's Magazine* 43 (January 1851): 75–90.

Bagehot, Walter. "Mr. Clough's Poems." *National Review* 9 (October 1862): 310–26.

———. Unsigned review of Tennyson's *Idylls of the King*. *National Review* 9 (October 1859): 368–94.

Bowker, R. R. Unsigned review of *Daniel Deronda*. *International Review* 4 (January 1877): 68–75.

Brook, Stopford A. "Arthur Hugh Clough." In *Four Poets: A Study of Clough, Arnold, Rossetti and Morris* (1908), 26–47.

Brownell, W. C. "James's *Portrait of a Lady*." *Nation* 34 (2 February 1882): 102–3.

Chretien, Charles Peter. Review of Tennyson's *The Princess*. *Christian Remembrancer* 17 (April 1849): 381–401.

Condor, Josiah. Unsigned review of *The White Doe of Rylstone*. *The Eclectic* n.s. 5 (January 1816): 33–45.

Dallas, E. S. Unsigned review of *Felix Holt*. *The Times,* 26 June 1866, 6.

Edmunds, C. Unsigned review of Browning's *Poems* (1849) and *Sordello* (1840). *The Eclectic Review* 26 (August 1849): 203–14.

Fox, William Johnson. Unsigned review of Tennyson's *Poems, Chiefly Lyrical. Westminster Review* 14 (January 1831): 210–24.

Francillon, R. E. "George Eliot's First Romance." Review of *Daniel Deronda. Gentleman's Magazine* 17 (October 1876): 411–27.

Hay, John. "James's *The Portrait of a Lady*." Unsigned review. *New York Tribune,* 25 December 1881, 8.

Howells, W. D. "Henry James Jr." *Century Illustrated Monthly Magazine* 3 (November 1882): 25–29.

Hutton, R. H. "Arthur Hugh Clough." In *Literary Essays.* London: Macmillan and Co., 1888.

———. "George Eliot's Moral Anatomy." Unsigned review of *Middlemarch,* Book VI. *Spectator* 45 (5 October 1872): 1262–64.

———. Unsigned review of *North and South. National Review* 6 (October 1855): 336–50.

———. Unsigned review of *The Portrait of a Lady. Spectator* 54 (26 November 1881): 1504–6.

———. Unsigned review of *The Princess Casamassima. Spectator* 3053 (60) (1 January 1887): 14–16.

James, Henry. "*Daniel Deronda:* A Conversation." *Atlantic Monthly* 38 (December 1876): 684–94.

———. Unsigned review of *Daniel Deronda. The Nation* 23 (24 February 1876): 131.

———. Unsigned review of *Felix Holt. Nation* 3 (16 August 1866): 127–28.

———. "The Life of George Eliot." *Atlantic Monthly* 55 (May 1885): 668–78.

Kingsley, Charles. Unsigned review, "Thoughts on Shelley and Byron." *Fraser's Magazine* 48 (November 1853): 568–76.

Lewes, G. H. Review of Clough's *Poems* (1862). *Cornhill Magazine* 6 (September 1862): 398–400.

Mallock, W. H. Unsigned review *of Impressions of Theophrastus Such. Edinburgh Review* 150 (October 1879): 557–86.

McDowell, A. S. "On Osborne's *Arthur Hugh Clough.*" *The Times Literary Supplement* (4 March 1920): 153.

Robertson, John Mackinnin. "Clough" (1887). In *New Essays towards a Critical Method.* London: The Bodley Head, 1897.

Roscoe, W. C. Review of Arnold's *The Strayed Reveller and Other Poems* (1849*)*, *Empedocles on Etna and Other Poems* (1852), and *Poems* (1853), and Alexander Smith's *Poems* (1853). *Prospective Review* 10 (February 1854): 99–118.

Sellars, W. Y. Review of Clough's *Poems* (1862). *North British Review* 37 (November 1862): 323–43.

Sidgwick, Henry. Consideration of Clough's life and work. *Westminster Review* 92 (October 1869): 363–87.

Simpson, Richard. Unsigned review of Robert Browning's *The Ring and the Book.* *North British Review* 51 (October 1869): 97–126.

Smith, William Henry. "Mr. Thomas Trollope's Italian Novels." Unsigned review in *Blackwood's Edinburgh Magazine* 93 (January 1863): 84–98.

Symonds, John Addington. "Arthur Hugh Clough." *Fortnightly Review* 10 (1 December 1868): 589–617.

Waller, J. F. (pseud. Anthony Poplar). "Midsummer Muses." Review of Matthew Arnold, Gerald Massey, and others. *Dublin University Magazine* (June 1854): 736–52.

Wedgewood, Julia. Review of *The Princess Casamassima. Contemporary Review* 1 (December 1886): 899–901.

Other Works

Arendt, Hannah. *The Human Condition.* Chicago: The University of Chicago Press, 1958.

———. *The Life of the Mind.* New York: Harcourt Brace, Jovanovich, 1978.

Aristotle. *The Basic Works of Aristotle.* Ed. and intro. Richard McKeon. New York: Random House, 1941.

Armstrong, Isobel. *Arthur Hugh Clough.* London: Longman, 1962.

———. *Victorian Poetry: Poetry, Poetics and Politics.* London: Routledge, 1993.

———, ed. *The Major Victorian Poets: Reconsiderations.* London: Routledge and Kegan Paul, 1969.

———, ed. *Victorian Scrutinies: Reviews of Poetry, 1830–1870.* London: Athlone Press, 1972.

Armstrong, Nancy. *Desire and Domestic Fiction: A Political History of the Novel.* Oxford: Oxford University Press, 1987.

Arnold, Matthew. *On the Classical Tradition.* Vol. 1 in *The Complete Prose Works of Matthew Arnold.* 11 vols. Ed. R. H. Super. Ann Arbor: University of Michigan Press, 1960–77.

———. *Culture and Anarchy.* Vol. 5 in *The Complete Prose Works.* Ed. Super. Ann Arbor, University of Michigan Press, 1965.

———. *The Letters of Matthew Arnold to Arthur Hugh Clough.* Ed. H. F. Lowry. London: Oxford University Press, 1932.

———. *The Poetical Works of Matthew Arnold.* Ed. C. B. Tinker and H. F. Lowry. London: Oxford University Press, 1950.

Arnold, Thomas (Jr.). *Passages in a Wandering Life*. London: E. Arnold, 1900.

August, Eugene R. "*Amours de Voyage* and Matthew Arnold in Love: An Inquiry." *Victorian Newsletter* 60 (Fall 1981): 15–20.

Austin, J. L. *How To Do Things With Words*. Oxford: The Clarendon Press, 1975.

Bagehot, Walter. *The English Constitution*. Intro. R. H. S. Crossman. Ithaca: Cornell University Press, 1966.

———. "Letters on the French Coup d'Etat of 1851." In *Literary Studies: Volume Three*. London, 1898.

———. *Physics and Politics*. Ed. and intro. Roger Kimball. Chicago: Ivan R. Dee, 1999.

Bakhtin, M. M. *The Dialogic Imagination*. Ed. Michael Holquist, trans. Caryl Emerson and Michael Holquist. Austin: University of Texas Press, 1981.

Bamber, Linda. "Self-Defeating Politics in George Eliot's *Felix Holt*." *Victorian Studies* 18 (June 1975): 419–35.

Barzun, Jacques. "Henry James, Melodramatist." In *The Question of Henry James*. Ed. F. W. Dupee. New York: Holt, 1947.

Beer, Gillian. *Darwin's Plots: Evolutionary Narrative in Darwin, George Eliot and Nineteenth-Century Fiction*. London: Ark, 1985.

Benjamin, Walter. *Illuminations*. Ed. and intro. Hannah Arendt, trans. Harry Zohn. New York: Schocken Books, 1969.

Bersani, Leo. *A Future for Astyanax: Character and Desire in Literature*. Boston: Little, Brown and Co., 1976.

Biswas, R. K. *Arthur Hugh Clough: Towards a Reconsideration*. Oxford: Oxford University Press, 1972.

Bloom, Harold. *Wallace Stevens: The Poems of Our Climate*. Ithaca: Cornell University Press, 1977.

———, ed. *Joseph Conrad's Nostromo*. New York: Chelsea House Publishers, 1987.

Bodenheimer, Rosemarie. *The Politics of Story in Victorian Social Fiction*. Ithaca: Cornell University Press, 1988.

———. *The Real Life of Mary Ann Evans: George Eliot, Her Letters and Fiction*. Ithaca: Cornell University Press, 1994.

Bodichon, Barbara Leigh Smith. *Reasons for the Enfranchisement of Women* (1866). In *Victorian Prose: An Anthology*. Ed. Rosemary J. Mundhenk and LuAnn McCracken Fletcher. New York: Columbia University Press, 1999.

Bostetter, Edward. *The Romantic Ventriloquists*. Seattle: University of Seattle Press, 1963.

Briggs, Asa. *A Social History of England*. New York: The Viking Press, 1983.

Bristow, Joseph. "'Love, let us be true to one another': Matthew Arnold, Arthur Hugh Clough, and 'our Aqueous Ages.'" *Literature and History* 4.1 (Spring 1995): 27–49.

Bromwich, David. *Disowned By Memory: Wordsworth's Poetry of the 1790s*. Chicago: University of Chicago Press, 1998.

Brooks, Peter. *The Melodramatic Imagination: Balzac, Henry James, Melodrama, and the Mode of Excess*. New York: Columbia University Press, 1984.

———. *Reading for the Plot: Design and Intention in Narrative*. New York: Vintage, 1985.

Browning, Robert. *The Poetical Works of Robert Browning*. 7 vols. to date. Ed. Ian Jack and Margaret Smith. Oxford: The Clarendon Press, 1982–.

Browning, Oscar. *Life of George Eliot.* London: Walter Scott, Limited, 1892.

Buchele, Nicholas. "Renunciations in James's Late Novels." In *Henry James and Homo-Erotic Desire.* Ed. John R. Bradley, intro. Sheldon M. Novick. New York: St. Martin's Press, 1999.

Burke, Edmund. *Reflections on the Revolution in France.* Ed. Conor Cruise O'Brien. London: Penguin Books, 1982.

Burke, Kenneth. *A Grammar of Motives.* Berkeley: University of California Press, 1969.

Buzard, James. *The Beaten Track: European Tourism, Literature, and the Ways to Culture, 1800–1918.* Oxford: The Clarendon Press, 1993.

Byron, George Gordon, 6th Baron. *Don Juan.* Ed. T. G. Steffan, E. Steffan, and W. W. Pratt. London: Penguin Classics, 1986.

Cargill, Oscar. "*The Princess Casamassima:* A Critical Reappraisal." *PMLA* 71 (1956): 97–117.

Carlyle, Thomas. "Characteristics" (1831). In *Critical and Miscellaneous Essays in Six Volumes: Volume Five.* Volume 10 of *The Library Edition of the Collected Works of Thomas Carlyle.* 30 vols. London: Chapman and Hall, 1869.

———. *Chartism.* In *Critical and Miscellaneous Essays in Six Volumes: Volume Three.* Volume 8 of *The Library Edition.* London: Chapman and Hall, 1869.

———. *The French Revolution.* 3 vols. Volumes 2–4 of *The Library Edition.* London: Chapman and Hall, 1870.

———. *Heroes and Hero-Worship* (1840). Volume 12 of *The Library Edition.* London: Chapman and Hall, 1869.

———. *Past and Present.* Volume 13 of *The Library Edition.* London: Chapman and Hall, 1870.

———. *Sartor Resartus.* Volume 1 of *The Library Edition.* London: Chapman and Hall, 1870.

Carroll, David, ed. *George Eliot: The Critical Heritage.* London: Routledge and Kegan Paul, 1971.

Caserio, Robert. *Plot, Story, and the Novel: From Dickens and Poe to the Modern Period.* Princeton: Princeton University Press, 1979.

Chandler, James K. *Wordsworth's Second Nature: A Study of the Poetry and Politics.* Chicago: University of Chicago Press, 1984.

Chorley, Katherine. *Arthur Hugh Clough, the Uncommitted Mind.* Oxford: Clarendon Press, 1962.

Clayton, Jay. *Romantic Vision and the Novel.* New York: Cambridge University Press, 1987.

Clough, Arthur Hugh. *Amours de Voyage.* Ed. Patrick Scott. St. Lucia: University of Queensland Press, 1974.

———. *The Bothie of Tober-na-Vuolich.* In *Arthur Hugh Clough: Everyman's Poetry.* Ed. John Beer. London: J. M. Dent, 1998.

———. *Clough's Selected Poems.* Ed. J. P. Phelan. London: Longman, 1995.

———. *Correspondence of Arthur Hugh Clough.* 2 vols. Ed. F. L. Mulhauser. Oxford: Clarendon Press, 1957.

———. *The Oxford Diaries of Arthur Hugh Clough.* Ed. Anthony Kenny. Oxford: Clarendon Press, 1990.

———. *The Poems and Prose Remains of Arthur Hugh Clough.* 2 vols. Ed. and intro. Blanche Clough. London: Macmillan and Co., 1869. (*PPR*)

——. *The Poems of Arthur Hugh Clough.* 2nd ed. F. L. Mulhauser. Oxford: Clarendon Press, 1974.

——. *Selected Prose Works of Arthur Hugh Clough.* Ed. Buckner B. Trawick. University: University of Alabama Press, 1964.

——, trans. and rev. *Plutarch's Lives: The Translation called Dryden's.* 5 vols. London: John C. Nimmo, 1893.

Cohn, Dorrit. *Transparent Minds: Narrative Modes for Presenting Consciousness in Fiction.* Princeton: Princeton University Press, 1978.

Coleridge, Samuel Taylor. *Biographia Literaria.* 2 vols. Ed. James Engell and W. Jackson Bate. Vol. 7 in *The Collected Works of Samuel Taylor Coleridge.* General ed. Kathleen Coburn. London: Routledge and Kegan Paul, 1983.

——. *The Collected Letters of Samuel Taylor Coleridge.* 6 vols. Ed. Leslie Griggs. Oxford: Oxford University Press, 1956–71.

——. *The Friend.* 2 vols. Ed. Barbara E. Rooke. Volume 4 in *The Collected Works of Samuel Taylor Coleridge.* London: Routledge and Kegan Paul, 1969.

——. "The Character of Hamlet." In *Lectures 1808–19 on Literature.* 2 vols. Ed. R. A. Foakes. Volume 5 in *The Collected Works of Samuel Taylor Coleridge.* Princeton: Princeton University Press, 1987.

——. *The Notebooks of Samuel Taylor Coleridge.* 4 vols. Ed. Kathleen Coburn. London: Routledge and Kegan Paul, 1957–90.

Collins, Wilkie. *The Moonstone.* Ed. and intro. Sandra Kemp. London: Penguin, 1998.

——. *The Woman in White.* Ed. and intro. Harvey Peter Sucksmith. London: Oxford University Press, 1975.

Comte, Auguste. *Introduction to Positive Philosophy.* Ed., trans., and intro. Frederick Ferré. Indianapolis: The Bobbs-Merrill Company, 1970.

Conrad, Joseph. *The Collected Letters of Joseph Conrad: Volume 3 (1903–1907).* Ed. Frederick R. Karl and Laurence Davies. Cambridge: Cambridge University Press, 1988.

——. *The Secret Agent.* Ed. Roger Tennant. Oxford: Oxford University Press, 1998.

——. *Nostromo.* Ed. Martin Seymour Smith. London: Penguin Books, 1990.

Craik, Dinah. "Something To Do." In A *Woman's Thoughts about Women.* Philadelphia: T. B. Peterson and Bros., n. d.

Cross, J. W., ed. *George Eliot's Life, As Related in Her Letters and Journals.* 3 vols. Boston: Dana Estes & Company, n.d.; republished Grosse Pointe, Mich.: The Scholarly Press, 1968.

Dallas, E.S. *The Gay Science.* 2 vols. New York: Johnson Reprint Corporation, 1969.

Darwin, Charles. *The Origin of Species and The Descent of Man.* New York: Modern Library, 1936.

Descartes, René. *Meditations on First Philosophy, With Selections from the Objections and Replies.* Trans. John Cottingham, intro. Bernard Williams. Cambridge: Cambridge University Press, 1986.

Dewey, John, and James H. Tufts. *Ethics.* New York: Henry Holt, 1908.

Dicey, A. V. *The Statesmanship of Wordsworth: An Essay.* Oxford: The Clarendon Press, 1917.

Dickens, Charles. *Bleak House*. Ed. and intro. Nicola Bradbury. London: Penguin, 1996.

Disraeli, Benjamin. *Lothair*. Westport, Conn.: Greenwood Press, 1970.

——. *Tancred, or, The New Crusade*. London: Peter Davies, 1927.

Dostoevsky, Fyodor. *Demons*. Trans. Richard Pevear and Larissa Volokhonsky. New York: Knopf, 2000.

Dupee, F. W., ed. *The Question of Henry James: A Collection of Critical Essays*. New York: Henry Holt, 1945.

Edel, Leon. *Henry James*, 5 vols. Philidelphia: J. B. Lippincott, 1953–72.

Eliot, George. *Adam Bede*. Ed. Valentine Cunningham. Oxford: Oxford University Press, 1996. (AB)

——. *Daniel Deronda*. Ed. Graham Handley. Oxford: Oxford University Press, 1988. (DD)

——. *Felix Holt, The Radical*. Ed. Fred C. Thomson. Oxford: Oxford University Press, 1988. (FH)

——. *The George Eliot Letters*. 9 vols. Ed. Gordon S. Haight. New Haven: Yale University Press, 1954–78. (*Letters*)

——. *Impressions of Theophrastus Such*. Ed. Nancy Henry. Iowa City: University of Iowa Press, 1994.

——. *Middlemarch*. Ed. David Carroll. Oxford: Oxford University Press, 1998. (M)

——. *The Mill on the Floss*. Ed. Gordon S. Haight. Oxford: Oxford University Press, 1996. (MF)

——. *Romola*. Ed. Andrew Brown. Oxford: Oxford University Press, 1994. (R)

——. *Scenes of Clerical Life*. Ed. Thomas A. Noble. Oxford: Clarendon Press, 1985.

——. *Selected Critical Writings*. Ed. Rosemary Ashton. Oxford: Oxford University Press, 1992.

——. *Silas Marner, The Lifted Veil, and Brother Jacob*. Ed. Peter Mudford. London: Everyman, 1996.

——. *The Spanish Gypsy*. In *The Complete Poems of George Eliot*. New York: Frederick A. Stokes Co., n.d. (SG)

Ellis, Sarah Stickney. *The Women of England, Their Social Duties, and Domestic Habits*. 2 vols. Philadelphia: A. L. Carey and A. Hart, n. d.

Emerson, Ralph Waldo. "Shakspeare; or, the Poet." In *Representative Men*. Ed. and intro. Wallace E. Williams and Douglas Emory Wilson. Vol. 4 of *The Collected Works of Ralph Waldo Emerson*. Cambridge, Mass.: Harvard University Press, 1987.

Epstein, Hugh. "*Victory*'s Marionettes: Conrad's Revisitation of Stevenson." In *Conrad, James and Other Relations*. Ed. Keith Carabine, Owen Knowles, and Paul Armstrong. Boulder: Social Science Monographs, 1998.

Erdman, David. "Wordsworth as Heartsworth; or, Was Regicide the Prophetic Ground of Those 'Moral Questions'?" In *The Evidence of the Imagination*. Ed. Donald Reiman, Michael Jay, and Betty Bennett. New York: New York University Press, 1978.

Faulkner, Peter. "*The Princess Casamassima* and the Politics of Betrayal." *Durham University Journal* 80 (June 1988): 287–93.

Ford, George F. *Dickens and His Readers: Aspects of Novel Criticism since 1836.* Princeton: Princeton University Press, 1955.

Forster, E. M. *Two Cheers for Democracy.* London: Edward Arnold and Company, 1951.

Forster, John. *The Life of Charles Dickens.* 2 vols. London: J. M. Dent and Sons, 1927.

Fraser, Robert. *Victorian Quest Romance: Stevenson, Haggard, Kipling and Conan Doyle.* Plymouth: Northcote Publishing House, 1998.

Freadman, Richard. *Eliot, James and the Fictional Self: A Study in Character and Narration.* London: Macmillan, 1986.

Gard, Roger, ed. *Henry James: The Critical Heritage.* London: Routledge and Kegan Paul, 1968.

Gill, Stephen. *Wordsworth: A Life.* Oxford: Oxford University Press, 1989.

——. *Wordsworth and the Victorians.* Oxford: Clarendon Press, 1998.

Godwin, William. *An Enquiry Concerning Political Justice.* Ed. and intro. Isaac Kramnick. London: Penguin, 1985.

Goethe, Johann Wolfgang. *Römische Elegien.* In *Gedichte 1.* Vol. 1 of *Goethes Werke.* 12 vols. Ed. Jochen Golz. Leipzig: Aufbau-Verlag Berlin und Weimar, 1981.

——. *Faust: Erster Teil.* In *Die natürliche Tochter, Pandora, Faust.* Vol. 4 of *Goethes Werke.* Ed. Jochen Golz. Leipzig: Aufbau-Verlag Berlin und Weimar, 1981.

——. *Wilhelm Meister's Apprenticeship.* Ed and trans. Eric A. Blackall, with Victor Lange. Princeton: Princeton University Press, 1995.

Goethe, Johann Wolfgang, and Friedrich Schiller. "On Epic and Dramatic Poetry" (1797). In *Goethe's Literary Essays.* Ed. and trans. J. E. Spingarn, intro. Viscount Haldane. New York: Harcourt, Brace and Company, 1921.

Goode, John. "*Amours de Voyage:* The Aqueous Poem." In *The Major Victorian Poets: Reconsiderations.* Ed. Isobel Armstrong. London: Routledge and Kegan Paul, 1969.

——. "1848 and the Strange Disease of Modern Love." In *Literature and Politics in the Nineteenth Century.* Ed. John Lucas. London: Methuen, 1971.

Graham, Wendy. "Henry James's Subterranean Blues: A Reading of *The Princess Casamassima.*" *Modern Fiction Studies* 40.1 (1994): 51–84.

Green, Martin. *Dreams of Adventure, Deeds of Empire.* London: Routledge and Kegan Paul, 1980.

Greenberg, Martin. *The Hamlet Vocation of Wordsworth and Coleridge.* Iowa City: University of Iowa Press, 1986.

Greenberger, Evelyn Barish. *Arthur Hugh Clough: The Growth of a Poet's Mind.* Cambridge: Harvard University Press, 1970.

Hadley, Elaine. *Melodramatic Tactics: Theatricalized Dissent in the English Marketplace, 1800–1885.* Stanford: Stanford University Press, 1995.

Haight, Gordon S. *George Eliot: A Biography.* London: Penguin, 1986.

Halliwell, Stephen. *Aristotle's Poetics.* London: Duckworth, 1986.

Hansard's Parliamentary Debates. 41 vols. London: H.M.S.O, 1804–1908.

Hardy, Barbara. "Clough's Self-Consciousness." In *The Major Victorian Poets: Reconsiderations.* Ed. Isobel Armstrong. London: Routledge and Kegan Paul, 1969.

———. *The Novels of George Eliot*. London: The Athlone Press, 1959.

———, ed. *Critical Essays on George Eliot*. London: Routledge and Kegan Paul, 1970.

Hardy, Thomas. *Tess of the D'Urbervilles*. Ed. Tim Dolan, intro. Margaret R. Higonnet. London: Penguin Classics, 1998.

Harris, Wendell V. *Arthur Hugh Clough*. New York: Twayne Publishers Inc., 1970.

Hartman, Geoffrey. *Wordsworth's Poetry, 1787–1814*. New Haven: Yale University Press, 1964.

———. *The Unremarkable Wordsworth*. London: Methuen, 1987.

Harvey, W. J. *Character in the Novel*. London: Chatto and Windus, 1965.

Hay, Eloise Knapp. *The Political Novels of Joseph Conrad*. Chicago: University of Chicago Press, 1963.

Hayes, Kevin J., ed. *Henry James: The Contemporary Reviews*. Cambridge: Cambridge University Press, 1996.

Hazlitt, William. *Character of Shakespeare's Plays*. Intro. Arthur Quiller-Couch. Oxford: Oxford University Press, 1952.

———. *An Essay on the Principles of Human Action*. London, 1805. Reprinted by Gainsville, Fla.: Scholars' Facsimiles and Reprints, 1969.

———. *Selected Writings*. Ed. Jon Cook. Oxford: Oxford University Press, 1991.

Hegel, G. W. F. *Introduction to the Philosophy of History*. Trans. and intro. Leo Rauch. Indianopolis: Hackett, 1988.

Hochberg, Shifra. "*Daniel Deronda* and Wordsworth's *The White Doe of Rylstone*." *English Language Notes* 31 (March 1994): 43–53.

Horne, Philip. *Henry James and Revision: The New York Edition*. Oxford: Clarendon Press, 1990.

Horrell, Joyce Taylor. "A 'Shade of Special Sense': Henry James and the Art of Naming." *American Literature* 42 (1970): 203–20.

Houghton, Walter E. *The Poetry of Clough: An Essay in Revaluation*. New Haven: Yale University Press, 1963.

———. *The Victorian Frame of Mind, 1830–1870*. New Haven: Yale University Press for Wellesley College, 1957.

Howe, Irving. *Politics and the Novel*. New York: The Horizon Press, 1957.

Jacobus, Mary. *Romanticism, Writing, and Sexual Difference*. Oxford: Clarendon Press, 1989.

James, Henry. *The Art of the Novel*. Ed. R. P. Blackmur. New York: Charles Scribner's Sons, 1934. (Blackmur)

———. "The Beast in the Jungle." In *Great Short Works of Henry James*. Intro. Dean Hower. New York: Harper and Row, 1966.

———. *The Future of the Novel*. Ed. Leon Edel. New York: Vintage, 1956.

———. *Henry James: Literary Criticism*. 2 vols. Ed. Leon Edel and Mark Wilson. New York: Library of America, 1984.

———. *Letters to A. C. Benson and August Monod*. Ed. E. F. Benson. London: Elkin Matthews and Marrot, 1930.

———. *The Letters of Henry James*. 4 vols. Ed. Leon Edel. Cambridge: Harvard University Press, 1974–84. (*HJL*)

———. *The Letters of Henry James*. 2 vols. Ed. Percy Lubbock. New York: Charles Scribner's Sons, 1920.

——. *Henry James: A Life in Letters.* Ed. Philip Horne. New York: Viking, 1999.

——. *The Notebooks of Henry James.* Ed. F. O. Matthiessen and Kenneth B. Murdock. New York: Oxford University Press, 1947.

——. *Notes of a Son and Brother.* In *Henry James: Autobiography.* Ed. and intro. F. W. Dupee. New York: Criterion, 1956.

——. *Partial Portraits.* London: Macmillan and Co., 1888.

——. *The Portrait of a Lady.* Ed. Robert D. Bamberg. New York: W. W. Norton and Co., 1975.

——. *The Princess Casamassima.* Ed. Derek Brewer. London: Penguin, 1986.

——. *Roderick Hudson,* Volume 1 of *The New York Edition of the Novels of Henry James.* New York: Augustus M. Kelley, 1971.

——. "The Story in It." In *Daisy Miller, Pandora, The Patagonia, and Other Tales,* Vol. 18 of *The New York Edition of the Novels of Henry James.* New York: Augustus M. Kelley, 1971.

——. *The Tragic Muse.* London: Rupert Hart-Davies, 1948.

James, William. *Pragmatism.* Ed. Bruce Kuklick. Indianapolis: Hackett, 1981.

——. *The Principles of Psychology.* 2 vols. New York: Dover Publications Inc., 1950.

——. *The Will to Believe; Human Immortality.* New York: Dover Publications Inc., 1956.

Jewett, William. "Action in *The Borderers.*" *Studies in Romanticism* 27.3 (Fall 1988): 399–410.

Johnston, Kenneth. *William Wordsworth: Poet, Lover, Rebel, Spy.* New York: W. W. Norton and Co, 1998.

Judd, Catherine. *Bedside Seductions: Nursing and the Victorian Imagination, 1830–1880.* New York: St. Martin's Press, 1998.

Kant, Immanuel. *Critique of Judgement.* Trans. J. H. Bernard. New York: Hafner Press, 1951.

——. *Foundations of the Metaphysics of Morals.* Trans. Lewis White Beck. Indianapolis: Bobbs-Merrill, 1959.

Keats, John. *The Letters of John Keats: A Selection.* Ed. Robert Gittings. Oxford: Oxford University Press, 1970.

Kenny, Anthony. *God and Two Poets: Arthur Hugh Clough and Gerard Manley Hopkins.* London: Sidgewick and Jackson, 1988.

Kettle, Arnold. "Henry James: *The Portrait of a Lady.*" In *An Introduction to the English Novel.* London: Hutchinson's University Library, 1953.

——. "Felix Holt the Radical." In *Critical Essays on George Eliot.* Ed. Barbara Hardy. London: Routledge and Kegan Paul, 1970.

Krook, Dorothea. *The Ordeal of Consciousness in Henry James.* Cambridge: Cambridge University Press, 1962.

Kucich, John. *Repression in Victorian Fiction: Charlotte Brontë, George Eliot, and Charles Dickens.* Berkeley: University of California Press, 1987.

Lamb, Charles. "On the Tragedies of Shakspeare Considered With Reference to their Fitness for Stage Representation." In Volume 1 of *The Collected Works.* 8 vols. Ed. E. V. Lucas. London: Methuen, 1912.

Langbaum, Robert. *The Language of Experience.* New York: W. W. Norton and Co., 1963.

Leavis, F. R. *The Great Tradition: George Eliot, Henry James, Joseph Conrad.* London: Chatto and Windus, 1948.

Levine, George. "Determinism and Responsibility in the Works of George Eliot." *PMLA* 77 (June 1962): 268–79.

———. "Isabel, Gwendolen, and Dorothea." *ELH* 30 (September 1963): 244–57.

Levy, Leo B. *Versions of Melodrama: A Study of the Fiction and Drama of Henry James, 1865–1897.* Berkeley: University of California Press, 1957.

Litvak, Joseph. *Caught in the Act: Theatricality in the Nineteenth-Century English Novel.* Berkeley: University of California Press, 1992.

Longinus. *On the Sublime.* Ed., intro., and commentary by D. A. Russell. Oxford: The Clarendon Press, 1964.

Lucas, John. "Conservatism and Revolution in the 1880s." In *Literature and Politics in the Nineteenth Century.* Ed. and intro John Lucas. London: Methuen, 1971.

———, ed. *Literature and Politics of the Nineteenth Century.* London: Methuen, 1971.

Lukács, Georg. *The Historical Novel.* Intro. Frederic Jameson. Lincoln: University of Nebraska Press, 1983.

MacIntyre, Alasdaire. *After Virtue.* Notre Dame: University of Notre Dame Press, 1984.

———. *Whose Justice? Which Rationality?* Notre Dame: University of Notre Dame Press, 1988.

Mackenzie, Manfred. *Communities of Honor and Love in Henry James.* Cambridge: Harvard University Press, 1976.

Maixner, Paul, ed. *Robert Louis Stevenson: The Critical Heritage.* London: Routledge and Kegan Paul, 1981.

Marshall, David. "The Eyewitnesses of *The Borderers.*" *Studies in Romanticism* 27.3 (Fall 1988): 391–98.

Martin, Graham. "Daniel Deronda: George Eliot and Political Change." In *Critical Essays on George Eliot.* Ed. Hardy. London: Routledge and Kegan Paul, 1970.

Matthiessen, F. O. *Henry James: The Major Phase.* New York: Oxford University Press, 1944.

Mazzella, Anthony. "The New Isabel." In Henry James, *The Portrait of a Lady.* Ed. Bamberg. New York: W. W. Norton and Co., 1975.

Meredith, George. *Beauchamp's Career.* Oxford: Oxford University Press, 1950.

———. *Diana of the Crossways.* New York: The Modern Library, 1931.

Mermin, Dorothy. *The Audience in the Poem: Five Victorian Poets.* New Brunswick: Rutgers University Press, 1983.

Mill, John Stuart. *Autobiography.* Ed. and intro. John M. Robson. London: Penguin, 1989.

———. "Civilization." In *Essays on Politics and Society.* Ed. J. M. Robson, intro. Alexander Brady. Vol. XVIII of *The Collected Works of John Stuart Mill.* Toronto: University of Toronto Press, 1977.

———. *A System of Logic: Raciocinative and Inductive.* 2 vols. London: Longman's, Green, and Co., 1879.

Milton, John. *Complete Poems and Major Prose.* Ed. Merritt Y. Hughes. New York: Macmillan, 1957.

Mintz, Alan. *George Eliot and the Novel of Vocation.* Cambridge, Mass.: Harvard University Press, 1981.

Moers, Ellen. *The Dandy, Brummel to Beerbohm.* New York: Viking Press, 1960.

Moorman, Mary. *William Wordsworth: A Biography.* 2 vols. Oxford: Oxford University Press, 1957–65.

Myers, William. "George Eliot: Politics and Personality." In *Literature and Politics in the Nineteenth Century.* Ed. John Lucas. London: Methuen, 1971.

Newman, John Henry. *Fifteen Sermons Preached before the University of Oxford, between A. D. 1826 and 1843.* 3rd ed. London: Longmans Green, 1919.

Nietzsche, Friedrich. *The Use and Abuse of History.* Trans. Adrian Collins, intro. Julius Kraft. New York: Macmillan, 1957.

Nightingale, Florence. *Cassandra and other selections from Suggestions for Thought.* Ed. Mary Poovey. London: Pickering and Chatto, 1991.

Novick, Sheldon M. Introduction to *Henry James and Homo-Erotic Desire.* Ed. John Bradley. New York: St. Martin's Press, 1999.

Preyer, Robert. "Beyond the Liberal Imagination: Vision and Unreality in *Daniel Deronda.*" *Victorian Studies* 4 (September 1960): 33–54.

Price, Leah. "George Eliot and the Production of Consumers," *Novel: A Forum on Fiction* 30.2 (Winter 1997): 145–69.

Price, Martin. *Forms of Life: Character and Moral Imagination in the Novel.* New Haven: Yale University Press, 1983.

——. "Imagination in *The White Doe of Rylstone.*" *Philological Quarterly* 33.2 (April, 1954): 189–99.

Pritchett, V. S. "George Eliot." In *Discussions of George Eliot.* Ed. and intro. Richard Stang. Boston: D. C. Heath and Company, 1960.

Przybylowicz, Donna. *Desire and Repression: The Dialectic of Self and Other in the Late Works of Henry James.* University, Ala.: University of Alabama Press. 1986.

Quintilian. *The Loeb Classical Library: Quintilian.* 4 vols. Ed. and trans. H. E. Butler. Cambridge: Mass.: Harvard University Press, 1969.

Radcliffe, Evan. "Wordsworth and the Problem of Action: *The White Doe of Rylstone.*" *Nineteenth-Century Literature* 46.2 (September 1991): 157–80.

Reed, John R. *Victorian Will.* Athens: Ohio University Press, 1989.

Richardson, Samuel. *Clarissa.* Ed. and intro. Angus Ross. London: Penguin, 1985.

Roe, Nicholas. *Wordsworth and Coleridge: The Radical Years.* Oxford: Clarendon Press, 1988.

Rzepka, Charles. *The Self as Mind: Vision and Identity in Wordsworth, Coleridge, and Keats.* Cambridge, Mass.: Harvard University Press, 1986.

Sacks, Claire, and Edgar Whelan, eds. *Hamlet: Enter Critic.* New York: Appleton-Century-Crofts, 1960.

Said, Edward. *Beginnings: Intention and Method.* New York: Basic Books, 1975.

Schopenhauer, Arthur. *Essays and Aphorisms.* Selected and trans. R. J. Hollingdale. London: Penguin, 1970.

Sedgwick, Eve Kosofsky. "The Beast in the Closet." In *Henry James: A Collection of Critical Essays.* Ed. Ruth B. Yeazell. Englewood Cliffs, N.J.: Prentice Hall, 1994.

Seltzer, Mark. "Surveillance in *The Princess Casamassima.*" In *Henry James: A Collection of Critical Essays.* Ed. Ruth Bernard Yeazell. Englewood Cliffs, NJ: Prentice Hall, 1994.

Shakespeare, William. *The Riverside Shakespeare.* Ed. G. Blakemore Evans. Boston: Houghton Mifflin Co., 1974.

Shelley, P. B. *Shelley's Poetry and Prose.* Ed. Donald H. Reiman and Sharon B. Powers. New York: Norton, 1977.

Sherry, Norman, ed. *Conrad: The Critical Heritage.* London: Routledge and Kegan Paul, 1973.

Showalter, Elaine. *Sexual Anarchy: Gender and Culture at the fin de siècle.* New York: Viking, 1990

Shuttleworth, Sally. *George Eliot and Nineteenth-Century Science: The Make-Believe of a Beginning.* Cambridge: Cambridge University Press, 1984.

Slinn, E. Warwick. *The Discourse of the Self in Victorian Poetry.* Houndmills: Macmillan, 1991.

Smiles, Samuel. *Self-Help with Illustrations of Conduct and Perseverance.* Intro. Asa Briggs. Centenary edition. London: John Murray, 1958.

Spiegelman, Willard. *Wordsworth's Heroes.* Berkeley: University of California Press, 1985.

Stang, Richard. *The Theory of the Novel in England, 1850–1870.* New York: Columbia University Press, 1959.

Stevens, Hugh. *Henry James and Sexuality.* Cambridge: Cambridge University Press, 1998.

Stevenson, Robert Louis. *Kidnapped.* Ed. Donald McFarlan. London: Penguin Books, 1994.

———. *R. L. Stevenson on Fiction: An Anthology of Literary and Critical Essays.* Ed. Glenda Norquay. Edinburgh: Edinburgh University Press, 1999.

———. *Treasure Island.* Intro. R. H. W. Dillard. New York: Signet Classic, 1998.

Stoehr, Taylor. "Words and Deeds in *The Princess Casamassima*." *ELH* 37 (March 1970): 95–135.

Strachey, Lytton. *Eminent Victorians.* London: Penguin, 1948.

Sypher, Eileen. "Anarchism and Gender: James's *The Princess Casamassima* and Conrad's *The Secret Agent*." *The Henry James Review* 9.1 (Winter 1988): 1–16.

Taylor, Charles. *Sources of the Self: The Making of the Modern Identity.* Cambridge, Mass.: Harvard University Press, 1989.

Tennyson, Alfred Lord. *Tennyson's Poetry.* Ed. Robert W. Hill Jr. New York: W. W. Norton and Co., 1971.

Thompson, E. P. "Disenchantment or Default? A Lay Sermon." In *Power and Consciousness.* Ed. Conor Cruise O'Brien and William Dean Vanech. London: University of London Press, 1969.

Thorpe, Michael, ed. *Arthur Hugh Clough: The Critical Heritage.* London: Routledge, 1995.

Tillotson, Kathleen. *Novels of the Eighteen Forties.* Oxford: Clarendon Press, 1956.

Timko, Michael. *Innocent Victorian: The Satiric Poetry of Arthur Hugh Clough.* Athens: Ohio University Press, 1966.

Trilling, Lionel. *Matthew Arnold.* New York: Columbia University Press, 1949.

———. *The Liberal Imagination.* London: Secker and Warburg, 1964.

———. "The Morality of Inertia." In *The Moral Obligation to be Intelligent.* Ed. Leon Wieseltier. New York: Farrar Straus, Giroux, 2000.

Turgenev, Ivan. *Virgin Soil.* Trans. Constance Garnett, intro. Charlotte Hobson. New York: New York Review Books, 2000.

Veeder, William. *Henry James—The Lessons of the Master: Popular Fiction and Personal Style in the Nineteenth Century.* Chicago: University of Chicago Press, 1975.

Veyriras, Paul. *Arthur Hugh Clough.* Paris: Didier, 1964.

Watt, Ian. *Joseph Conrad: Nostromo.* Cambridge: Cambridge University Press, 1988.

Weinstein, Mark A. *William Edmonstoune Aytoun and the Spasmodic Controversy.* New Haven: Yale University Press, 1968.

Weinstein, Philip. *Henry James and the Requirements of the Imagination.* Cambridge: Harvard University Press, 1958.

Welsh, Alexander. *George Eliot and Blackmail.* Cambridge: Harvard University Press, 1985.

———. *Hamlet in His Modern Guises.* Princeton: Princeton University Press, 2001.

———. *The Hero of the Waverley Novels, With New Essays on Scott.* Princeton: Princeton University Press, 1992.

White, Allon. *The Uses of Obscurity: The Fiction of Early Modernism.* London: Routledge and Kegan Paul, 1981.

Wilson, Edmund. "The Ambiguity of Henry James." In *The Triple Thinkers: Ten Essays on Literature.* New York: Harcourt, Brace and Company, 1938.

Winters, Yvor. *In Defense of Reason.* London: Routledge, 1960.

Wollstonecraft, Mary. "Letter on the Present Character of the French Nation." In *A Wollstonecraft Anthology.* Ed. Janet Todd. Bloomington: University of Indiana Press, 1977.

Wordsworth, Christopher. *Memoirs of William Wordsworth.* 2 vols. Ed. Henry Reed. London, 1851. Reprinted by New York: AMS Press, 1966.

Wordsworth, William. *The Borderers,* Ed. Robert Osborne. Ithaca: Cornell University Press, 1982.

The Cornell Wordsworth. General editor Stephen Parrish. Volumes (in order of date of publication): *The Salisbury Plain Poems.* Ed. Stephen Gill. Ithaca: Cornell University Press, 1975.

———. *The Excursion.* In *William Wordsworth: The Poems.* 2 vols. Ed. John O. Hayden. New Haven: Yale University Press, 1981.

———. *The Fenwick Notes of William Wordsworth.* Ed. Jared Curtis. London: Bristol Classical Press, 1993.

———. *Home at Grasmere.* Ed. Beth Darlington. Ithaca: Cornell University Press, 1977.

———. *Letters of William and Dorothy Wordsworth.* Ed. Ernest De Selincourt. *The Early Years, 1785–1805.* Revised by Chester L. Shaver. Oxford: The Clarendon Press, 1967. *The Middle Years, 1806–1811.* Revised by Mary Moorman. Oxford: The Clarendon Press, 1969.

———. *Lyrical Ballads, and other Poems, 1797–1800.* Ed. James Butler and Karen Green. Ithaca: Cornell University Press, 1992.

———. *The Oxford Authors: William Wordsworth.* Ed. Stephen Gill. Oxford: Oxford University Press, 1984.

———. *Poems, in Two Volumes.* Ed. Jared R. Curtis. Ithaca: Cornell University Press, 1983.

———. *The Poetical Works of William Wordsworth.* 5 vols. Ed. Ernest De Selincourt and Helen Darbishire. Oxford: The Clarendon Press, 1940–49.

———. *The Prelude 1799, 1805, 1850.* Ed. Jonathan Wordsworth, M. H. Abrams, and Stephen Gill. New York: W. W. Norton & Co., 1979.

———. *The Prose Works of William Wordsworth.* 3 vols. Ed. W. J. B. Owen and Jane Worthington Smyser. Oxford: The Clarendon Press, 1974. (Prose)

———. *The Ruined Cottage and The Pedlar.* Ed. James Butler. Ithaca: Cornell University Press, 1979.

———. *Shorter Poems 1807–1820.* Ed. Carl H. Ketcham. Ithaca: Cornell University Press, 1989.

Yeats, William Butler. *The Collected Works of W. B. Yeats.* Ed. Richard Finneran. New York: Scribners, 1977.

Yeazell, Ruth Bernard. *Language and Knowledge in the Late Novels of Henry James.* Chicago: University of Chicago Press, 1976.

———. "Podsnappery, Sexuality, and the English Novel." *Critical Inquiry* 9 (December 1982): 339–57.

———. "Why Political Novels Have Heroines: *Sybil, Mary Barton,* and *Felix Holt.*" *Novel* 18 (Winter 1985): 126–44.

———, ed. *Henry James: A Collection of Critical Essays.* Englewood Cliffs, N. J.: Prentice Hall, 1914.

INDEX

abstinence. *See* inaction

accident (action as), 88–89, 115, 116–17, 139, 143, 155–56, 191n. 10

acting (theatrical): in *Daniel Deronda,* 112–15; in James's works, 138, 155, 217n. 97; and politics, 124. *See also* drama (theater)

action (incident): as accidental, 88–89, 115, 116–17, 139, 143, 155–56, 191n. 10; and belief, 153–57, 164; betrayals into, 9, 14, 16, 20–22, 34, 37, 187n. 63; vs. character, 1–10, 38–39, 43, 48, 57, 65, 68, 83–86, 92, 102–3, 129, 130–32, 165–70, 173, 179n. 9, 184n. 29; choice as, 52, 95–96, 131–32, 134, 139–40, 143; vs. consciousness, 3, 4, 6, 10, 15, 23, 29, 33, 40, 54, 132–33, 146, 168, 171, 198n. 119; as dangerous, 10, 74, 116, 126–27, 135, 137, 145; defined, 5–6, 108; demise of, as entailing demise of character, 10, 167, 169–70, 221n. 141; evil as mobilizing, 21; and feelings, 1, 3–4, 11, 68, 76–77, 85, 107,

123, 163; inaction as frustrated external, 4, 6, 75–76, 106, 166; internalization of, 1, 4, 9, 10, 25, 32, 48, 65, 68–71, 73, 89, 95–104, 107, 118–20, 130, 132–33, 136, 138–40, 168–69, 178, 210–11n. 24; irreversibility of, 92, 95, 98, 109, 112; as leading to unintended consequences, 91–92, 95, 96–97, 100, 101, 112–13, 124, 139; as natural and unmeditated, 50, 175–76, 190n. 10; nineteenth century as providing decreased scope for, 1–10, 48, 50, 53–54, 57, 60, 61, 63–68, 78, 86, 102, 106, 119–20, 156, 172, 210n. 16, 214n. 58; nineteenth-century uses of word, 64; offstage occurrences of, in literature, 136, 212n. 30, 220n. 140; past, as determining present and future, 91–92, 107–8, 112, 115, 117, 119, 120, 170, 192n. 18, 209n. 131; political implications of word, 6; vs. reaction, 8, 210n. 8; risk-free substitutes for, 10, 90–95, 98–100, 106–8, 110, 116, 121–27, 188n. 74, 205n. 82, 207n. 109, 218n. 110; and

commerce. *See* laissez-faire economics

community. *See* individualism: vs. collective action

Comte, Auguste, 111

Conan Doyle, Arthur, 220n. 141

Congreve, Mr. and Mrs., 99, 100

Conrad, Joseph, 6, 8, 158–59, 171, 177–78, 217n. 96

conscience: and consciousness, 7, 23, 27, 126, 186n. 52; and inaction, 11, 23. *See also* guilt

consciousness (self): vs. action, 3, 4, 6, 10, 15, 23, 29, 33, 40, 54, 132–33, 146, 168, 171, 198n. 119; action's role in shaping, 19, 21, 23; and conscience, 7, 23, 27, 126, 186n. 52; and dandyism, 162–63; defined, 6–7; Eliot's emphasis on, 97, 100, 124–28, 132; and inaction, 23, 26, 49, 56, 84, 121, 123, 207n. 109; James on, 10, 132–33, 142–43, 147–48, 168; memory as basis of, 19, 21–22, 27, 34, 37, 40, 45; multiple, in Wordsworth's works, 16–17, 19–20, 27, 30, 31, 37, 40, 43, 45, 142; novels of, 7–8, 123; suffering as entailing, 21–22, 28, 34, 100, 161. *See also* character; memory; novels: psychological; thought; "underconsciousness"; will

consequences: action as leading to unintended, 91–92, 95, 96–97, 100, 101, 112–13, 124, 139; James as interested in pursuing, of characters' actions, 131, 143, 158–59; past, as determining present and future, 91–92, 107–8, 112, 115, 117, 119, 120, 170, 192n. 18, 209n. 131; past, as shaping character, 17, 20, 21

convention, 75. *See also* habit

The Convention of Cintra (Wordsworth), 33, 38

courtship plots. *See* marriage plots

Craik, Dinah, 104

Crimean War, 172, 199n. 124, 214n. 58

crimes: in *Amours de Voyage,* 62, 78; biblical, 55; in *The Borderers,* 23–25, 28, 34, 90; in Eliot's works, 95, 109, 112, 115, 116–18, 126, 185n. 36, 207n. 109; in James's works, 144, 145, 168; of omission, 22–25, 28, 34, 37–38, 90, 185n. 36; revolutionary, 158–59. *See also* regicide; transgression

Critic, 146

critics, 8; psychological, 65–67, 69–71; on psychological novels, 88; responses of nineteenth-century, to crisis of action, 9, 48. *See also names of specific critics*

Cross, John, 95, 96, 106

Culture and Anarchy (Arnold), 59–60

daguerreotype photography, 70

Daisy Miller (James), 146

Dallas, E. S., 65–67, 101–3, 156, 201n. 9, 221n. 2

dandyism, 65, 161–63, 178, 221n. 2

Daniel Deronda (Eliot), 108–28; crisis of action as theme in, 10, 89–90, 108–12, 142, 147, 149; female characters in, 106, 108–15, 125, 128, 130, 132, 136, 140, 164; on gender roles, 103; male characters in, 115–24, 127, 136, 140, 163, 176, 216n. 79; as political novel, 107, 108–9, 119, 124, 147, 192n. 18, 200n. 7, 208n. 117

darkness metaphor, 64–65. *See also* invisibility

Darwin, Charles, 153, 202n. 34. *See also* evolution

Darwinism. *See* evolution

Defense of Poetry (Shelley), 121

Defoe, Daniel, 172